The
Ballad
of
Britain

Also by Will Hodgkinson

Guitar Man
Song Man

Published by Bloomsbury

First published in the United Kingdom in 2009 by
Portico Books
10 Southcombe Street
London
W14 0RA

An imprint of Anova Books Company Ltd

Copyright © Will Hodgkinson, 2009

The moral right of the author has been asserted.

ISBN 9781906032548

A CIP catalogue record for this book is available from the British Library.

10 9 8 7 6 5 4 3 2 1

Typeset by SX Composing DTP, Rayleigh, Essex
Printed and bound by Printed and bound by Athenaeum Press, Ltd., Gateshead, Tyne & Wear

This book can be ordered direct from the publisher at anovabooks.com

To hear more songs, view photos and find out further information on Will's journey please visit www.myspace.com/theballadofbritain

The
Ballad
of
Britain

How Music Captured
The Soul Of A Nation

Will Hodgkinson

PORTICO

Contents

Preface   1

chapter one   *Before the Journey Started*   3

chapter two   *Morris Dancing in Oxford*   25

chapter three   *Cornwall*   38

chapter four   *Devon, Somerset and
                   The English Air*   65

chapter five   *By the Light of the Magical
                   Moon: Gypsies in Sussex*   90

chapter six   *The Garden of England: Kent*   110

chapter seven   *London, Part One:
                   Pop in Suburbia*   130

chapter eight   *London, Part Two:
                   The Underground*   151

chapter nine   *The Ancient Spirit, Part One:
                   Robin Hood's Bay, Yorkshire*   170

chapter ten   *A Town of Bob Dylans:
                   Anstruther in Fife, Scotland*   194

chapter eleven   *The Ancient Spirit, Part Two:
                   Edinburgh to Bradford*   210

chapter twelve   *Sheffield*   228

chapter thirteen   *Why Does Everyone*
                      in Liverpool Love
                      Pink Floyd?   251

chapter fourteen   *The Dyfed Triangle,*
                      West Wales   267

chapter fifteen   *The Ballads of Britain*   294

                      Bibliography   303

                      Acknowledgements   305

                      Tracklisting   307

To Otto and Pearl

Preface

A HUNDRED YEARS AGO, BRITAIN WAS ALIVE WITH SONG. Town and city-dwelling families gathered around the piano to share in a rendition of the latest music hall number. Farm labourers sang laments to lost loves. Everybody came together in churches and pubs to sing the hymns and ballads of the land. As much as language itself, music was an inevitable form of communication and expression. There was no better way to get a sense of a place and its people than to listen to the songs that came from them.

Then something happened. With the growth of the music industry in the 20th century, a myth built up that music was something best left to the professionals. Record sales mushroomed. Classical and, later, rock concerts became million-pound concerns. A handful of people became very rich indeed. The average Briton accepted they were rubbish at singing, as they were at most things in life, and simply stopped doing it. The churches and the pubs emptied. The choirs dispersed. People stayed in to watch *Pop Idol* on television.

This had to change. Roughly since the dawn of the new millennium, British culture has been heading towards a more organic, anarchic, localised state. We've seen it happen with food: the idea of growing your own vegetables and keeping chickens has become acceptable, even fashionable. Now it is happening with music. Once more, landscape and folklore are shaping the songs that we sing.

The Ballad Of Britain is the story of a journey through

a small island with a portable, digital recording studio called a Zoom. To this day I have only learned how to press play and record on the thing, but that was enough to make a series of field recordings that have, I hope, captured something of the British people.

Some of those I recorded sang ancient ballads passed down through the generations. Others sang songs known only to themselves and their mums. The journey lasted from a spring to an autumn, covered a handful of places in England, Scotland and Wales, and was made in a truly unpleasant off-white Vauxhall Astra. Along the journey I met a few dangers, the odd moment of loneliness, and life-affirming levels of generosity and imagination. Most of all, I found that everyone has a story to tell; everyone has a story worth hearing.

Will Hodgkinson
London, March 2009

Chapter One

Before the Journey Started

IT WAS A SPRING MORNING IN PECKHAM, SOUTHEAST London, a Saturday, and there was that rare wonderful feeling of not having to do anything at all. 'Lord And Master' by Heron melted out of the speakers of the spillage-stained portable CD player in our kitchen. 'See the waters drifting by, on a winter's day in the cold,' whispers Tony Pook, lead singer of this short-lived and obscure band from the early seventies, who recorded their debut album in a field in Berkshire. 'I am the lover of everything, and I walk with a friend of the trees.'

To an acoustic guitar, mandolin and accordion accompaniment Tony Pook (graduate of Reading University, part-time musician, full-time dreamer) creates a gentle vision of a rustic, peaceful Britain. 'Lord And Master' is redolent of hedgerows and muddy fields, of dappled sunlight on a forest floor. You can hear birdsong in the background, and at one point what sounds like a tractor. The words speak of being at one with the land, of soaking into the eternity of nature. It makes you think about the mysteries of British life, and it makes you want to be in the countryside, preferably with a jug of ale, sitting in the shade of an oak tree beside a flaxen-haired English rose, the laces of her bodice slightly loosened. The nineteenth-century French historian Hippolyte Taine claimed that the first music of England is the patter of rain on oak trees. Listening to Heron, you know what he means.

Our house is a modern semi in one of London's less bucolic neighbourhoods, and it sits in the shade not of an oak but of a large brick wall with broken glass along the top. The transformative power of 'Lord And Master' is such that the ancient spirit of the land soaked through the house that morning. Music twinned with imagination has a transcendent quality. If William Blake could see angels in the trees of Peckham Rye then I don't see why we shouldn't hear the scrambling of woodland creatures in our privet hedge, even if it was only the rustle of crisp packets being stuffed into it by the boys from the school across the road.

The coffee bubbled up. I poured it into a large mug and added enough hot milk to turn it the right shade of golden brown. I rubbed my eyes and stretched and thought about the pleasant dream of a life lived close to the earth. Suddenly a bass boom of the kind that has been known to cause involuntary bowel movements among the elderly exploded into life on the street outside. The boys that live in the house opposite spend every weekend tinkering with their Audi TX and they had just successfully installed two enormous speakers. The rustic whimsy of Heron was smashed into oblivion by the dominant sound of Peckham: electronic beats, heavy bass, incidental whoops and a rap in a growled, ultra-masculine voice that was saying something about wanting to scare dem bad. Then the Doppler effect of a police siren waxed and waned. Then our children attacked each other. Then our flame-headed neighbour ran down the pavement shouting, 'Ya facking carnt!' as she chased her husband with a cricket bat.

What is British music? It's a question the musician Cecil Sharp sought to find an answer to when, in 1903, he embarked on a 21-year quest to notate traditional English songs that were otherwise in danger of dying out. Concentrating mainly in Somerset, Sharp wound his way through pubs, farms and vicarages in search of songs passed down through oral history that captured the story of the land and its people. Many were based on ballads written down on single sheets of paper called broadsides, sold by pedlars from the sixteenth century onwards and describing in narrative form a current event like a military victory or a society scandal; but now these were the organic songs of the people, changing lyrically and musically as they travelled from village to village and telling the story they needed to tell.

Sharp believed that such songs offered 'the expression of aims and ideals that are primarily national in character'; unconsidered utterances that exposed the real nature of the people and the land they were a part of. This was the organic music of rural England; the music that, according to the composer and fellow collector Ralph Vaughan Williams, lived 'in the minds of unlettered country men, who unknown to the squire and the parson were singing their own songs'.

Sharp grew up in Denmark Hill in Camberwell, about a mile from our house, and made a living as a conductor, pianist and teacher. It was a middle-class suburb then, with the kind of high terraced houses, now mostly broken up into flats, which had enough space for servants' quarters. He had passed forty before he discovered there was such a thing as English folk music. 'It was generally assumed that the English peasant was the only one of his class in all Europe who was unable to express himself in terms of dance or song,' writes Sharp in *English Folk Songs: Some Conclusions*, which was published in 1907, a time when the idea that rural England could produce its own culture of value was something of a novelty.

Even morris dancing, that staple of village fetes the country over that has its roots in the ancient seasonal pageants known as mummers' plays and possibly the Moorish traditions brought back from the Crusades, was almost extinct in Sharp's day. He had never come across it until Christmas 1899, when he was staying with his wife's mother in Headington, near Oxford. Bad-tempered, tired and suffering from eye-strain considerable enough to cause him to wear shades during daylight hours, he looked out of the window to see a strange procession of eight men in white, garlanded with ribbons and bells, carrying sticks and handkerchiefs. A concertina player and a man dressed as a fool – tattered ribbons, odd-coloured leggins and a stick – accompanied the procession, which formed into two lines in front of the house, jumped high into the air, and danced with springs and capers on the frosty ground.

Sharp was transfixed. He introduced himself to the concertina player, a 27-year-old called William Kimber, who told Sharp that they were called The Headington Quarry Side and were performing a dance called 'Laudnam Bunches'. They were touring around town in the hope of making a little money to help their families get through Christmas. Enraptured and fascinated by this aspect of rural Britain he never knew existed, Sharp notated the five tunes to which the dancers performed. So began a mission to capture the folk traditions of Britain that continued for the rest of his life.

Sharp's second eureka moment came on 22 August 1903, when he was visiting the vicarage of his friend Charles Marson in the village of Hambridge in Somerset. Marson's gardener, a local man called John England, was singing a song called 'The Seeds Of Love' to himself as he mowed the vicarage lawn.

> I sowed the seeds of love
> And I sowed them in the spring
> I gathered them up in the morning so soon
> While the small birds do sweetly sing.

According to his assistant and fellow collector Maud Karpeles, Sharp whipped out a notebook and wrote down the tune there and then, before getting England to repeat the words. He harmonised the song and persuaded a fellow guest to sing it at dinner that evening. As Karpeles wrote: 'The audience were delighted . . . it was the first time the song had been put into fancy dress.'

For England, a labourer's son from Hambridge's neighbouring village of Westport, father of eight children and husband to the fragrantly named Rose Morris, 'The Seeds Of Love' was a nice tune to accompany his work, probably learned when he was working in Dorset as a young man. To Sharp it was a revelation. Over the next two years he collected 1,500 songs in Somerset alone, which he then published in the five-volume edition, *Somerset Folk Songs*. In 1911 he founded The English Folk Dance Society. It remains in operation to this day, continuing Sharp's goal of preserving the sword dances, morris dances, folk tunes and ancient pagan traditions of England that had, until Sharp and his contemporaries came along, often existed only in the shared memory of the people that performed them.

Sharp came with an agenda, though. He did want to preserve the folk music of rural Britain, but only in a version that could be taught in schools without fear of reprisals from outraged parents or churchmen – and a song like 'The Seeds Of Love' is quite obviously about sex. 'When every English child is, as a matter of course, made acquainted with the folk songs of his country then, from whatever class, the musician of the future may spring in the national musical idiom,' he writes in *English Folk Songs: Some Conclusions*. But he could hardly offer a traditional Somerset ballad like 'The Keeper', which celebrates rape, to the music teachers of primary schools the country over in the hope of getting their young wards to perform it at the end-of-term pageant. So he sanitised the words, turning what was once organic into something refined and fashioned, and sharpened up the melodies which, having previously only existed in the oral

7

tradition, changed according to the person singing them. By notating English folk songs and writing piano parts he created a body of national music for schoolchildren to learn, thereby strengthening the artistry and identity of England itself.

Not so long ago NJ (my wife, whose actual name is Nichola Jane) and I were invited to a centenary celebration of the English Folk Dance and Song Society at their headquarters at Cecil Sharp House on the corner of Regent's Park Road and Gloucester Avenue in Camden, North London. The invitation came out of the blue. I knew nobody at Cecil Sharp House. But the fact that the letter had clearly been written on an old typewriter by the society's secretary in an age when even Christmas cards from one's parents take the form of an email intrigued and charmed me. So we duly turned up to the high-windowed red-brick hall at half past seven to be met by a lanky man with large glasses who welcomed us with effusive enthusiasm. First he took us into the building's basement, where a tiny, youth-hostel-like bar was manned by a ruddy-cheeked fellow with a lustrous beard who served real ale with ebullience and wine with resentment, and then to a hallway upstairs where a woman was standing behind a trestle table stacked with CDs and leaflets. The atmosphere was more like that of a jumble sale in a village hall than a major event in the centre of London.

Our host took us into the main room. It was full of mostly middle-aged and elderly people sitting on the kind of stacking chairs used for school assemblies. We took our seats and watched as one astonishing scene after another unfolded before us.

Cecil Sharp House is in the heart of Camden, London's alternative-music neighbourhood. Dank, black-walled venues are filled every night with an endless parade of image-conscious young people hoping their next gig will be the one that propels them towards the dazzling heights of fame and glory. In Cecil Sharp House, processions of men with beer guts and beards danced with sprightly glee around swords and whacked at each other with clubs. At one point a teenager in tight white trousers and gelled hair was wheeled out for a special solo dance. A woman in the audience fainted.

A man dressed as a crocodile – large green head, snapping wooden jaw – prowled up the aisle and attacked an innocent-looking girl who could not have been more than twelve. A tiny, fierce-looking woman with enormous owl-like glasses, who was standing entirely still on the stage and had been intermittently barking orders and admonishments at audience members for arriving late or talking during performances, bellowed, 'Leave that virgin alone!' A man dressed as a Victorian milkmaid stumbled about as if drunk. A timid-looking boy of eight or nine sprinkled talcum powder onto the hall's wooden floorboards, only to be interrupted by a solid-bodied woman who, with her lank brown hair, swaying foot-length tasselled skirt and sensible jumper, looked rather like my old sociology teacher. 'Not like that, darling, not like that!' she bellowed in a piercing, teacherly voice, grabbing the talcum powder from the cowed child and shaking the stuff with a rhythmic samba-like swing of her impossible-to-ignore bottom. Then a group of men leaped out and attacked each other with brooms.

The evening had been made up of dances and songs that belong to the ancient traditions of Britain; traditions that NJ and I, like most people in Britain, had scant knowledge of. We had both seen morris dancers, but this tended to be on a Saturday morning in a town quadrant outside a branch of Mothercare and hence didn't make too much of an impression on us. Growing up in Cornwall, NJ took for granted bizarre rituals such as the Padstow 'Obby'Oss (a man dressed as an ornate decorated horse, a remnant of the goddess Epona, leads a procession through the town of Padstow on May Day) and Flora Day in Helston (an evolution from the medieval feast day of Saint Michael, featuring a garlanded parade that cuts right through people's houses whether they like it or not on 8 May), but even she was amazed by the evening's entertainment.

'It's so elemental and mysterious, yet so domestic,' she said as we walked to the Underground. 'It's just like *The Wicker Man*.'

The performances at Cecil Sharp House were indeed reminiscent of the cult British musical horror comedy from 1972 in which a seemingly cosy world – a Scottish island – is revealed to be filled with erotic murderous foreboding and pagan exoticism after a policeman from the mainland goes there to investigate the disappearance of a girl. The islanders are seemingly happy living close to nature, in communion with the rites of fertility and the changing of the seasons, and not too worried about sacrificing the odd virgin to ensure a good harvest. The songwriter Billy Bragg once described the film as 'a terrible juxtaposition of sad folk songs we sung at school, and Britt Ekland's tits'. The film does indeed feature Britt Ekland's tits, but not her bum – that was supplied by a bum double.

What really astounded us about the evening was that, however parochial and unsophisticated it might have seemed, it had an abundance of character – and theatre. This was the world that had fascinated Cecil Sharp a hundred years previously: an anarchic world where distant memories of mysterious pagan rituals blend into the familiar and everyday, and which was in Sharp's time totally divorced from urbane middle-class life. It was a world the quintessentially English composer Vaughan Williams turned into national property. He based his melody for 'To Be A Pilgrim', which every child of my generation would be made to sing in school assembly, on that used in an old Suffolk seduction-and-desertion ballad variously known as 'The Blacksmith' and 'Our Captain Calls'. And yet at the beginning of the 21st century this localised world occupied such a small patch on the landscape of the British imagination.

If Cecil Sharp was the great chronicler of English music, Ralph Vaughan Williams was and remains its greatest exponent. Vaughan Williams, born into upper-middle-class gentility in Gloucestershire, had been exploring the music of Henry Purcell and English hymns when in 1903 he began his own quest to rescue traditional rural songs from extinction after embarking on the ancient ceremony of taking tea with a vicar. It was in the market town of Brentwood in Essex, and the vicar had invited an old labourer called Charles Pottipher along. Pottipher began to sing an old tune called 'Bushes And Briars', and although Vaughan Williams had never heard it before he later wrote of having 'a sense of familiarity . . . something peculiarly belonging to me as an Englishman'.

It wasn't just the delicate melody of 'Bushes And Briars' that entranced the composer; it was the way it captured something of the dreams and concerns of anonymous people. He felt that this was our real national music, not the national anthem or music from a military brass band. Vaughan Williams, a confirmed atheist, sought to distil the spirit of English life in his music whether that meant borrowing ideas from the Elizabethan organist Thomas Tallis, taking a melody from an old folk song or finding inspiration in a walk on the Sussex Downs. It was that blend of the commonplace and mystical, the melancholic and hopeful, that he rightly identified as lying at the heart of the national character; at the heart of the national music.

There's no single word to describe the type of yearning sorrow you can hear in Vaughan Williams' 'Pastoral' Symphony or 'Fantasia on a Theme by Thomas Tallis', but I think it is something intrinsic in the English character: of dreaming of things as they fade and die, of the constant battle against attachment to all things transient. It's a reflective, comforting type of sadness. There is a Brazilian term for this mood, forever found in the words of sambas: *saudade*. It's that feeling of being in a glorious place and knowing you can't stay there for ever; of being in love and aware that you are creating a fantasy for yourself. Vaughan Williams probably knew, consciously or not, that the magic of his music, and of English music as a whole, lay in this idea of something intangible and impossible to capture; the paradox of a living past.

There's a *controlled* sadness to the English – and possibly British – character. We may not throw ourselves over to drama and tragedy, at least not during working hours, but it seems that so many of us are forever battling a sense of loss. 'Hanging on in quiet desperation is the English way,' wrote Pink Floyd on 'Time', from 1973's *The Dark Side Of The Moon*. You can hear it in British music from 'Greensleeves' to Radiohead: a sound, or an underlying mood, which suggests everything isn't simply going to work out for the best. But that doesn't mean we're all doomed either. We keep calm and carry on.

Not everyone felt the patrician, educated approach of Cecil Sharp and Ralph Vaughan Williams was in the interests of the British people. In 1944 A L 'Bert' Lloyd, a journalist, broadcaster, folklorist and committed communist who was born in Wandsworth in 1908 to an AA patrolman father and a mother who mimicked the songs of the Gypsy singers she heard in her childhood, published a pamphlet called 'The Singing Englishman'. Lloyd argued that the early-twentieth-century collectors presented a sanitised version of traditional British music that was a travesty of the real thing. 'Englishmen who only know their own folk songs through cultured arrangements of the more insipid melodies will be surprised to hear that, really, English traditional music is among the very best in Europe,' he wrote. 'Hungary has her Bartok, Spain her Pedrell and Torner. The USSR has the collaborators at the folklore institute in Leningrad. But the best we can produce are Cecil Sharp and the Rev. Baring Gould (who wrote of English agricultural labourers as 'the peasantry'). The old traditions exist, as a rule, merely as something artificial. Folk-dance means a prancing curate in cricket flannels. Folk song means the BBC Singers cooing quaintly in the accents of Palmers Green and Ealing.'

Lloyd claimed that rural folk-song was a fantasy. It had been appropriated by the bourgeoisie who found it to be charmingly romantic, much like the Pre-Raphaelite painters re-imagining the myths of old Albion. A year after 'The Singing Englishman' was published Lloyd went even further, claiming that traditional music in England was completely dead. 'There's no two ways about it: in England folk music has to be looked on as a thing of the past,' he concluded in an article in the magazine for the Workers' Music Association. 'The series has long since been discontinued and all we have are the back numbers.'

In the years that followed Lloyd discovered that the situation was not as bleak as he had painted. In Newcastle he was introduced to the lost heritage of mining songs of north-east England; in East Anglia he was reacquainted with Harry Cox, a farmer with a huge repertoire of traditional songs. Lloyd went on to become a key figure in the folk-song revival of the late fifties and sixties, staging concerts by Anne Briggs and The Watersons and recording albums of traditional English and Scottish ballads with the hard-line communist actor, playwright and songwriter Ewan MacColl.

He formed Centre 42, a touring arts festival that aimed to ensure folk music was performed throughout the working-class towns of Britain. His goal was to promote the kind of urban folk-song found in America at the time, music that spoke of the realities of working-class life in a post-industrial climate. He believed that unless British music lived in the moment and reflected the realities of the people involved in it, it would die.

I could understand Bert Lloyd's concerns. The evening at the English Folk Dance and Song Society, fascinating as it was, had more than a touch of the museum piece, like a preservation society containing something the rest of the world couldn't care less about. Most of what we call folk song has its roots in the countryside of a pre-industrial Britain, which is a very different place from the Britain we live in today. But Lloyd had as much of an agenda as Cecil Sharp did. In viewing traditional folk as the music of the British people he politicised what was formerly a mostly unselfconscious expression of daily realities, hopes, dreams and loves. MacColl started The Singers' Club, where performers were only allowed to sing songs from the places they came from in an attempt to instil purity of purpose; a joke considering MacColl was from Salford but sang in a Scottish accent in honour of his ancestral roots. The Scottish guitarist Bert Jansch got thrown out of The Singers' Club in the early sixties for daring to perform 'Anji', an instrumental classic that every would-be guitar maestro across the land was currently trying to master, making it the folk tune – the shared experience that had entered into public ownership – of the moment.

For Lloyd and MacColl British music had to be about joining unions and squaring up to exploitation and most of all about *rules*: they saw a right way and a wrong way of approaching the music of the people. For all his immense talent and evangelising zeal MacColl was more like a trade union leader than an artist, which helps explain why the one-time leader of the National Union of Mineworkers Arthur Scargill held him in such high esteem: on MacColl's seventieth birthday in 1985 Scargill presented him with a miner's lamp inscribed, 'To Ewan MacColl for outstanding service to the British working class'. But there's a reason why there are a lot more love songs in the world than songs about working in a factory: because artistic expression is far more likely to be an emotional pursuit than a political one.

A hundred years on from the days when Sharp was collecting songs like rare butterflies and Vaughan Williams was dissecting and reworking them into something of his own, British music is as different and varied as the country itself. Listening to Heron on a CD on a Saturday morning as the far more urban sounds of young Black Britain blast out of a car stereo outside goes some way to show how much things have changed. Vaughan Williams and Sharp were searching for music that was affecting because it had a deep truth to it, but I was listening to what would generally be called folk music in an environment that was alien to it, while the music that came out of the car across the road, which nobody in their right mind would call folk, was producing a far more prescient soundtrack to the reality of life in a notoriously crime-ridden if nonetheless charming (you have to live here to feel it) neighbourhood.

Sharp was notating the songs of the rural working classes at a time when Britain was predominantly white, and when people travelled far less and had a much narrower access to global information. He believed that even different parts of the same county developed their own musical style, just as those who lived and died in the countryside could probably tell which town and village somebody came from according to the intonations of their accent. 'Tunes from West Somerset are partly Celtic and are smoother and more polished than those from East and Mid-Somerset,' Sharp concluded. '"Bruton Town" is forceful and rugged and typifies the Anglo-Saxon, one in whom the need for self-expression is the dominant feeling.'

Bruton Town in South Somerset is just off the A303, which cuts past Stonehenge and features some of the most dilapidated Little Chef transport cafés known to humanity. It is also the name of a mournful if elegant song, possibly dating back to the fourteenth century, that tells the story of two brothers, sons of a farmer, who murder the family servant sleeping with their sister. In some versions of the song his ghost comes to the sister in the dead of night to tell her where she can find his bloodied body (in a ditch alongside a bush); in others she finds the body herself. Are these stories and the melodies they are couched in still a reflection of whatever it is that gives Britain its identity? Beguiling as they are, they only make up a part of a bigger picture.

Listening to Heron in the unlovely environs of Peckham on a Saturday morning in spring got me thinking about the forces that shape music: history, place, characters, stories, and most of all the land itself. If you take note of the accent of someone from a large city like London or New York the chances are they'll talk in a fast, clipped tone without too many drawls or long pauses. The further away from the city you go, the deeper into the countryside you venture, it seems the people speak slower and slower. A few years ago I visited some small towns in Mississippi and noticed that the people I met spoke in drawled tones without too much variation in pitch. They spoke like the blues – the music that Mississippi gave birth to – sounded.

Surely the same rules apply to British music. There must be a reason why Sheffield, a city I hardly know but associate with large factories and brutalist architecture, has produced erudite, observant, slightly cynical bands from the nineties and 2000s like Pulp and The Arctic Monkeys alongside a welter of futuristic, experimental groups from the seventies and eighties: ABC, Heaven 17, The Human League, Clock DVA and Cabaret Voltaire. Presumably there's something in the water that makes everyone in Liverpool go mad for Pink Floyd, one of the most archetypal southern products of melancholy-indulging privilege there is. Why is everyone in Cornwall a hippy? And what is the folk music of London, a city that is more cosmopolitan, diverse and aspirational than anywhere else on the planet?

The idea to try and answer these questions, and the bigger one of what British music is, germinated in our kitchen in Peckham to the combined sounds of rural hippy folk and urban grime, and took flower in the fastnesses of rural England over an early-summer weekend. Our friends Will and Stacey had invited us to come away to the tiny cottage in Bedfordshire that Stacey's family had been renting for a nominal amount since the 1960s. Once there had stood nearby a grand stately home called Battlesden House, which the ghost of a dishonest steward atoning in death for the misdeeds he committed in life is said to have haunted. There's very little about the cottage to reveal we are no longer in 1972, making it one of my favourite places in the world. You need to get a coal fire going to have hot water, the games cupboard is stacked with such decidedly non-21st-century diversions as Boggle and Mastermind, and the old brick walls are sparsely decorated with paintings Stacey's hippy uncle did forty years ago. Best of all is the collection of LPs that goes with the Dansette in the corner: *Are You Experienced* by Jimi Hendrix, *Led Zeppelin III*, *The Basement Tapes* by The Band and the debut by the American-born, Britain-based singer Madeleine Bell are played on rotation whenever we visit. They made up the soundtrack to this idyll. And Will and Stacey are about as English as it gets. Will has a permanent frown and an ability to make the simplest things complicated. Stacey hates the sun, loves cold rainy days, and will crease up at the mention of anything fart-related. Both are very kind. All of this contributed towards a rather British experience, especially when added to our national preoccupation: the weather.

The weekend we went to the cottage it did little but rain. This meant we did little but eat, read, drink whisky and listen to records as the children played games and drew pictures. 'This could be an advertisement for rustic content-ment,' said Will as the children read Richard Scarry books on the old sofa and we sat around the aged wooden table flicking through 35-year-old copies of *House And Garden* magazine, 'if it were 1971.'

Will and I did manage to take my son Otto and daughter Pearl out on a kite-flying expedition, through yellow fields of the unfortunately named rape crop. The wind was high and flying the kites was easy; for about a quarter of an hour I lay down in the rape and attached the single string of a kite to my belt buckle, dreaming of English bliss. We walked through the field and along a path that passed a single oak tree filled with birdsong, and then by the side of a small stream that ran alongside a field with rather large cows with horns. It was only when we had left the field that we realised they were actually bullocks. We arrived at a church, cold with its 800-year-old stone walls, high stained-glass windows and empty pulpit and pews. I had to tell the children not to go up to the altar where the cross stands aloft.

'Why not?' asked Pearl, who was five.

'Because it's disrespectful,' I replied.

'Why is it disrespectful?' asked seven-year-old Otto.

'Because it . . . it . . . it . . . do what you're told.'

I sat down at a pew and flicked through a hymnbook, my head filling with never-to-be-forgotten melodies as I read the words to 'All Things Bright And Beautiful' and 'To Be A Pilgrim'. When William Tyndale's New Testament was distributed and published in 1526 a significant step towards the creation of a Church of England was made. The absolute power of the Catholic Church and the Pope at its head was undermined for the first time. Hymns about being British became known in the centuries that followed. Catholics and witches were persecuted; in 1642 a Protestant parliament declared war on a Catholic-sympathising king. Oliver Cromwell banned Christmas. The English made God one of their own.

We took a small road back to the cottage garden, where apple and pear trees break up the lawn and strawberries and broad beans and potatoes grow in a vegetable patch next to a derelict caravan that was up until a few years previously occupied by an elderly man with no teeth and a back-to-front wig. Will put the kettle on and I dropped *Led Zeppelin III* onto the Dansette. I listened to the strange distant blues of 'Bron-Y-Aur Stomp', and read the portentous sleeve notes inside the gatefold: they explained how the band had written much of the album at a derelict cottage in Snowdonia, which helped in 'painting a somewhat forgotten picture of true completeness which acted as an incentive to some of the musical statements'. It was a reminder of what a strange achievement Led Zeppelin made. They took traditional English songs and American blues, envisioned a mystical Arcadia, sprinkled in a dash of the occult and became the biggest band in the world. When I was at university a girlfriend from the Midwest told me that most American kids in the eighties grew up listening to Led Zeppelin. That means soaking in old, anonymous tunes like 'Gallows Pole' and 'Blackwaterside' (which found its way onto the band's first album with a Jimmy Page writing credit as Black Mountainside) without realising it; tunes that had been almost forgotten in this country.

It was raining again by now. Rivulets of water made snaking patterns on the window pane, while Will did his best to make a fire in the hearth out of damp wood and newspaper as thick smoke mingled with the twisting steam rising from the large brown teapot that Stacey had just filled. The children made a line of discarded raincoats and boots that went from the front door to the back room, where they had discovered a wooden box filled with prehistoric Lego. We sat by that gnarled wooden table, moved from cups of tea to tumblers of whisky, played one Led Zeppelin record after another and talked about what made British music.

'It's the post-war, music-hall tradition of Alma Cogan and The Andrews Sisters,' offered Stacey, who has always had a weakness for this sort of thing – chirpy pop made by desexualised, unthreatening elder-sister types. 'And Kate Bush and Morrissey.'

'Of course, that's nonsense,' said Will, closing his eyes, leaning backwards and scratching his head in the way he does when he's feeling mildly irritated by and intellectually superior to everyone around him. 'It's George Formby and his ukulele.'

'Everyone knows British music is The Zombies and The Kinks,' I announced, haughtily. 'It's that combination of whimsy, childishness, surrealism and cynical humour that all those sixties bands did so well. Big truths are captured in a small-minded way. Even the songs of The Who were based on everyday observation – I think they only became a stadium rock band by mistake. Syd Barrett sang about a man who stole knickers from washing lines on Pink Floyd's "Arnold Layne", and there's a sense of loneliness to it all. It's not grandiose – it's eccentric. Even when it gets pompous and overblown, as happened in the early seventies with progressive-rock bands like Yes and King Crimson, there's still something rather absurd about it. I mean, Rick Wakeman staging a musical called *The Myths And Legends Of King Arthur And The Knights Of The Round Table On Ice* and then having so much dry ice that all the dwarves kept crashing into each other . . . it's ridiculous.'

'Why don't you go off around Britain and make field

recordings?' said NJ, who until now had been reading a magazine, declining to take part in the debate. 'That would give you an answer to the question.'

'What do you mean?'

'Who was that guy who travelled across America making recordings of all the old blues and country singers? Alan Lomax? You could do the same thing here in Britain. Find the real Britain. After all, you have the gear for it.'

Alan Lomax was one of the great collectors of folk music. The son of the musicologist John Lomax, he travelled not only across America but also through Europe and the West Indies, recording interviews and songs with the people he met everywhere he went. He understood that everyone has a story to tell; everyone has a song worth singing. Lomax and the young Sussex folk singer Shirley Collins travelled through the southern states of America in 1959 and discovered Mississippi Fred McDowell, now rightly regarded as one of the giants of country blues, alongside hundreds of other singers and musicians both black and white – a significant gesture given that they were moving through the South at a time of high racial tension. He understood the value of musical expression from any place in the world. He promoted multiculturalism before there was such an idea. He was a heroic figure. Who wouldn't want to walk in his footsteps?

As for the gear NJ mentioned, she had bought me an eight-track portable recording studio for my birthday six months previously as a way of encouraging me to write songs. It was called a Zoom MRS-8. It was less than a foot long, but I found I could record an entire album on it. Technology had moved on so much that, while Lomax had to lug a weighty reel-to-reel tape machine through the fields of Mississippi to capture authentic moments of spontaneous musical expression, you could take a Zoom in a supermarket carrier bag to pretty much anywhere. It ran on batteries and had a built-in microphone. Lomax had to make sure his subjects were ready before recording them since tape was finite and expensive, and this destroyed spontaneity somewhat. With the Zoom's digital memory you could record as many times as you wanted and it cost nothing – if the recording went wrong you could just wipe it out and start again. But so far I had done little more than take it out of the box. I fear technology, and the instruction manual for this complex piece of machinery was an inch thick.

'Cecil Sharp went around Britain collecting songs, but that was a hundred years ago,' she continued. 'It's been fifty years since Alan Lomax did his recordings. Things have changed. You could try and update what they did. You know, get a sense of Britain now.'

Making field recordings meant that it wouldn't be necessary to get to grips with the portable studio's multiple functions. One track was all it took. Surely even I could manage to press play and record and point the thing in the direction of someone singing.

'Why do you want me to do that?' I asked. 'Are you trying to get rid of me?'

'I'm trying to get you to use that bloody thing I saved up to get you for your birthday,' NJ replied. 'It cost a fortune.'

Summer was about to begin. It was the festival season. The cash-rich era of the music industry was over and a new haphazard model was taking its place. We could be returning to an age where the pub and the church became the temples of the land once more, where people were rediscovering the simple joys of singing together, of making music for its own sake, of representing the reality of their lives through song. And I had got through half a bottle of whisky and wasn't thinking straight.

Slamming my fist down on the table, I said, 'OK, I'll do it.'

'You could make a musical document out of it,' said NJ, biting into an apple. 'A portrait of Britain. Maybe record something from each place you go to.'

'Yes! And I can travel around on bicycle, just like Cecil Sharp.'

'You still haven't fixed the puncture on the back wheel that happened about four months ago,' interjected Will, who is the kind of man who thinks nothing of cycling from London to Brighton and back again after work – in a corduroy suit.

'All right then, by car.'

We owned an extremely unpleasant white Vauxhall Astra, bought for £500 from my mechanic because he was dying and I couldn't say no. (He's dead now.) We never washed the car and the back seat was covered in the kind of sickly detritus only children are capable of producing. Shards of lollipop, chocolate wrappers, crayons, plastic toy parts and comics with titles like *Sparkle Girl* combined to turn the rear half of the car into a sugary hell. NJ hated it with a passion. In what I think might have been an unconsciously deliberate gesture she drove it into a wall a month after I returned from the garage with it and so, my regular, reliable mechanic now being dead, I had to take it to the one at the top of our road in Peckham. He welded a black side panel on what is otherwise a white car. When I pointed out his quite noticeable mistake he shrugged, blew a cloud of smoke into my face, and asked for a hundred pounds.

'Are you going to include Ireland?' asked Stacey.

'I don't think so,' I said. 'It'll have to be contained by car journeys and the island we live on, and the music of Ireland is such a huge story in its own right. But I don't really know what I'm going to include or where I'm going to go yet. NJ only just came up with the idea five minutes ago.'

'As long as you don't leave the kids for months on end or make me sleep in a tent I don't mind what you do,' said

NJ. 'But I think it will be a good project for you. You've been moping around the house for too long now.'

She was right. It was time to get out there and, as tourist boards the nation over implore us, discover Britain. For the next hour or so we worked out a plan. Half-term was coming up and NJ wanted to visit her parents in Cornwall. This is the isolated, wind-ravaged county she had grown up in, despite appearances to the contrary: NJ's chief interests are fashion and glamour while the rest of her family enjoy growing vegetables and dismantling tractors. It would be a good place to start making field recordings. NJ wanted to travel down with the children a few days ahead of me by train, in part I think because she was ashamed to be seen in the Astra.

London to Cornwall would thus be the first leg of the journey. But en route I would make my first field recording at the place where it all began: in that little village in Oxfordshire where Cecil Sharp first saw the rather odd, uniquely British phenomenon that is morris dancing.

Chapter Two

Morris Dancing in Oxford

'I ALWAYS THOUGHT COUSIN MIKE WAS THE TYPE TO become a morris dancer,' said my father, who lives on a spiritual commune near Oxford, where I was to stay for the first night of the journey. 'Morris dancers seem to present such a delightful image of rural England, but then you meet a few and discover that they're total psychopaths.'

I had only met Cousin Mike (unmarried) once, when I was twelve. He had a neatly clipped beard and he tucked his mother-knitted jumper into his trousers. We had sat in his mother's heavily furnished living room in total silence for an entire afternoon.

Morris dancers, rather than being heralded as the keepers of a great and ancient British tradition, are largely written off as a national joke. In Brazil muscular young men act out the ancient dance rituals of *capoeira* on the beaches and in the streets to cheers and adoration; in Spain flamenco dancers are heroic figures embodying that perfect balance of discipline and passion the country holds in such esteem. In Britain even ascetics who have given up all worldly goods and dedicated their lives to meditation and spiritual reflection in the pursuit of soul-consciousness dismiss morris men as socially disabled maniacs. Why is this?

It transpired that the Headington Quarry Side in Oxfordshire, the group of morris dancers that had first exposed Cecil Sharp to the folk traditions of rural England, were still active. 'If you hurry, you might be in luck,' came back the reply from Bill Partridge, one of the Side's members, when I asked him if I could come and make a recording of the team in action. 'We're having a session next Tuesday in Headington Quarry. We're not advertising it or anything. It's what you might call secret.'

'Where shall I meet you?' I asked Bill, after calling him up.

'We'll be outside The Mason's Arms at seven-thirty,' he told me in a lowered voice. 'Come and find me – ask anyone who I am and they'll tell you. The Headington Quarry morris men are the ones in the cricket caps.'

So it was that, two days after making contact with Bill Partridge, with the rest of the family already in Cornwall, I packed the little Zoom eight-track digital recording studio and a pair of headphones into an Asda shopping bag and made the two-hour journey from Peckham to Headington Quarry in Oxfordshire to penetrate the dark heart of the underground morris scene. Partridge's detailed instructions had taken in three pubs in quick succession: 'When you see The Six Bells swerve to the right, then keep going until you come to Chequers. Go to the left of it, taking a left at the old school, and then go straight until you come to The Mason's Arms.' It sounded like Headington Quarry was quite a big place. Actually, all of these pubs are within a few hundred yards of each other. The village doesn't contain much else, which might help explain why it is morris dancing's spiritual home.

Headington Quarry is just off the multi-lane Oxford ring road, but it is still very much the archetype of an English hamlet. The Mason's Arms is down a small lane and opposite a church with a garden shadowed by a huge and ancient weeping willow. Streets are cobbled and walls are made of slate and stone. Modern houses, uniform in their neatness, make rows along the streets around the pub. Everything is small, quaint, unthreatening.

It was one of those warm English evenings blessed with an orange sky and a breeze, and there must have been at least thirty morris men – all men – standing outside The Mason's Arms, drinking ale out of metal flagons garlanded with ribbons.

If ever there was evidence that the English temperament is a product of the twin forces of conservatism and eccentricity, it was to be found here. The men, mostly but by no means all either middle-aged or elderly, were in favour of hair: beards grew in abundance, eyebrows were tangled, and going bald was no bar to wearing your hair down to your waist. Images of werewolves came to mind. One man was carrying a green watering can painted with images of flowers and the multicoloured legend 'Thirst Aid'; I only realised when he poured the can into his tankard that it was filled with ale. Legs were garlanded with bells. Some of the men wore ragged, flower-laden top hats with pheasants' feathers, others were clad head-to-toe in ribbons, like multicoloured yetis, and an old man was struggling to control a huge circular snapping hobbyhorse. One of the younger morris dancers kept blinking furiously and looking at me from sideways on.

'Where's Bill Partridge?' I asked a bearded man in a cricket cap.

'He's the one bossing everyone about,' the man replied. Bill Partridge, a no-nonsense type with sandy hair and wire-framed glasses, was getting the morris men to shift en masse from outside The Mason's Arms to outside Chequers, where the dancing would begin. I introduced myself. 'Ah, you're the fellow from London,' he said, raising his head up to take a good look. 'Right then, follow me.'

As he rounded up his brightly coloured dancing army Bill explained how the three morris sides present at the meeting, two from Oxfordshire and one that had come all the way from Minnesota, would provide examples of how the dances differed from place to place. 'I could take you to every village in Oxfordshire and each one would have its own dance,' he explained in the kind of good-humoured, authoritative and slightly belligerent tone that is so particular to British middle-aged men. 'Cecil Sharp discovered that all of these dances were variations on a theme, and his studies took him to the Appalachian Mountains where morris dancing had flourished. It's amazing to see how the tradition has travelled to America, and how they religiously follow the dances. With the Minnesota lot I was eager to see how they interpreted the English dance in America because so many things are corrupted over there, but this is *true to the tradition*.' Then he raised his voice and turned to the men. 'Right then, you lot. Look lively.'

A car pulled out of the driveway of Chequers, where the morris faithful had gathered, causing a seagull-like cry of 'car, car, car' that reverberated through the crowd and mingled with the ever-present shaking of bells that accompanied their every movement. Bill introduced me as 'a chap from London that's here to do some recordings', which inspired a few grunts. This was the first time I had tried to make a recording, and in the last few days I had actually managed to get through a fair bit of the instruction manual. It sounded simple enough: there were a few things like levels and settings to get right, but beyond that it was just a case of making sure the internal microphone was working before hitting record.

I crouched down on the gravel of the Chequers car park, a few feet away from the dancers, headphones on in the hope that I would be able to hear what was being recorded, and then pressed the buttons. It seemed to be working: on the display panel are various digital meters that flicker up and down as the Zoom is picking up sounds, and these were flickering away like mad as the morris men made whoops and hollers to psychologically prepare themselves for their big moment. Then the dancing began. To a penny whistle, accordion and drum accompaniment the Headington Quarry Side danced to 'Laudnam Bunches', moving in double-file formation with a spring in their step as the bells around their legs jingled. It was carefully choreographed, with the men shifting about in patterns which ensured that, at the correct intervals, they lined up opposite one another to whack large sticks together before going on their way. Some were smiling; others had faces fixed stern with concentration. Knobbled knees were raised high as they followed the dance like children in a playground game.

The music was cheerful and unthreatening with simple merry-go-round melodies in major chords, and the dances were jolly. The bells on the legs of the morris men jingled with history as the sun set on this pretty village. It certainly made a change from the police sirens and traffic roars I had grown used to in Peckham, but I couldn't help but wonder if my father was right. There was a subtle underlying tension to the whole affair, buried deep under layers of good cheer, warm ale and facial hair. Should it all kick off I'd stand no chance, crouched as I was over the Zoom not far from the dancers' hopping feet. What if one of them should take sudden objection to my presence, and do a jig over the Zoom itself? I made a silent prayer that it would remain peaceful.

Bill took a break to tell me about the epic moment Cecil Sharp first saw morris dancing. 'It all started right here, on Boxing Day, 1899,' he said, pointing at the ground. I looked down and stared at the discarded wrapper of a chocolate bar called Chomp! 'The Quarry Side didn't normally go out on Boxing Day, but they did that year because most of them were bricklayers and stonemasons and there was no work, so they were off to try and raise a few shillings. They were outside Sandfield Cottage in Headington, there was snow about, and Cecil Sharp got into conversation with William Kimber who was playing the accordion. It prompted Sharp to go around the country and record every tune he could get his hands on. He recorded the songs and the footwork in book form and that's what we rely on.'

I told Bill that I understood morris dancers came from mummers' plays, the ancient pageants that combined pagan myths with early Christian stories like that of St George and the dragon. 'There are lots of silly theories about where it came from,' he replied, hotly. 'Nobody knows where it started, but there was a dance that came from the Crusaders so the name is probably a corruption on "Moorish". That became one of the dances in the Tudor court, and there are records of the lord of the manor in Curtlington paying a morris side to dance in 1500. And although Bill Kimber died in 1961 he taught a young chap called John Graham, who is playing accordion for us tonight. So we have that direct link.'

The young chap playing accordion looked like he might have seen active service in the Great War.

As I squatted down with the Zoom and got near to John Graham as he led the dancers through a tune called 'The Rigs Of Time', I wondered if this living tradition could really keep going, and what aspect of British reality it was a part of. It had almost died out in Sharp's time; the fact that he had never even heard of it until that Boxing Day in 1899, when he was already in middle age, proves how obscure it had become.

The Great War almost wiped out morris dancing for good. Not only was a significant part of the male population killed off; so was the idea of Britain as a green, pleasant and above all noble place. The unswerving confidence in the

British way of life built up during the Victorian Empire was shot asunder. The natural order, and the old ways of hierarchy and deference according to class and birth, no longer made sense when so many people were put through such extreme suffering for no noble purpose – my history teacher believed the Great War was a result of Archduke Franz Ferdinand's car taking a wrong turn down a side street, giving a chance for the young Bosnian assassin Gavrilo Princip to shoot the presumptive heir to the Austro-Hungarian throne and his wife Sophie. The folk dances of the morris men and the tunes that went with them celebrated the land, the changing of the seasons, rites of nature and the rigours of time. If all of that is thrown out of kilter by a man-made re-ordering of life expectancy and the replacement of nature with destruction for political gain, how can the morris-dancing vision of Merry England have relevance any more?

But the old dances and tunes survived, just as pubs, hymns and cricket on the village green survived. Whether morris dancing had a glory age – perhaps in the 1950s, before the revolutions of youth made it seem hopelessly irrelevant once more – is hard to tell, but the faithful were in agreement that it was suffering another crisis. 'It's a living tradition, isn't it?' I said to Bill as the Minnesota Side leaped about, waved white handkerchiefs at one another and made the occasional yelp.

'It is, and we keep going – just,' said Bill, raising an index finger meaningfully. 'That's the tragedy of it. We've got to keep it alive somehow, but the youngsters don't want to know.' He dropped his voice and leaned towards me. 'You just can't get them to join. It's the computer age and everything. I could hardly go into this pub on a Monday night and say, "Come on then, lads, let's go dancing," could I? They'd tell me to eff off.'

On that note, Bill rounded everyone up to return to

The Mason's Arms for a few more dances and a rousing finale. 'You should come here on Boxing Day. Now that's really something to behold,' he said proudly if a little grumpily, bells jiggling as we walked the remarkably short distance from one pub to another. 'We do a mummers' play and a sword dance and everything. We have King George and the Turkish Knight, and the doctor who brings him back to life, and the Fool, and Big 'Ead, and the devil – he turns up. You come here on Boxing Day and every pub will be packed. It's a well-known tradition.'

It is a strangely English thing that mysticism and exoticism come wrapped in the cloak of parochialism. Morris dancing has a dowdy image, but its roots are in the *Moresque*, the fifteenth-century Spanish dance that was based on romantic memories of the Moorish period in southern Europe. Morris is a display of vigour and fertility, with the high leaps and shouts of the dancers and the phallic power of the Fool's stick, yet its main practitioners are not exactly lusty youths.

It was getting dark, giving that peculiar type of orange glow, with its gentle romance, that you only get in the British countryside. The Minnesota Side, who I couldn't help but feel were just a little bit more exuberant than the British troupes, were starting a dance filled with leaps and shouts and it occurred to me that this wasn't the preposterous anachronism it is so often written off as. These were men who presumably found morris dancing a great way to connect with their roots, wear exotic, elaborate costumes – something the English have always enjoyed doing and, as Mick Jagger once rightly surmised, British men need very little encouragement to get dressed up as women – and leap about for no other reason than they enjoy it. Morris dancing belongs to a time before overwhelming personal ambition. There are few stars in the morris firmament; these were working men who, whatever they did in civic life, were of equal rank once the old costumes were donned. It's all lads together, dancing in tandem and drinking a lot of ale while they're at it. And the ale was taking its toll.

'Well done, chaps,' slurred Bill as the Minnesota Side finished an impressive, potentially finger-busting stick dance. 'True to the tradition, true to the tradition . . .'

Somebody shouted: 'Maid Of The Mill!'

'Watch this,' said Bill, swaying gently. 'The maid of the mill involves an unsuspecting young lady. She has no idea what will happen to her. She'll find out sooner or later . . .'

One of the sides, the Eynsham lot I think it was, got hold of a teenage girl in a tracksuit top who had wandered out of a nearby house with her mother to see what was going on. She looked a little unsure at first at being manhandled by these strangely dressed men, but the excess of metal tankards and beards appeared to put her at ease and before long she was yieldingly allowing the morris men to dance around her as some of their number sang the following lusty chorus:

> The maid of the mill is a sweet pretty girl,
> The maid of the mill is for me.
> The maid of the mill is a sweet pretty girl,
> The maid of the mill is for me.
> She's as straight and as tall as a poplar tree,
> And her cheeks are as red as a rose,
> She's one of the fairest young girls that you see,
> When she's dressed in her Sunday clothes.

Then the dancers closed in on the young girl, and for a moment it looked like it might all get a bit dark – I had heard of virgins being sacrificed to the nature gods of England to secure a good harvest, and if the pagan dances were still with us there seemed no reason why the pagan killings might not be too – but all they did was raise the girl high into the air. She whooped with joy and ran back to her mother triumphantly. She had arrived at the scene of the morris activity a nondescript tracksuit-wearing local and she left as the sweet and pretty maid of the mill.

'She'll pop out a kid nine months from now,' said one of the morris men, cocking a thumb in her direction.

The dances continued, and I recorded as many as I could before the batteries ran out. Nobody seemed to mind, although a couple of the morris men kept craning their necks and attempting to read my notes when they thought I wasn't looking. It gave me a chance to overhear their conversations.

'Condoms are EU regulation now,' said one.

'I wouldn't be surprised if health and safety bans the stick dances soon,' muttered another. 'Another freedom lost in Nanny State Britain.'

'Of course the Eynsham Side think they're the bee's knees, but at least they know their spring from their caper . . .'

It was late now. Yet still the dances came.

'From the Headington tradition, "Trunkles",' announced a bleary-eyed Bill, waving an arm wildly. 'Google it and find out what Trunkles means.'

If a car drove along the lane and needed to get past, it had to wait. The rituals of the land and its people were taking precedence over modernity that night. There were only ever a few curious onlookers; being the mecca of morris the village of Headington Quarry was apparently used to this kind of activity and turned a blind eye to it. And I was beginning to recognise its value as a joyful shared experience. A few weeks later I discovered that the Maudsley in Camberwell, one of London's largest high-security mental institutions, has its own morris side. To connect with something bigger than yourself, to lose your ego and neurosis in the comfort of a shared activity, and most of all to dress up in bizarre costumes and make strange whooping sounds while leaping about brandishing large sticks and white hand-kerchiefs on which you can blow your nose in the event of being overwhelmed by the emotion of it all, must be far more beneficial to the average troubled mind than a double dose of Mogadon.

The problem with the morris men, I thought as I packed the Zoom in the Asda bag and put it in the boot of the Astra, was that in their enthusiasm to stay 'true to the tradi-tion' they appeared to be taking the historical re-enactment approach. They were concentrating on the physical details and routines of the ancient English dances at the cost of connecting with the wild spirit that makes these rites so fasci-nating in the first place. But it brought back a sense of community that, in an age when evenings for vast swathes of the population are spent in front of the television and the computer, is valuable.

Now it was time to visit an actual commune: the one my father lives on. It is only a few miles away from Headington, in a gothic former stately home now occupied by the Indian spiritual organisation he fell in thrall to about twenty years ago and has remained loyal to ever since. He hasn't drunk a beer, missed a 6 a.m. meditation session, or lost his temper in that time. By the time I arrived it was well past his bedtime (nine o'clock), but we went down to the communal kitchen in the basement nonetheless to drink a cup of spiced tea and see what fruits my first field-recording session had yielded.

'How exciting!' said my father as I placed the Zoom on one of the kitchen tables, turned it on, and prepared to listen back to the evening's worth of material.

I put on the headphones, waiting for what should have been a recording of 'Laudnam Bunches'.

There was silence.

If you listened very carefully, you could hear a slight hissing.

'May I have a go?' said my father with wide-eyed enthusiasm.

'Gladly,' I said, glumly, handing him the headphones.

His face dropped as he listened.

'Oh,' he said. 'Oh dear.'

I had no idea what had gone wrong. I had done exactly as the instructions commanded – press play and record. 'It's a complete failure,' I said, disconsolately. 'The whole project was doomed before it even began. I can't be trusted with technology.'

My father continued to listen to the tiny hiss on the headphones. I padded over to the hot-water urn to make us another cup of tea and reflect on whether I should just cut my losses and head down to Cornwall, return to Headington Quarry to see if a few drunken morris men were still at it, or give up entirely. 'I should stick to what I'm good at, what-ever that is,' I said, shoulders slouched as I poked at an infusion. 'It was a mistake to meddle with forces I couldn't understand.'

But my father couldn't hear me. He had the head-phones on, and was still listening to the lack of recording on the Zoom. He now had his eyes closed, a look of blissful contentment on his face. What was he doing? Then I realised – he was meditating! That bastard was using my recording disaster as an excuse to take another step towards enlightenment!

But then his eyes popped open in shock, like a monk

who had just sat down on a whoopee cushion. 'They've started!' he said, bopping his head from side to side. 'It's very lively. Have a listen.'

Fifteen minutes in – and I'm really not sure what button I must have pressed – the Zoom decided to pick up the sounds of the Morris dancers and their accompanying music with crystal clarity. I had missed 'Laudnam Bunches', the tune that Cecil Sharp first heard on that life-changing Christmas morning in 1899, but there were other morris tunes there alongside the heavy jangling of bells, the sound of middle-aged feet hopping up and down on gravel, and, occasionally, the odd beery burp.

'It worked after all,' said my father. 'It sounds like the world of country pubs, doesn't it? I've forgotten what they're like.'

'When was the last time you were in one?'

'Well, let me see . . . what is it, April? So that's January, February, March . . . about twenty-five years ago. But this brings it all back.' He stifled a yawn and took the headphones off. 'Well, I'd better turn in. So had you, if you're driving all the way to Cornwall tomorrow.'

That night I went to bed in one of the small, clean, white-walled guest rooms at the top of the house, visions of bearded men with fierce staring eyes and bells on their legs lulling me into sleep. Then at six o'clock the following morning came the gentle sounds of Indian meditation music piping through loudspeakers: the commune's call to prayer. I didn't manage to make a field recording of it. Instead, I checked that the recording of the morris men really had worked, packed up the Zoom, and prepared to take off to a place that holds a far wilder reality than that of the morris men or my father's spiritual commune: Cornwall.

Chapter Three

Cornwall

CORNWALL IS A PLACE WHERE DISTANCE FROM THE capital, a particular kind of light, a wild landscape, a jagged coastline and a friendly if somewhat detached people have produced a culture distinct from anywhere else in Britain.

NJ grew up in Cornwall and had every intention of leaving at the first opportunity. Her parents are of the seventies generation of provincial-to-urban, working-to-middle-class people – her mother is from Cardiff, her father from Paisley – who had a dream of the countryside as a place to build a better life. After a short spell in suburban north London they moved to Penryn, a then-poor town near the south coast of Cornwall where they could afford to buy a large dilapidated house ideal for bringing up three children. They were typical of what the Cornish call incomers – a well-intentioned family from 'up country' searching for some kind of rural freedom. NJ's youngest brother discovered music and the world of the shuffling, guitar-playing, hemp-wearing, dreadlock-sporting provincial bohemians the county is filled with. Her other brother was driving a tractor by the age of twelve. NJ was in her room, cutting out pictures from *Vogue* and saving up for her first pair of high heels. She came to London and has stayed there ever since, and if I ever make vague suggestions that we should move out of the city and into the country she makes rather less vague ones that should we do so I can expect to come home one evening to find her hanging from the rafters of whatever quaint little cottage we sold our house in the capital for.

As the shamefully ugly Vauxhall Astra passed Stonehenge on the A303, a little line of modern-day pilgrims in brightly coloured kagoules making the clearly designated sacred walk around the standing stones, I reflected on what experiences over the last few years had taught me about the nature of Cornwall and its people.

Perhaps unsurprisingly, given my wife's oft-given assertion that life in the country is not the image of bucolic bliss that much of British identity is built on but in fact for the most part is crashingly dull, I had always assumed that nothing happened in Cornwall. You could go surfing there, and there were the strange old folk traditions, Celtic crosses, burial stones and a few nice pubs, but the most you could expect by way of cultural enrichment would be a set by The Rockin' Tomcats at The Pandora Inn. Then, one Christmas Eve, we were in a pub called The Jacob's Ladder in Falmouth, a town that is given a degree of ragged glamour by its art school. Two pretty, long-haired young women with the air of Pre-Raphaelite muses, all braids, bangles and floor-length dresses with tight bodices, took to the tiny stage while two hairy men, who turned out to be their boyfriends, played various strange instruments at the back. The music was charming: folk-tinged tunes with the rough elegance of Cornwall itself. 'We shall dance among the trees, and I shall give myself to thee,' sang these gently swaying, tambourine-shaking, latter-day Ophelias in high-pitched tones reminiscent of the mice from the seventies children's television series *Bagpuss*. It was all rather thrown together, but captivating.

We got talking to the band after they had finished their set. The girls, whose names were Lydia and Tiffany, had met at art college, liked the way each other looked and decided to form a band. Tiffany was living on an old wooden boat called *Rosemarie* at the creek in Penryn with her boyfriend Jarvis, while Lydia was in a flat in Falmouth with her boyfriend Ben. They had a large knowledge of obscure folk-rock from the late sixties and early seventies and collected albums by mostly forgotten bands like Cob, The Sun Also Rises, Loudest Whisper, Mellow Candle and Fresh Maggots. The Jacob's Ladder gig was their first, and they had written only a handful of songs. They claimed they had no financial ambition for their band, which was called Thistletown; it was simply a way of playing the music they loved and giving them the creative challenge of writing lyrics and coming up with melodies.

All had fallen in love with the rough beauty of Cornwall and moved there from elsewhere across the country, and thought of London as one of the worst places in the world. They did casual jobs, grew vegetables, smoked rolled-up cigarettes and drank beer in nearby pubs when they had enough money to do so. There was romance to their vision of the world.

A few weeks later I went to visit Jarvis and Tiffany on their boat, the wooden cabin of which was dominated by harmoniums, trumpets, drums and bongos. 'We first met at a party, right here,' said Tiffany, the youngest of the four. 'Jarvis was completely drunk and he fell off the side of the boat and into the mud, which I've since found out is quite normal for him. I was sitting on the deck when suddenly this mud monster came towards me. It was quite scary, but then it opened its mouth and said, "Will you look after me?" We've been together ever since.'

I later found out that Jarvis's dad Steve, originally from the North, had followed his son down to Cornwall. He was living in a low-ceilinged, thick-walled cottage in a village called Mabe that had a garden filled with the kind of exotic tropical plants and flowers the county's temperate climate allows for; sculptures in metal and glass sat among the palms and ginkgos like a miniature Barbara Hepworth exhibition. Jarvis and Tiffany had been putting on evening concerts in the garden, finding local bands that combined traditional British folk with the avant-garde and creating sounds that were as far-reaching as anything going on in the capital, yet with a Cornish tinge. It was a long way from The Rockin' Tomcats, and a signifier of Cornwall's secret: hidden away from the bay windows of the tea shops and B&Bs, a little further down the country lanes than the average visitor would normally go, the county is alive with expression.

I envisaged great things for Thistletown. Their songs had something of the spirit of the land. Their lifestyle was an attractive one, and I could see impressionable young music fans falling in love with the girls. Around the time of meeting them I was starting up a tiny record label. Tiffany, Jarvis, Ben and Lydia seemed like such easy-going, gentle, hippy types. Would they like to record an album?

From that moment the dream began to crumble, appearing like a tiny crack on a car windscreen and slowly spreading until the whole thing fell apart. It started when I got them a slot at a free festival in Devon. About an hour before they were due on stage Tiffany refused to come out of her tent, apparently stricken with nerves, in floods of tears and (justifiably) upset about an indiscreet comment I had let slip about her family. A couple of months later I arranged for the band to come up for their first ever gig in London. It was on a boat on the River Thames, which looked out onto the Houses of Parliament.

They arrived, looked around, and said, 'It's not very large, is it?'

'What do you want, Wembley?'

Then the time came to make the album. We decided to record it in the garden of the cottage at Mabe with a friend of ours called Michael Tyack, an early-music enthusiast who fronts a psychedelic-medieval rock band called Circulus. Michael was so stoned that he kept forgetting to press the record button at the right time, and on the rare occasions he did manage to capture something he usually deleted it sooner or later. Somehow – and I'm really not sure how – the whole thing got finished, and perhaps even more incredibly it sounded great. I put the album out and it was warmly received. It sold a decent amount of copies and got good reviews. Then the band split up.

There had been all kinds of simmering tensions between the two couples for months, but things reached a head when one of the girls took a well-aimed right hook at the other girl's boyfriend, sending him crashing into the drum kit about ten minutes before the band were due to begin their triumphant homecoming concert in Penryn. At that point, it was agreed, Thistletown had better call it a day.

The short history of Thistletown is the history of Cornwall, in which dogged resistance clashes with good intentions and creativity to thwart wider ambitions of making it in the world. The two couples in the band self-sabotaged their career: to let it continue and succeed would mean bringing an end to the comfortable if frugal life they had built for themselves in a remote corner of Britain, and none of them wanted that. Cornwall is filled with people that have gone in search of isolation as well as artistic inspiration, to create their own world and to lose themselves. These are people who for the most part have rejected the standardisation of civilisation.

There's something about Cornwall that welcomes, even encourages, eccentricity. The Cornish are proud of local saints like St Gennys who, with typical West Country resilience, walked around holding his head in his hands after being decapitated by heathens. St Keyne helped deal with the ever-present problem of adders by turning them into stones. Hermits are heroic rather than pitiful figures in Cornwall: St Roche cured several people of the plague before catching it himself and withdrawing into a wood so as not to infect others, where a kind dog brought him a loaf of bread every day.

Sir James Tillie, who lived in St Mellion near the River Tamar, built a tower called Mount Ararat that, following the instructions in his will, was his place of burial after his death in 1712. He was to be dressed in his best clothes and hat, strapped to a chair and placed near to all of his books and papers because he was planning to rise again two years after his death and return to his castle. His executors duly returned to Mount Ararat at the appointed time, but a skeleton was all that remained of the hopeful lord.

Christianity can only ever sit alongside the old religions and superstitions rather than stamp them out of existence; the isolation and unchanging landscape means the ancient is always present. If you pass the Men-an-Tol near Lanyon, a standing stone with a large hole in its centre, climb through the hole nine times with your back facing the sun and you should be able to ward off disease. Milk turns sour not because it has been left in the warm but because piskies, a troublesome breed of household fairy, have been meddling with it again. Don't ever mention rabbits or hares on a fishing boat – it will ensure no fish will be caught. In Padstow on May Day the baiting of the 'Obby'Oss drives winter out. A giant called Cormoran built St Michael's Mount, the famous castle on a jutting outcrop turned into an island by high tides. The Cornish claim Arthur, the most mythologised of all British folk heroes, born in the castle of Tintagel and killed at Slaughter Bridge near Camelford, as their own. As late as the seventeenth century they were still waiting for his second coming. Perhaps it's the constant rain, the mild winters or the early blooming of primroses and daffodils, but something about Cornwall inspires the fantastical.

Cornwall has been a bohemian destination since the late nineteenth century. That's when a group of painters called the Newlyn School relocated there to make use of the brilliant light (a product of having a thin strip of land surrounded by ocean) and to take inspiration from the county's vitality and exoticism. The St Ives School, a generation of artists that included Barbara Hepworth and Ben Nicholson, followed in the 1930s. The traditional Cornish industries are tin and copper mining and fishing, physically demanding jobs that make few people rich, and this has shaped a place far less welcoming and cosy than the dingle-dell valleys and farms of neighbouring Devon. The mining died out in the seventies while tourism picked up, leaving a two-tiered society of desperately poor towns in inland Cornwall and a handful of increasingly wealthy holiday towns and villages by the sea – one on the north coast, Rock, even became the favoured destination for partying Royals and their privileged chums.

The bohemian tradition developed throughout the twentieth century, giving Cornwall a unique artistic landscape. Alongside the generations of visual artists flocking to St Ives, Land's End and the Lizard Peninsula, musicians of a freewheeling temperament made Cornwall a busking destination from the fifties onwards. The pioneers were guitarists like Wizz Jones, Donovan and Clive Palmer, displaced urbanites who loved folk and blues, were horrified at the prospect of getting jobs, and attracted by the county's mild weather conditions and less than sophisticated adoption of capitalism. Add to this the fact that Cornwall's untameable landscape of palm trees and wind-ravaged moors are still awash with the mysteries of the old religions and you have a fertile breeding ground for a special kind of musical endeavour. It's not surprising that raves – those hastily organised, ritualistic parties in which people take ecstasy, dance around, and say that they love each other – were hugely popular in Cornwall in the early nineties. At the time it was NJ's father's unfortunate job, as environment officer of Carrick County Council, to close down raves held in remote fields – whether his daughter was at them or not.

It may sound fanciful, but there is some strange Celtic mystical quality to Cornwall. No wonder the Cornwall-dwelling novelist Daphne Du Maurier felt inspired to write *The House on the Strand*, in which a dissatisfied Londoner escapes to Cornwall for a holiday to take an LSD-like drug that propels him into the fourteenth century, following a steward of the Lord Of Tywardreath and discovering murder, adultery and the encroaching horror of the plague in the very village he is staying at. Somewhere between the barren, dirt-poor towns of the interior and the clotted cream and rosy cheeks fantasy of the coastal towns there exists an Arthurian Eden. The Roseland Peninsula is a densely wooded stretch of land accessible by the King Harry Ferry, which is pulled along by foot-thick chains across a creek. There is a miniature castle on the peninsula where empty, circular rooms have slits in the walls that look out onto the misty valley below – it was built in the reign of Henry VII in preparation for French invaders who never arrived. Further towards the tip of Cornwall are villages like Porthcurno and Crean, accessible only by tiny, twisting single-lane roads barricaded by high hedgerows and apparently oblivious to whatever changes might be going on any further than five miles up the road. Outside the village of Mylor, where NJ's parents live, there are old woods alive with fecundity, rotting fungus-filled trunks and moist moss turning the forest floor into a seething mass of organic activity. Footpaths cut through fields where signs casually announce the presence of randy bulls. Along the creek Mylor is built on, oversized gunnera plants look like they should have a few fairies – an outdoor variant on piskies, perhaps – hopping about on them.

It is in the woods of Mylor that a unique, if little-known, development in British music took root. In the early seventies, living in a caravan on so little money that they subsisted for a week on a packet of digestive biscuits between them, the three members of the mostly unheard, unheralded folk-rock band Cob fashioned their ancient, entwined-with-nature vision of the world. Led by the defiantly singular Clive Palmer (the name stands for Clive's Original Band), Cob managed to release two albums on major labels, CBS and Polydor's short-lived Folk Mill, respectively, *Spirit Of Love* and *Moyshe McStiff And The Tartan Lancers Of The Sacred Heart*. Both sold no more than a few hundred copies. Perhaps it's unsurprising. They sound nothing like anything that came before or has been made since.

Cob's singer Mick Bennett has a voice that's strong but mournful, like a knight returning from a battle that has been lost. The music itself is like an etching by Durer or a painting by Brueghel: full of detail, but barren too, like a frozen field or an orchard filled with trees shorn of their leaves and beginning to bud. The songs have a medieval quality, but this isn't medieval music. Mostly acoustic instruments – congas, banjos, guitars, balalaikas – create a mood that's poignant. Cob's two albums are from the edge of British culture, yet they couldn't have come from anywhere but here.

I first heard about Cob through the guitarist Bert Jansch, a kind and likable if rather surly man who doesn't have much good to say about most music by most people, but he couldn't praise this obscure band highly enough. 'Clive's got some sort of ancient quality about him,' he said as a song about the eternity of the seasons called 'Chain Of Love' lilted out of his stereo. 'It really does seem like he belongs in another century.'

Moyshe McStiff, of which 'Chain Of Love' is a part, sounds like Cornwall. It isn't traditional, although there are hints of Breton and Celtic influences, but it creates an impression of the place. It has the same atmosphere and timelessness as England's savage western peninsula. The words are about the birds singing, and the winter chill, and about how 'autumn comes so slowly you don't know that it is here'. One song is about a miserable encounter with a prostitute, another is about the Lion of Judah, and yet somehow they are all reminiscent of this outpost of Britain that feels like another world.

Clive Palmer, born in North London, was a banjo player whose childhood polio had left him with a severe limp, a disjointed education and a mistrust of authority. A proto-beatnik who left school at fifteen with the conviction that he would do what he could to avoid conventional employment, Clive hitchhiked to Edinburgh and hooked up with the city's burgeoning underground scene that revolved around the reasonably innocent pursuits of smoking dope and writing poetry – the heroin-ravaged nihilism depicted by Irvine Welsh in *Trainspotting* was still another two decades away. Clive started a folk club, formed a group (The Incredible String Band) and lived a life free from such bourgeois concerns as making money or looking out for one's health. Bert Jansch recalled attempting to go skiing with Clive in the Scottish Highlands: Bert's decrepit Morris Minor broke down, forcing the two of them to survive in the snow on nothing but hashish for three days until being rescued by an unimpressed crofter.

In his sixties memoir *White Bicycles*, the American producer, impresario and former manager of The Incredible String Band Joe Boyd describes Clive as 'a true rebel. He rejected any attempts by me to turn the band into a commercial entity.' Clive left after the first album, deciding he would rather travel to Afghanistan than become famous. He told the rest of the band that they could do what they liked with the songs he had written; he couldn't be bothered to seek any financial or creative return for them.

When Clive returned to England he headed to Cornwall, where he hooked up with a fellow displaced Londoner called Mick Bennett and a local musician called John Bidwell. He also met a somewhat legendary Cornish family called the Val Bakers. The patriarch, Denys Val Baker, was a writer, poet, pacifist, early vegetarian and freethinker with a sympathy for the recent wave of incomers searching for some kind of elemental freedom in Cornwall, who he frequently allowed to live rent-free in the chalets at the

47

bottom of the garden of his house in Crean, at the far western end of Cornwall known as West Penwith. His widow and one of his daughters still live there. Clive formed a band called The Temple Creatures with fifteen-year-old Demelza Val Baker, a very good conga player; when they split he formed Cob and enlisted the even younger Genevieve Val Baker, who could only just about play the congas but did offer the valuable attribute of being extremely pretty.

Once they started recording it looked like the band might get somewhere. They landed a support slot with the then-huge jazz-folk-medieval fusion band Pentangle, and the singer Ralph McTell, a star after having a huge hit with the busker's favourite 'The Streets Of London', produced the albums. But they went nowhere.

Perhaps Clive Palmer's character is such that success in the conventional sense could never happen. I very much wanted to meet him. Bert Jansch thought that he was living in Brittany, but Thistletown's Ben remembered meeting him in a pub in Falmouth not so long ago, extremely drunk and on the verge of being chucked out. Bert suggested I try Martin Val Baker, son of the late Denys and brother to Demelza and Genevieve, who had been putting on concerts in Cornwall for decades and knew every artistically inclined person in the county. It turned out that Clive was indeed back, living in St Ives and even playing the occasional gig. Martin suggested I come and meet him in the gallery he ran on the high street, and we would see if we could get hold of Clive while I was there.

Since the demise of Thistletown Lydia and Ben had returned to a world of day jobs and part-time degree courses. Jarvis and Tiffany, however, were increasingly dedicating themselves to music, and I felt that what they were doing with their new, two-person group The Rosemarie Band might well capture something of the spirit of the land. They were utilising the piping melodies of the flute and the

eternal unwavering om of the harmonium and using elec-
tronics to loop them into cyclical patterns, adding other
instruments as they went to build up washes of sound. Some
songs borrowed the words and melodies of traditional tunes
and others were meandering, repeated ideas without any
beginning or end. This was their joy, and not their liveli-
hood. Both worked for an opera-loving farmer in the
daytime, Jarvis making cheese and Tiffany helping out
wherever she was needed. The music they made was like the
lifestyles of so many people in Cornwall: in the moment and
rarely working towards any real goal.

───────────◆─◆───────────

As the Astra rolled up NJ's parents' drive in Mylor after the
six-hour drive from Oxford the children hopped out from
the garden with excitement and innocent joy. NJ's mother
Gill, as jolly and domestic as NJ is willowy and distant, took
my luggage – the Asda bag, with the Zoom eight-track in it
– out of the car. After commanding me to sit down and let
her make a cup of tea, she mentioned that she had joined a
women's choir.

'Actually, men are welcome to join,' she said, bustling
from kitchen to dining room. 'But none of them seem to
want to. And young people just aren't interested, which is a
shame because singing together is a lovely thing to do. We
sing all kinds of songs – hymns, show tunes, music hall . . .
it's great fun.'

'Could I make a recording of you?'

'Good gracious, no!'

The following morning I took the children and the
dog out for a walk up a hill on the outskirts of Mylor that
passed a field with two horses in it. As Otto and Pearl

climbed to the top of a gate and tried to make the horses eat sods of earth I wondered where exactly the Cob caravan had been. Mylor is a wealthy place now. The houses along the creek conform to the image of the country cottage the average city-dweller has: roses around the door, thick uneven walls painted white, a thatched roof if you're lucky, and an inbred labrador panting with inane good humour by the garden gate. In the early seventies it was just another deprived Cornish hamlet. The harsh reality of the caravan life of Clive Palmer and his gang was not so unusual, nor was the closeness with which they lived to the land.

A few hours later I drove down to St Ives, still an artistic stronghold in Cornwall even if it is overrun with holidaymakers in St George's cross T-shirts. The Rainy Day Gallery is on the cobbles of Castle Jew Street, which cuts through the centre of the town, and on most days Martin Val Baker can be found behind the counter there, frequently talking to the local artists who are darting in to see if anyone has bought one of their paintings, and less frequently selling one to a member of the public. He has the standard Cornish greeting of 'right' for everyone who comes in or leaves the gallery. He has also been the point of reference for visiting musicians since being a teenager in the early sixties. In 1964 the singer Donovan was filmed loafing about in Cornwall with a group of proto-hippies for a documentary on the beatnik phenomenon. Martin Val Baker is, as he will tell anyone that asks, 'the thin one at the back'.

After reminiscing on the impact of meeting the first guitar-playing buskers that came to Cornwall back then, Martin did his best to describe Cornish music. 'Going up the Celtic line would be wrong,' he said after I suggested there must be a lot of traditional music around. 'What defined Cornish music was the folk boom in the sixties when you had a lot of creative musicians like Wizz Jones and Michael Chapman coming down to play here, sleeping on people's floors and making just enough to get them to the next place. I ran the Mast Club at St Ives, a Cornish singer called Brenda Wootton ran the Pipers Folk Club, and you had a lot of fifteen-year-old local guitarists coming along to watch the fingers of all the great players. That created a terrific bank of people producing stuff, and by the seventies they had learned to play their instruments. None of this was significant on a national scale but it was very exciting.'

Martin told me about some of the more noteworthy characters who have captured Cornwall in one way or another. There was a singer called Chrissy Quayle whose father billed her as The Mermaid Of Zennor, from the Cornish fairy tale of a mermaid who falls in love with a human after hearing him sing in the local church (he ends up joining her in the sea). There was a songwriter called Mike Silver who was once slated for big things but messed it all up after turning down an American tour with Elton John because he thought Elton was after his body. And then there was the cautionary case of Ella Knight, a singer who ran a now-legendary venue called The Folk Cottage in Mitchell, near Newquay and the victim of a freak morris-dancing accident. One of the sticks went out of control and bashed her on the head.

Martin staged gigs by all the (relatively) big names of the British folk revival of the sixties and seventies, Anne Briggs, Steeleye Span, Bert Jansch and Fairport Convention among them. But his greatest admiration went out for Clive Palmer. 'He's ahead of his time, really,' said Martin in a gentle, rolling burr. 'Somebody should give Clive a few thousand pounds and just let him get on with it because he's the kind of person that could still do something amazing given the chance.' Did Martin know where I could find Clive? 'He lives about five minutes from here. I'll give you his number.'

Martin also suggested that I speak to Murray and Zoe Young, a couple of about my age (mid or, if you're being pedantic, late thirties) who put on a folk club called

Patchwork and were artists in their own right: Murray was a poet who had notoriously received a million-pound advance from EMI for writing poetic commentaries on decadent *fin de siècle* English life with titles like 'Everybody's On Cocaine', while Zoe had a number-one hit back in the early nineties with a hand-waving anthem called 'Sunshine On A Rainy Day', which was played at a lot of outdoor raves as the sun rose at five or six in the morning and everyone was coming down from whatever they had taken and in need of a bit of hope for the future. They had escaped London for rural family life ten years previously, first settling in Sussex, then Ibiza, and finally in St Ives. And perhaps unsurprisingly, given the narrow gene pool of musical creativity in Cornwall, they were friends with the members of Thistletown.

There was no answer from Clive Palmer's number. I called Murray and it turned out he and Zoe were a couple of streets away, packing up as they left St Ives for a house in West Penwith not far from the Val Baker stronghold. A few minutes later I met a good-looking couple in the process of strapping the final box of books onto the roof of their mud-splattered Land Rover. We went for a coffee and they told me about the first, disastrous time they put on their folk night. 'We underestimated how popular a local band called Men-An-Tol were,' said Murray. 'It had got late and all the stewards wanted to go home and close the place, and Men-An-Tol ended up only playing for twenty minutes. The crowd, which for the most part was made up of bearded hippy types, went mad. It was a folk riot.'

Zoe talked of how strong busking was in Cornwall. 'There's a tradition of people turning up for a couple of months in a year and then wandering off somewhere,' she said. 'There's a banjo player who does the whole *Deliverance* thing of super-fast playing every summer. It becomes part of the fabric of the society down here. Everyone gets to know these buskers and becomes fond of them.'

'There's a giant with a ukulele who appears in St Ives every now and then,' added Murray. 'But more than anything, the land itself is inspiring. There is the savagery and nobility of being stuck on a rocky peninsula with a huge weather system beating away, and at the same time you have woodland creeks and two very different seas surrounding you. It's unique.'

'Everyone has their own expression of the life down here,' said Zoe, casually. 'If you go out walking you start hearing melodies in the way the birds are singing, while the sea will create a totally different mood. It's affecting you constantly whether you acknowledge it or not.'

'Cornwall has a hard edge,' said Murray. 'You're talking about people that have survived on very little for thousands of years. But Donovan came down in the early sixties and found a ready supply of hipsters whose free-thinking parents came to places like Newlyn and St Ives in the thirties and forties, and then you have a combination of daffodil pickers, musicians and artists to add to it all. That blend of influences is what it's all about – the hardness of the landscape, the people that have always survived here, and the incomers with their bohemian attitudes creating the biggest artistic community outside of London. You certainly don't feel that this is a backward place. There are all kinds of people hiding out down here doing interesting things.'

Murray was trying to reclaim the folk tradition in his poetry. 'I've been writing a bunch of songs about modern folk practices, and if you like I'll sing one for you tomorrow down at our new place,' he offered. 'It's my attempt to show how the old traditions and styles can adapt for the modern age.'

In the meantime there was the elusive Clive Palmer to track down, and somehow convince that it was a good idea to let a total stranger come to his house to talk about the Cornish musical landscape. I called again, and this time he answered. I offered a brief and ultra-polite précis of my mission and asked if we could meet over the next couple of days. 'Yeah, whatever you like,' came back the rough cockney reply. 'Come round now if you like.'

Five minutes later (St Ives isn't very big) I was in the sparse, tiny front room of a nondescript house around the back of a row of shops at the top of a hill in the centre of town. The walls were bare, the television was on, and a yellow-haired man with large black-rimmed glasses and wide red braces was sitting next to a pretty middle-aged woman who was entirely motionless and wore an enigmatic half-smile.

The house looked like a squat. An offcut of carpet didn't quite cover bare floorboards, and the sofa Clive and the woman (who I later found out is Clive's wife, Gina) sat on looked like it had been pulled out of a skip. Here was a home occupied by people who didn't lose too much sleep over décor.

'Sit yourself down, then,' said Clive in a booming voice, and I found myself strangely terrified. I was with a man in his mid-sixties, pretty much unknown to the world at large, not rich, welcoming me into his home, and I was star-struck. I couldn't believe I was sitting in the same room as him. It was like meeting William Burroughs or Richard Brautigan.

Over the last few years of playing *Moyshe McStiff* so constantly I had built up an arsenal of questions I wanted to ask Clive: what inspired the songs, what was his lifestyle like at the time, who was going out with that foxy girl in the photograph on the back cover (she was Genevieve Val Baker)? Now I couldn't think of anything to say. Clive and Gina just sat there, smoking rolled-up cigarettes. 'Put the kettle on, would you, love?' said Clive, eventually. Gina glided upwards in silent grace and reappeared with three cups of tea a few minutes later. The strong brew had a restorative effect. My power of speech returned. I asked Clive how Cornwall shaped those two albums he made almost forty years ago.

'There was an underlying influence,' he said, still staring at the television. 'I first came to Cornwall in 1958, just busking, and I've been coming back and forth ever since. We were nomadic then, to an extent. I went up to Scotland and formed The Incredible String Band and then went off to India and Afghanistan and when I came back there was no question of being in the band again. So then the Cob thing started in Cornwall.'

I asked Clive how he came up with the unique sound of the band, of the things that inspired songs like 'Bright Eyed One' and 'Chain Of Love'.

'We didn't have any idea for the music. We just started playing together and coming up with ideas,' he replied. 'We were quite high on creativity. At that age it comes easily – all of my songs are written in a rush. I get images. Not so long ago Gina was playing a tune on the piano and for some reason I remembered being in Paris and the words for a song called "Paris" came out in one go.'

Clive didn't appear to care in the slightest that the albums were total commercial failures. 'The thing is, the only reason the albums got made was because the labels they were on were sloshing money around and giving all these musicians the chance to produce an album by a band they liked, so they approached Ralph McTell and he suggested us. I think the label thought the albums might sell because of the String Band connection. They didn't, but they were appreciated. People have liked those records.'

Gina stared at me in curious, inscrutable silence.

'I don't listen to music very much. Never have done,' continued Clive, looking like a wizened mystic enveloped in a cloud of cigarette smoke. 'My brother and mother were musical and I was encouraged from an early age to sing and play banjo, but I hardly ever listen to other bands because I like to make the music that I hear in my own head. Bits and pieces wander in from what I've heard and it all gets mixed up, like scraps of food that go together to form a stew. I've never based myself on anything. I think that's a big mistake. If you try to make a sound you think will be successful you're generally behind the times. It's far more useful to be yourself.'

Some might argue that Clive was behind the times – by about 500 years. There is something about Cob that sounds like it belongs to an age when the enclosure system was still in practice and crumhorns were all the rage. He would have done well as the time-travelling hero of *The House On The Strand*. But with Clive that's an impression more than a style. This strange, unique man didn't study court music, or traditional folk, or anything else as far as I could work out. He was off on his own. I asked him why he moved to Cornwall.

'I liked its smallness,' he replied. 'You're never more than four miles away from something or someone. Things grow that don't grow anywhere else, wild flowers coming out of walls and so on, and the land is so narrow that you get the famous double light from the two seas that all the painters like. It gets pretty Stone Age round here. In the winter you go back to a real desolation. It's wild.'

I couldn't help it. I had to blurt out in an uncool way about how much I loved those albums.

'They're *all right*,' said Clive with a Steptoe-like snarl. 'The truth is, it's for other people to decide whether they like them or not. But I'm very good at waiting. People say you've got to push yourself, but if there are opportunities for you they'll come sooner or later. I've hardly played for the last five years. I don't miss it at all. I'm not a one-track person – I come from a family of French-polishers and I like making things as much as music. I can take it or leave it but when I feel like doing it, great. It's the best way, the waiting game. Just wait until people want you to do something. I remember watching a guy on telly, and the idea was to produce a highly desirable, trendy restaurant. He hid the place away in the back streets, made it look really exclusive, and it was only open at certain times. It was packed out. It's best not to push yourself too hard; it's better to let people come across you. Look at Bert [Jansch]. Nobody was interested in what he was up to until recently. But then, Bert is very insular and he's not a team person. He's a bit of a recluse. He's very talented, although I'm not a great fan of his music because I don't understand it.'

'I love it,' said Gina. It was the first time she had said anything all afternoon. She would only say two more words in the hours I spent with her.

Clive said he liked bagpipe music, recalling the time he went into Heligan Woods in west Cornwall and chopped down a tree to make a set of bagpipes. 'The idea with what I do is to be elemental,' he said, talking in a way that suggested he was announcing everything to a large audience. 'It's hard to explain. I make things that look or sound old when they're in fact new, even though I'm creating whatever happens to be on my mind at the time. I mean the songs are about nothing in particular. I did a ballad called "The Skranky Black Farmer" that has an umpah, umpah thing going on in it. It's based on a traditional tune but it's totally ridiculous. Sorry, but that's got to be worth a fortune.'

The seventeenth-century sewing box that had just appeared on *Antiques Roadshow* had grabbed Clive's attention. He stared at the television, enraptured. 'You see, I write a song using these old elements . . . look at that. It's beautiful. Is that embroidery on it? When you think that it's survived for so long . . .'

Gina disappeared into the kitchen and came back with three more cups of tea. She and Clive appeared to chain-smoke rolled-up cigarettes, but the strange thing was that I never saw them rolling one. Perhaps they spent an hour each morning making enough to get them through the day.

'Somebody would recite a story in the Bronze Age and before you know it someone else would be playing a harp alongside the story, and as people settled down and stopped killing each other quite as much they became more sophisticated. If you look at old Brueghels you will see crowds of people dancing outdoors. Later on they started dancing indoors. Shepherds built bagpipes because they had to spend a lot of time hanging around on hills and they got bored. Everything evolves to meet the situation.'

Clive jumped backwards and forwards in his conversation regardless of anything I said, hopping from anecdote to advice to general ramblings about Cornwall. The silent Gina stared at me as her husband held forth. 'There is something primeval about Cornwall,' he said, looking like a cloud of smoke that had developed the ability to talk. 'You feel it when you go out onto those cliffs, and the great thing is that in winter you can have it to yourself. I mean you need to avoid the queues. I've never been part of the normal thing. I think life is a spiritual journey and we haven't lost that sixties kick of looking for nirvana. The modern world is so materialistic, especially the people that come here for their holidays. Look at all these great big cars that everyone's got now that we really can't afford to keep on running. We're going through a crisis. When you first came to Cornwall the only people you found were artists that bought up old cottages nobody wanted to live in. Now the prices have gone through the roof. I recommend West Penwith. That's still wild.'

West Penwith is where Murray and Zoe's new house was, where I would be visiting the next day. 'I'm an old beatnik, really,' Clive continued. 'Me and my friends are people who are quite happy sleeping on a floor, or in a hedge, or wherever. People say to me, "Oh, you paid too much for that," and I say, "Coffins don't have pockets." As I get older I get even happier. The last year and a half I've been in and out of hospital, but that's been a good experience too. I certainly never get bored. I'm very lazy, though. My advice to people is to be incredibly lazy and then get going when you've got something to get going about. The only time I practise is just before the gigs.'

This was Clive and Gina's life: drinking tea in the daytime and beer in the evening, smoking cigarettes, going for walks along the beaches and moors, watching television, making things and occasionally playing music. They seemed content. Clive claimed that he was thinking of getting Cob back together. John Bidwell was now a teacher in Thailand, which made his plan slightly complicated, but he was sure there would be a way round this. He had come up to London not so long ago to play a solo concert, but he wasn't a fan of the place and avoided it as much as possible.

'Oh, I always hated it, even though I was born in Edmonton,' he confirmed. 'I just need more space. I'm a restless soul. We went for a walk this morning and the sea is right there . . . marvellous.'

Clive Palmer may well have been the ultimate embodiment of the spirit I felt could be Britain's saving grace: spontaneity, individuality and doing things for their own sake. 'I've got no desire for money or fame – none whatsoever,' he said. 'Fame is highly overrated and I think money is too. At the moment I've got it made. From the moment I get up in the morning I can do exactly what I like. Exactly. I've always been like that, which is why life hasn't always been easy for me. I'm very rebellious, even at my age. I'm an anarchist deep down. I'd like to see the whole thing ripped up.'

This was going to the heart of my conviction that we were on the wave of a new age of localised creativity and musical activity. There was something about the strange rituals played out at the night NJ and I spent at Cecil Sharp House that felt timeless, even relevant, and it did seem that we were coming to the end of an age in which status came through acquisition of product. Perhaps people really were beginning to involve themselves more in the immediate world around them, rather than the one that was being sold to them. Out of ecological and economic necessity we would see a return to an age of productivity, creativity and self-sufficiency. We would reach an understanding that everything we need is right there in front of us. Or perhaps this was hopelessly wishful thinking. I presented my theory to Clive.

'But most people aren't creative,' he said. 'They can't entertain themselves or live on that level of consciousness. They like having famous people to queue up for.'

The sound of Cob must have been a product of this wayward soul letting whatever is inside him come out in an unfettered way, and a product also of a group of people making whatever music came out of their being together. It was a part of Cornish life that had always been there, but which I had never been privy to in the fifteen years NJ and I had been coming down to see her family. All of these people – the Val Bakers, Clive Palmer, Thistletown, Murray and Zoe Young, the Mermaid Of Zennor, even the poor unfortunate morris-dancing enthusiast Ella Knight – were hidden behind the bushes and briars, taking inspiration from the land and becoming artists in a natural, unorganised way. I wondered where Gina fitted in to all of this. Just before I left I asked her if she was from Cornwall.

'I'm American,' she replied.

It turned out that Gina was once a Val Baker. She was married to Denys Val Baker's son Stephen until she met Clive and fell in love with him.

───────── ◆ ─────────

The following day I drove into the depths of West Penwith to meet Zoe and Murray at their new home. It was surrounded by fifty acres of land, all of it wooded, unfarmed. Getting there involved going down ever-smaller roads and lanes, and inevitably I got lost – a confusion between Polruan and Polperro. At the point at which a loss of bearings had been confirmed I went into a village shop to ask for directions. A bell tinkled as I pushed the door open and walked into a dark, dusty space filled with tins that looked like they were hoping to make it to preservation status. There was nobody else in there. There was a rustling from another room, the creak of a door, and the appearance of a cadaverous figure with sandy-white hair and eyes in permanent state of stare. He gave me the kind of look you might expect to get from someone who has just walked out of his or her bathroom naked to be confronted by a total stranger. Eventually he discovered the power to say: 'Yes?'

I grabbed a packet of pre-decimalisation crisps and slapped them on the counter. 'I'll have these,' I said, ' and can you tell me the way to Porthcurno?'

'Why do you want to go there?' said the man, in a tone that suggested to do so would be unwise. I told him who I was meeting.

'They do not live here,' he said. Then he gave me my change and disappeared into the back room. Oddly, he had a German accent.

I found Murray – in a muddy lay-by, off a narrow road that coursed up a hill leading to a wood. His folk song was about dogging, the seemingly unappealing practice where a bunch of people meet in a field or a car park in the dead of night and have sex in their cars while others look on. The lay-by seemed an appropriate place to record this tale of anonymous transgression, which was couched in the language and sung in the style of an old ballad, and the boot of my disgracefully filthy Astra an appropriate surface to place the Zoom to record it on. I put on the headphones, pressed record, and listened as Murray affected a West

Country accent and listed the various places he had engaged in this contemporary approach to voyeurism before concluding each verse with the refrain: 'And a-doggin' I will go'.

Murray stood on the narrow patch of gravel, which backed on to a field full of cows, and sang heartily with his head raised. No cars went past as we recorded, actually a shame since that would have made for relevant background noise, but a family of four tramped past in Wellington boots, engaging that brilliantly British trait of being entirely nonplussed at the sight of something strange happening – in this case a tall, curly-haired man singing the praises of illicit goings-on in a deserted lay-by while another tall, curly-haired man stands on, wearing large headphones.

'Dogging is a modern folk activity,' explained Murray, leaning on the roof of the Astra, exhausted by his performance. 'It's anonymous and rather seedy and anyone can join in.'

We drove through a field with thick ditches of mud in Murray's Land Rover to get to a pond recently built by a neighbour. The man was standing by the pond with Zoe, surveying his handiwork as Murray and Zoe's children splashed about on the muddy banks.

The man announced that he had enlisted the help of a labourer to build the pond, and that he had paid him with two boxes of pornography. 'Had to get rid of it anyway,' he said dismissively. 'Wife won't even have VHS in the house.'

'Was he a local man?' I asked of his presumably now-sated helper.

'Waren't local man,' he said, giving me a sideways look. You caren't pay local man in porn. He was from St Levan.'

St Levan is a few miles up the road.

That evening I made it down to the cottage in Mabe where Thistletown had recorded their album, and where

Jarvis and Tiffany spent their evenings when they weren't on the boat. Jarvis's dad had just finished crafting some chandeliers with enormous phalluses sticking out of them in all directions. He was hoping to sell them to a Parisian nightclub. We set up in the front room of the little cottage, where tiny quarter-panes look out onto the sculpture-filled garden and uneven white walls enclose a barely furnished space. I put the Zoom in the middle of the room, somewhere between Tiffany's flute and Jarvis's drum kit. What followed had nothing to do with Cornwall in any obvious way – electronic loops, jazz-inflected flute runs and a pounding 4-4 beat are quite hard to connect with Celtic traditions – but it sounded like Cornwall nonetheless. The track's name – 'Mabe Cloud' – betrayed its inspiration. There was lightness to the music, and an ambling sense of something without beginning or end.

This time the whole recording worked, and it actually sounded quite good. There was a real possibility that you could make portraits of places, and people, on a piece of digital equipment, just as Cecil Sharp did a hundred years earlier through notating songs. The music that Jarvis and Tiffany made said something of their contemporary reality, in which music and information from anywhere in the world were available to them through the Internet but also in which walking out of the front door of the cottage in Mabe or off the gangplank of their boat in Penryn meant crunching acorn shells underfoot and walking in the shades of hawthorn bushes and oak trees.

We sat outside the cottage on a low stone wall, drinking wine and talking about the little pockets of grass-roots activity that would be worth seeking out elsewhere in Britain. 'You should speak to the people that run a label called Singing Knives in Sheffield,' said Tiffany. 'They're doing similar things to us – seeing how they can take folk music and throw it into the future. Sheffield seems like an interesting place. Why do all those electronic bands come out of this tough northern city?'

'What about old English court music? "Greensleeves" and so on?' asked the softly spoken Jarvis, whose long hair and thin beard was illuminated by an orange sun sinking into a silhouette of trees behind us. 'Michael would be a good person to talk to about that kind of thing. He's like a medieval troubadour that has wandered into the twenty-first century by mistake.'

Michael Tyack had recorded Thistletown's album in this very cottage and then wiped it out after pressing the wrong button on a machine not so dissimilar from my own Zoom. Despite appearances – his fondness for tights, doublets and little pointed shoes that curled up at the toes might have held him back in a lifelong quest to be taken seriously – Michael was a diligent student of early music. One of his best friends was a man called Chris Goodwin, who held the esteemed position of Secretary of The Lute Society of Great Britain. The following evening in London they were staging what might prove to be a niche-interest event in some old vaults under London Bridge railway station: an early-music nightclub. It was called Early Nights. Michael and Chris would be ideal subjects for field recordings representing the English Renaissance tradition, but first I needed to visit a farm in Somerset, where a conductor called Charles Hazlewood was on a one-man mission to change people's perceptions of English classical music. And on the drive up from Cornwall, a chance encounter while visiting my brother in Devon gave me hope in the future of the British folk tradition.

Chapter Four

Devon, Somerset and The English Air

A FEW YEARS AGO MY BROTHER TOM AND HIS WIFE Victoria moved to an old farmhouse in North Devon. After a shaky start – Tom wrote a newspaper article about the quaintly irritating ways of country folk, enraging his neighbours so much they just stopped short of chasing him across the moor with burning torches – he has increasingly involved himself in the community, most notably helping set up a local festival that was due to start the day after I made the recording of Jarvis and Tiffany in the cottage at Mabe. NJ was going to stay down in Cornwall with her parents and our children for a few more days, so I decided to spend a night or two with my brother and see if the festival threw up any possibilities for field recordings.

The Astra wheezed into Lynton and Lynmouth, pretty coastal towns connected by a cliffside railway, surrounded by forest, and awash with shops selling fish and chips and rock. I had set out from my brother's house in a hamlet called Martinhoe, locally known to be haunted by the ghost of a cruel landowner called Sir Robert Chichester, through an equally phantasmagorical landscape of twisted rocky hills called the Valley of the Rocks. The rocks were once a band of (presumably enormous) beggars, led by a man called Ragged Dick. They found themselves exposed in the valley one cold night, so they started to dance to keep warm. The devil duly turned them to stone, as it was a Sunday and they should have been resting.

By the time I arrived near the main stage, which was on a flat patch of land next to the sea, Keith Allen was leading a group of fitfully employed fellow actors through a spirited if essentially terrible rendition of 'Anarchy In The UK' by The Sex Pistols. It was interesting to watch the diverse crowd – old ladies in deck chairs, British families on holiday, young farm labourers drinking cider – enter into the spirit of the thing and start spitting at each other. I did my best to record it, but the theatrical punk energy was too much for the little Zoom and Keith Allen's singing inspired it to protest with a rush of feedback.

'Big shout going out to a young lady called Megan,' said Keith Allen as 'Anarchy In The UK' came to a bellowing end. 'She's just won first prize for long-distance running in the Devon County Finals – well done, Megan.'

On a cliff above this scene of chaos and cream teas was a small stone church that was playing host to the festival's quieter acts. I took the little railway up the cliff and found the church, passed through a porch with a handful of weather-beaten leaflets pinned to a notice board announcing choir sessions and cake competitions, and pushed its creaking oak door open to reveal a small crowd politely sitting through one earnest singer-songwriter type after another. I crouched down towards a front pew and placed the Zoom onto the stone floor. I wasn't hearing anything that really inspired or felt connected to this place we were in, although there was something warming about all of these people giving it a go anyway.

Then a tall, vigorous young man with big teeth, wire brush hair and the kind of open face you instantly warm to stood before the altar and sang a haunting, lilting tune without accompaniment called 'The Lakes Of Shallin'. It was captivating, and he sang it sparsely, without affectation, but with a certain projection of theatre. It had mystery. It was a ghost of a song, belonging to an age long past and yet still around us. The Zoom served me well: it caught the song perfectly.

I introduced myself to the man, who was wearing a faded black T-shirt, a very short pair of shorts and some plimsolls on the point of collapse, once he was back in a pew. His name was Sam Lee, he worked for Cecil Sharp House in London, and he had spent the last year searching for British singers who had kept the oral tradition of storytelling through song alive.

'Everyone kept telling me that there was no oral tradition any more,' said Sam, when we went outside the church and sat on a patch of grass that looked out onto the ocean below. 'The general belief is that the last of the traditional singers, the ones that sang songs learned from their parents or grandparents, died in the sixties and seventies. I felt that it couldn't be true, so I went off in search of them.'

The awakening of interest in traditional British music that began in the late 1950s and died out, for the most part, by the mid-seventies is usually termed the folk revival. Singers like Anne Briggs and Sandy Denny and guitarists like Martin Carthy and Bert Jansch made use of the volumes of songs put together by Francis Child, Cecil Sharp and Percy Grainger and adapted them for the times. These weren't people who had grown up with the songs; they had discovered them and wanted to bring them alive. At the same time the men and women that sang songs passed down to them through the ancestral line were getting old, and dying out; men like the Shropshire stone-waller Fred Jordan and the East Anglia farmer Sam Larner. Communities sing songs to tell stories, to mark events, to relay the news and to bring poetry to the most mundane aspects of daily life. In Britain the belief was that we had all but lost that tradition.

But Sam Lee had found a group where the old songs were not only still alive; they remained the primary form of communication. It was a secretive community, and one that had good reason to be wary of outsiders, but he had gained the trust of some of its number. Would I like to meet them?

I would love to, I told him, and a week later I did – in the twilight shade of a wood in East Sussex. But the next stop on my trip was a farm in Somerset, to get a better understanding of something I knew very little about: English classical music.

———◆———

Charles Hazlewood is a conductor and pianist who sidelines as a musical evangelist. Forever popping up across the BBC, he's the most learned person I know when it comes to the history of English music, but he's far less precious than you might expect from a man of his discipline. He admires great pop songs as much as he admires sophisticated symphonies and is willing to argue long into the night on the merits of both. Apparently he's something of a controversial figure in classical circles, although, as is often the case with well-brought-up people, it's hard to see how.

Charles lives with his wife and (at last count) four children in a large and chaotic white house in the wilds of Somerset, not far from Glastonbury Tor. After a night at my brother's house I drove up from Devon, passing stretching suburbs that dissolved into the curved branches of elms, the sturdy trunks of oaks and the dappled bark of birches. On small bridges and riverbanks I passed men (and it usually is men) fishing, the ultimate British occupation: meditative and purposeful with an illusion of practicality. A little lost, I stopped in the car park of that kind of train station rural England specialises in: one that hardly exists. There were platforms, and some sort of a waiting-room/ticket-booth area, but that was all. Outside was a line of taxis, their owners leaning against cars and drinking tea from Thermos flasks, sharing jokes in the midday sun. I wondered how much business they had. Charles had forgotten to give me an address and I couldn't get through to him, so I asked them if they knew where the Hazlewoods lived, thinking that, although unlikely, it was worth a try.

Such is the way with local knowledge in country life that half an hour later the taxi bumped its way up the muddy track that leads to the house with the Astra following it. Charles appeared, waving his arms: he was on the phone making final arrangements for a concert he was conducting that evening with the BBC Symphony Orchestra.

'Terribly sorry, mate,' he said in an ebullient, enthusiastic manner. 'I have to do everything on the phone these days because I don't have a computer. A couple of years ago I was in New York with an orchestra and I hadn't checked my emails for a couple of weeks. Finally I opened my laptop and there were something like four thousand unread messages. So I closed the laptop without reading any of them and haven't opened it up since.'

We had lunch. The house had the messy-tasteful look specific to the artistic, unconventional upper-middle classes, who I think believe that to clean up and put everything in its place and to worry about details like wallpaper or even walls themselves is to miss the point of life. We went to Charles's barn, where he records BBC radio shows that feature exciting and unusual combinations of musicians improvising together. It was cavernous and cold and contained little more than a grand piano and a couple of guitars. We went to his office, an old caravan sitting inside a barn, which was the most chaotic quarter of all: piles of sheet music and books covered the floor, records and CDs were stacked in towers in what looked like no order whatsoever; navigating your way through all of this to ensure none of it came crashing down around you required no small degree of agility.

Charles had been looking into the nature of British music for years, in particular its ability to take on board foreign elements with open arms. 'There's this misnomer that we as a nation are incapable of producing our own music,' he began, once he was safely seated in one of the caravan's two chairs. 'When I tell people that the four great pioneers of English music are Purcell, Haydn, Handel and Mendelssohn, they say, well there you are. Three of them are European. I interpret it as a very positive sign that we are able to take on these outside influences and offer them safe haven.'

The eighteenth-century illustrator William Hogarth derided the English tendency to celebrate other cultures while putting down its own, in one etching depicting crowds of people excited about an Italian opera while the works of Shakespeare and Dryden are turned into 'waste paper for shops'. Charles saw a love affair with foreign art as a sign of confidence, of vigour.

'Like so many people, Haydn came here to find freedom,' he began in his justification at nominating a Viennese composer as part of the fabric of British music. 'At the behest of a man called Salamanzy he arrived in London, having spent years as an indentured composer writing music for the Esterhazy family. At the time – the late eighteenth century – London orchestras were the toast of Europe. It was the burgeoning of the middle class and these people had money to burn and a huge appetite for culture. So Haydn turned up and he was treated like a rock star. England was a wonderfully corrupt but free place at the time. Everyone had the pox, and yet the country could produce a freethinker like Newton and allow him to develop ideas about gravity. This would have been unthinkable in France where anything outspoken could only find an audience through slightly devious means.'

Haydn was fascinated by England's prosperity and liberal culture. He made friends with the astronomer William Herschel and visited his observatory near Oxford. He worked out how many lumps of coal were consumed by Londoners on a daily basis. And he recognised that money could be made in ways that it couldn't back home in Vienna. It was the onset of the parlour age, when the average middle-class household made music in their front rooms.

'Haydn saw that all these people could play reasonably well and wanted to buy a piece of music and perform it on their piano at home,' said Charles. 'A few decades later Mendelssohn noted that there was still a living, breathing folk tradition in Scotland – in England it was already in its death throes because we had industrialised so quickly that our songs about hay swains courting nymph-like lovers had receded as everyone ran to the cities – and at the same time Walter Scott was creating an image of Scotland as a misty, grey-dye world.'

Charles grew excited as he talked of the romantic notions Haydn had of the Scotland of old; of Mary, Queen of Scots, being crowned on a now-ruined altar amid the shrubs and the ivy creeping up over the stone. Realising that there was a market for this sort of thing, the canny German composer churned out Scottish 'folk songs', adding cod gestures to sound vaguely authentic: a bit of a drone here, some bagpipes there, a few bent and wavering notes scattered about. 'Of course, he markets these as the voice of Scotland and they sell like mad. He made it up as he went along and these songs sounded like they had been around for ever and now they are at the heart of what we term as classical.'

The deeper I got into the question of what British music is, the more I was realising how cloudy and best avoided is the whole question of authenticity. A year or so earlier I had met the singer Shirley Collins, born and raised in Sussex and deeply versed in the traditional music of her place and people. Shirley had sung folk songs all her life and was clear about what they are: anonymous tunes, passed down through oral tradition, that are the shared property of those that sing them. Nobody could write a folk song today, she believed; and there wasn't much good English music after Purcell either. The singer was just a vessel for the song. Their ego should not come into it.

I had a feeling that Shirley Collins didn't fully appreciate her own talent and originality. On her best albums, like her duet with the guitarist Davy Graham, *Folk Roots, New Routes* (1964), and the one she made with her sister Dolly, *Love, Death And The Lady* (1970), her own character and experience shine through and it sounds like these ancient songs are telling *her* story, even if she hadn't encountered the murderer that casually kills his lover in 'The Oxford Girl' and she wasn't the woman that met an ominous old man on a country road in 'Death And The Lady'. But Shirley appeared to be sure that there is a pure and true way of approaching these songs. 'Like a bird landing on a branch, you land on the note,' she said, somewhat poetically. I asked Charles about this approach to the old songs of the country.

'When John Gay wrote *The Beggars' Opera* in 1728 it had about seventy folk tunes in it, all of which were the pop songs of the day and everyone knew every fucking one of them. Then industrialisation happened and it all changed, almost overnight. The next big thing to happen to British folk music was Vaughan Williams and Cecil Sharp going around collecting songs in the early twentieth century. They were desperate to capture a lost tradition, and as soon as you utter that sentence you've lost it. Folk music is a living, breathing, oral tradition that is passed down through the centuries. It cannot be something you preserve in aspic. You know, "This is a song sung by farmhands in Gloucestershire, circa 1710." Already it's bollocks. If it doesn't somehow tell the story of the person singing it, what purpose does it serve?'

Charles's verdict on the state of British folk music and its part in the classical tradition was fashioned after his choral project brought him into close and frequent contact with communities in the townships of South Africa, where there are hundreds of songs for buying a beer and thousands for birth, circumcision, marriage and death ceremonies. Most are old, some are new, and all are the main artery of expression for the people they belong to. 'For whatever reason we have lost that tradition,' he said. 'Vaughan Williams was trying, charmingly or not, to harness traditional songs in his orchestral material. But it's like pinning a butterfly. The butterfly is only valuable, it only has beauty, when it's flying around.'

I felt that Charles was being too harsh. Vaughan Williams, Cecil Sharp and all the other song collectors of the time may have been chasing after a false dream, but in doing so they did harness aspects of the ancient line that are exquisite. Many of the old melodies that ran across rural Britain would have been lost had not Sharp notated them, even if the rendition of 'My Boy Willie' he heard from a 71-year-old drunken Warwickshire farmer was representative of nothing more than how that old fellow felt like singing it that night. Wasn't all that work of value?

'More of these songs might have died without Cecil Sharp, but it's rather like finding a piece of mosaic under the pavement: interesting but random. I just hate the aspect of the national psyche that has a passionate need to preserve everything and nail it all down. I was in the Hebrides recently and we went to Fingal's Cave on the Isle of Staffa, which is where Mendelssohn wrote the *Hebrides Overture*. There are all these people howling and screaming because the whole thing is falling into the sea as a process of natural erosion. There's a huge Save Staffa campaign, and the suggestion that it's a great tragedy that it's all collapsing, when in fact that's just the reality of time. That's why I like

Prague so much more than Paris. Paris is prissily cared for and it's boring as hell. Prague's real. It's falling down and nobody gives a crap because the city is so alive.'

What about Shirley Collins's suggestion that there is no such thing as a modern folk song?

'Clearly that's madness. There are four or five great stories and that's how many there have always been. Everything that has happened since has been a reworking of those stories. Folk music is a chronicling of our lives and so it's a continual, living, breathing thing. "Rehab" by Amy Winehouse is a brilliant folk song. These are the songs that tell the Martian who lands on Earth who we are and how we live.'

Despite all of this there is such a thing as British music, and an unassailable spirit that endures, irrespective of the details of tradition that die away with each new generation. Nursery rhymes such as 'Baa Baa Black Sheep' and 'Georgie Porgie' – the former dates back to the wool industry in fourteenth-century Britain and the latter refers to the notorious seventeenth-century courtier George Villiers, lover to both King James I and the Queen of France – have a solid, dependable aspect to them. French ones, like 'Frere Jacques' and 'A La Claire Fontaine' tend to be more floral . . . effeminate, really.

There is also a tendency for the 'dying fall' in British music. The tune builds up, reaches a shimmering climax that suggests hope and glory, and then dies away into melancholy and unease. 'Greensleeves', perhaps the archetypal British composition, is the perfect utilisation of the dying fall. Initially the tune is in a minor key, sad and yearning, and then there is the chorus, a time of celebration and release. But then we end up back in the minor key, directionless and mawkish and just a little bit shit. 'Greensleeves' captures the British soul. You can have your moment of catharsis, but you will inevitably return to your natural state, which is one of vague discontent and quiet, controlled despair.

'It's interesting to compare Russian and British music because they're quite similar,' said Charles on the point of 'Greensleeves'. 'Russia has the dying fall too, but the Russians don't just wallow in misery: they drown in it. It's all about fate dragging you down. At least the British get *glimpses* of hope. The chorus to "Greensleeves" is saying: "You know what? The world is fantastic right now!" The other point about the British psyche is that it is an essentially liberal one, probably because we're relatively comfortable as a nation. This is why Mendelssohn couldn't get enough of Britain. Here was a Jewish German boy coming to England and being treated as an equal. Look at France – Le Pen [leader of the French National Front] has a significant following. That wouldn't happen here.'

Charles was optimistic for British music. The backbone of British humour being self-deprecation, it's generally assumed that we are not musical, or indeed particularly good at anything. Charles cited the football song as the ultimate example of the song in action. 'Our football crowds are a living proof that we are a nation of songsters,' he stated, now in a state of extreme agitation. 'Croatian and Hungarian football crowds just chant. We sing! It's bizarre that our folk songs have become this little thing that a small crowd of people lamely, limply cling on to. I mean, morris dancing? For God's sake! It makes you think of child molesters. What passes for folk tradition has been taken over by dysfunctional men with bladder issues. It's become a thing that happens at the end of the corridor and smells faintly of warm beer and piss and nobody wants to go there.'

On that note, it was time to return to London and find some dysfunctional men with bladder issues. After navigating our way through the floor-based filing system of the caravan but before I took my off-white Astra onto the A303, Charles offered his summation of the great strength of the British character.

'We're practical, basic folk,' he said, leaning on the top of a wonky wooden gate that looked like it might come off the hinges if he put any more pressure on it. 'We like something and we take it on, wherever it comes from. Germanic culture has been pure and hence they're a bit of a fuck-up. They don't welcome outside influences. The Japanese are a bit like that, too. We may be a rather unstylish, unattractive race, but there's much to be celebrated here. There will be someone singing "Dirty Old Town" in five hundred years' time and you can guarantee that it will only bear a passing resemblance to the original song. The spirit of the thing endures.'

As the car cut through the rain-sodden Somerset and Wiltshire countryside and passed the familiar branded signs for Britain's slightly dreary attempts at uniformity – Little Chef, Costa Coffee, Welcome Break – I wondered if this search for the real Britain was a lost cause. This was a consumer age; consumption and the status that went with it had taken the place of production as a primary endeavour. But until the dawn of the record industry in the early part of the twentieth century, making music in Britain was as much of a community activity as going to church, dancing around the maypole and drowning the local witch. Stories were told through the songs passed down from father to son and mother to daughter, most families had at least one member that could play an instrument to a passable level, and communication through song was as ubiquitous as communication through prose.

In the medieval and Renaissance periods, religious and secular songs intermingled to the extent that it was impossible to say where one stopped and the other began. Romantic ballads doubled up as paeans to Christ. The clergy didn't mind. 'That woeren in thissen lande blissfulle songs,' noted the Worcestershire priest and poet Layamon back in 1189. Just as it was unthinkable that the church would not be a part of your life, so would it go against nature not to include music as part of the adventure of living.

A document of Britain through field recordings had to include something to represent the medieval-Elizabethan classical tradition, a high point in the development of the British sound and the capturing of the British character through music. Gustav Holst, excited by his recent discovery of the English madrigal, wrote that he considered it 'the real musical embodiment of the English composers'. Ralph Vaughan Williams and Frederick Delius borrowed extensively from their seventeenth-century forebears Thomas Tallis and William Byrd. Benjamin Britten took the songs of John Dowland as a starting point for his operas. All captured the national spirit of hope, resignation and romance . . . a happy sadness.

The ultimate Elizabethan instrument was the lute. It is the symbol of English, if not necessarily British, culture, learning and refinement. 'Now divine aire, now is his soule ravisht, is it not strange that sheepe's guts should hale souls out of men's bodies?' wrote Shakespeare in *Much Ado About Nothing*. While its brother the cittern, a precursor to the guitar, was best suited to bawdy taverns and barber shops, and frequently played, according to one outraged thirteenth-century clergyman, 'to getyer the stynkyng love of damselys', the lute made its way through the finest courts and houses of the land, turning stars out of its best players and making a handful of luthiers very rich indeed. But the lute's origins are a long way from England's hills and dales.

The history of British culture is the history of assimilation. Just as English pop, from the rock'n'roll of The Rolling Stones to the white stiletto soul of Spandau Ballet and Simply Red, is fashioned from the basic template of Black American music, and just as religious life in this country from the fourth century until Henry VIII wanted a divorce was imported from Rome, so English classical began with the borrowing of an instrument from the East. Whether it came via the Crusades, Moorish Spain or Sicily, where King Manfred Von Hohenstaufen was known to drive his thirteenth-century courtiers insane with endless extended solos on the thing, the Arabic oud made a big impression on British Renaissance-era musical life. The lute developed from this staple of Eastern music, and by the fifteenth century its players had worked out that it could be played with one's fingertips, allowing for the development of arpeggios and the picking out of notes. Being quiet, the lute was the instrument of choice throughout sixteenth- and seventeenth-century high society. John Dowland was its Elizabethan master. It became a symbol of harmony and angelic perfection in the paintings of the era, while a lute with a broken string, as in Holbein's *The Ambassadors*, was a symbol of the natural order of things being out of kilter.

Ultimately, though, the lute was a craze. And like all crazes it went out of fashion, even if it did take 150 years to do so. By the late seventeenth century orchestras were replacing lutes at all the best soirees and wealthy households bought keyboards, far easier to play and with a wider octave range, for their ongoing musical education and enrichment. The period also suffered a bout of dumbing down. Fewer people read classical Greek and Roman literature, meaning the lute's associations with instruments of Ancient Rome like the cithara and lira were no longer significant. But the lute survived, one way or another, and today there are a handful of enthusiasts keeping the golden age of English music alive.

Chris Goodwin is a cheerful, well-spoken man from Guildford in Surrey who divides his time between being secretary of The Lute Society and performing in The English Ayre, a duo that revive the music of Elizabethan England through lute and voice. I called up from the car park of a motorway service station somewhere near Reading and asked how he felt about my making a field recording of

The English Ayre. 'Well, I should be absolutely delighted,' came his response, delivered with the kind of exquisite manners the British are capable of. 'And I do hope we will be seeing you tonight.'

I was looking forward to Early Nights, a medieval disco in the dank arches underneath London Bridge that Michael Tyack was organising. The DJ would be spinning all the greatest fourteenth-century dance-floor smashes through a modern sound system, but the musicians would be performing without amplification in a nod to authenticity.

Medieval disco proved to be of limited appeal to the people of London. I arrived at Early Nights late after only getting the Astra into the drive at nine o'clock in the evening, but needn't have worried about talking my way past the maid on the door. You had to walk through half a dozen empty arches before coming to a candlelit corner with about thirty people in it. The English Ayre was on stage. Chris, smart and sober, with glasses and a benign smile, was plucking at his lute with his eyes closed while a pretty woman was singing with her hands clasped against her bosom. But amplification was invented for a reason. You couldn't hear a bloody thing. Then a medieval stripper loosened her wimple on a stage nearby and the crowd couldn't have shifted quicker if Chris announced he had caught the plague.

You couldn't help feeling a little sorry for The English Ayre – refined court musicians upstaged by a brazen strumpet – but they didn't seem to mind. They appeared to be of the mentality that to complain about one's lot was not done. Chris suggested we meet the following day at the North London flat of an actress friend called Kathryn who specialised in Elizabethan tragic-comedies, so I duly arrived at the address Chris gave me to be met at the door by a small, attractive, blonde woman dressed entirely in muted pink, who welcomed me into a little flat with a pink sofa and chairs, pink curtains, and pink fairy cakes on a silver stand. There was an enormous dog with doleful eyes padding about the place, despite the fact that his golden coat didn't fit in with the colour scheme. Chris was plucking away at his lute and the singer of The English Ayre was practising her scales, which she managed to carry on doing, wide-eyed and open-mouthed, as she waved hello. It was like walking into a scene from a Disney film. All that was missing was for Kathryn to sprout some wings and flutter away as a chorus of birds harmonised around her head.

There is a certain type of British person that is educated, gently impoverished, well mannered and very nice indeed. They tend to graduate towards low-paid, creative professions with a lot of freedom like teaching, music and acting. Sometimes they work for arts organisations. They are grounded in the values of the middle classes although they can come from any background; reading, learning and unostentatious living are among the things they hold dear. And they often have an ability to live in blissful ignorance of anything that does not concern them.

Kathryn was laying out small plates of buffalo mozzarella and cherry tomatoes with a graceful flourish, as if she might break out into an aria at any moment. Chris stopped plucking his lute as I entered to introduce me to The English Ayre's singer, whose name was Jeni Melia. In the corner sat Jeni's pretty nine-year-old daughter, quiet and uncomplaining. In fact she never said a word.

At one point the enormous dog made a leap for the mozzarella, threatening to upturn the table. 'Jupiter, no!' said Kathryn in a breathy bellow, and the dog went back to looking sorry for himself. 'I'm sorry to shout at you, darling, and I know you've been good,' she said, taking Jupiter's sad head in her hands, 'but that's no reason to start being naughty.' Then, turning to me, she asked, 'Would like coffee with your lunch or after?

Kathryn was too selfless to sit and eat herself. The table could only fit three people around it so she elected to glide in and out of the kitchen while Jeni's daughter sat on the pink sofa, eating from a plate on her lap in silence.

Jeni, a clear-voiced soprano, had no knowledge of popular culture whatsoever, but was remarkably articulate, well informed and wise on the English classical tradition, the romantic songs of John Dowland, Robert Johnson and Thomas Campion in particular. Chris had discovered the lute at the age of nineteen and never looked back. Any hope of a normal life for either of them had gone out of the window when they were seduced by the romance of the rich history of English court music. 'I heard the lute played at an historical re-enactment and I was entranced,' he explained. 'I've been deeply involved with it ever since.'

Jeni had a well-established career as a classical singer, performing solos in Purcell's *Dido And Aeneas* and Fauré's *Requiem* before discovering a natural affinity with lute music. 'It sounded like I had heard it all my life. Singing it felt like coming home,' she said. Since then The English Ayre had recorded albums in a thirteenth-century church in the village of Harrold in Bedfordshire. One of the albums, *The Lost Art Of Wooing*, honours the golden age of chivalry and romance when a gentleman only ever got his way with a woman after five or ten years of opening doors before her and laying cloaks over puddles. The album takes in a step-by-step guide to seducing a lady, and I couldn't help but wonder if Chris was still somewhere in the opening-doors stage with Jeni. They were clearly very fond of one another, but it was hard to tell if they were an item or not. Perhaps playing this refined, archaic music together was enough.

'We would like to do a song called "Oft Have I Sigh'd",' announced Jeni. 'It's about parting, and it comes from the golden age of the lute song – the early seventeenth century. It would have been performed in a wood-panelled room owned by a well-to-do couple, perhaps in front of half a dozen of their friends. This was not the music of the common people.'

I put the Zoom on the little table and hoped that Jupiter wouldn't mistake it for something edible and demolish it, then pressed record. Jeni began to sing with the utmost purity and pitch, perfectly poised as she did so. Chris came in with a gentle tune on the lute, then began singing with a look of wistful contentment. It was appealing, uplifting, and evocative of bowls at Hampton Court, and making low bows in a doublet and hose. Thomas Campion wrote the song. He was something of a purist of his day, and in 1602 wrote a treatise attacking 'the vulgar and unartificial' modern trend for singing words that rhymed. He was also accused of murder. In 1620 he caught the plague and died.

In Campion's day it was not unusual for a man to follow two or more professions. Born in London in 1567, Thomas Campion studied law at Gray's Inn before giving it up to become a doctor. Composing songs was something he did on the side for extra money. His 1601 song collection *A Book Of Ayres* made him famous, and by 1606 he was writing masques that were performed in the Court of St James. He was a product of the emerging upper-middle classes in early seventeenth-century Britain: erudite and with a propensity for pleasure.

'English music tends to be very key-aware,' said Chris. 'Typically it starts on the dominant note and goes to the tonic – D to G, for example – and that establishes the key very strongly. It is set up to fulfil the listener's expectation, unlike, say, Irish music, which is more garrulous and talkative.'

Campion was writing at the time of a craze for songs in English courtly life. 'They went absolutely mad for songs from 1597 to 1620 and the sale of lutes went through the roof,' explained Chris. 'The bigger lutes, such as the theorbo, started coming in from Italy and Germany around 1608. The first one that arrived was confiscated by customs because they thought it was a monstrous Popish machine designed to blow up the King. The Privy Council took it away and examined it.'

Jeni and Chris went all the way back to the thirteenth century with a tune called 'Edi Be Thu, Heven-Queene' (Blessed Art Thou, Virgin Mary), but unfortunately Jupiter was affected by its spiritual power and started howling. I recorded it nonetheless; perhaps having an enormous hunting dog wailing away in the background gave authenticity to the rendition. One thing hit me about these old songs: the power of the tunes. They stuck in your mind and were easy to sing. I asked Chris if that was something particular to English music.

'It's true that English lute music is not academic,' he said. 'Bach is highly constructed and extremely academic. The English lute composers didn't go in for fantasias or anything like that. They wrote in dance forms. They wanted to have a good time.'

Chris believed that the rhythms of seventeenth-century music are based on the rhythms of the iambic pentameter, the meter used in Shakespearean poetry and prose that creates stress patterns like this: da-DUM da-DUM da-DUM da-DUM da-DUM. 'When you have a text in iambic the natural rhythm is six-eight,' he explained. 'It makes sense that songs should be sung following the same pattern and it's a very English thing. "Greensleeves" is in six-eight, and so is the theme tune to *The Archers*.'

Eventually, everyone had to leave. Kathryn had a Shakespeare to act in, Jeni and Chris had a church to sing in. I left these polite people, having got just a glimpse of their early-music world. It was heartening that these people could follow their passion for something so outside of the mainstream and still get by, one way or another.

That afternoon, the house lonely without the happy noise of children filling it, I called up two old friends that have been equally involved in the recapturing of Britain's medieval

and Elizabethan musical heritage. Michael Tyack and Will
Summers perform as The Princes In The Tower, live together
in Will's featureless flat near Hampton Court, and appear to
have developed a rather odd co-dependent relationship.
Michael advises – dictates to – Will on all aspects of daily life,
from finding a girlfriend to decorating his flat to dressing in
the morning. Will looks after Michael, cooking him delicacies
like mashed-up carrot and hummus pasted onto fried bread,
eggs that have been on the boil for twenty minutes and – his
pièce de résistance – baked beans and broccoli. Michael, the son
of a Cornish tomato grower, has wilfully embraced eccentricity,
as a wardrobe full of capes attests. For Will, eccentricity is not
a choice. His parents gave him a record by David Munrow, the
late master of early music, when he was seven. That was
the beginning of the end as far as fitting into society was concerned. In 2003 the figure of a man in Tudor costume was
spotted on closed-circuit television. Ensuing reports gave the
figure's identity as the ghost of Henry VIII. Although he has
never admitted it, I am fairly convinced that it was in fact Will.

Two days later, with NJ and the children returned to
the house and turning it back into a home once more,
Michael and Will came over, an assortment of early-music
instruments filling the hessian sacks across their shoulders.

'I had an extended stay in hospital. From the ages of
seven to nine I was there pretty much permanently because
of hearing problems,' Will explained on his early conversion
to the medieval world. 'During that time I listened to David
Munrow obsessively. When I got out I joined a church choir
in Teddington and began to discover more about the world of
Elizabethan music. Hearing Renaissance classics like William
Byrd and Thomas Tallis was a religious epiphany. From then
on I knew that I had to dedicate my life to this kind of music.'

And dedicate it he did. While his classmates were
chasing after girls, kicking footballs around and listening to
pop music Will was in his bedroom, getting to grips with

seventeenth-century counterpoint. 'I avoided pop entirely. I was quite closed-minded then and felt that all that was good and valuable was in danger of drowning in a sea of crap.'

'Did you have any pop music at all in the house?' asked Michael.

Will stroked his little beard and stared up at the ceiling. Then he said, 'I did have "Variations" by Julian Lloyd Webber. But I was learning to play music more than I was listening to it. I picked up the violin when I was three. I didn't really take to it, though. When I was four I started to sing, and that's when I really connected to music. It wasn't something remote. It was a deep culture that I wanted to preserve.'

'At the age of four?' I asked. Michael sighed and lit a cigarette.

'At school it was like being the only boy in the class who was a member of a different religion,' he continued, large lips quivering at the memory. 'Nobody was interested in talking to me about John Dowland.'

He sniffed. 'It was hard.'

David Munrow's work introduced Will to strange Renaissance instruments like the crumhorn and the rauch pfeifer. Baroque music was his speciality throughout adolescence. 'I did get a little rebellious and have a dip into the eighteenth century for a while,' he admitted, 'but I always returned back to my natural home – the late sixteenth and early seventeenth century – sooner or later.'

Michael Tyack went in for rebellion of a more conventional sort. After playing in various bands in his late teens and early twenties he moved to New York aged 24 with his stripper girlfriend. It was there that he found a cassette tape of early music by chance. 'It blew my freaking mind,' he said, invigorated by the memory. 'It had so much passion, rhythm and melody. I tried to get lute lessons and couldn't find any in New York, so I moved to California and learned at the University of Palo Alto.'

Michael is an unusual candidate for an early-music obsessive. More common are quiet, well-behaved types like Chris and Jeni of The English Ayre; people that have found safe haven in recreating the past. Michael was a trouble-maker, if mostly charming with it: he never had any money, and enjoyed the hedonistic thrills of lost weekends and living without responsibility to anyone but himself – and perhaps Will. I pointed this out to him.

'Most early-music people are running away from something,' he said. 'There's a desire to escape from the modern age with a lot of them, but I can relate to that.' He went off into a long rambling monologue, variants of which I had heard over the years, on his dream of buying a castle in Brittany and starting up a commune of 'like-minded people' (acolytes) where there would be a lute player on every turret, flagons of ale in the larders and beautiful women in high-waisted dresses wafting around the court-yard. 'Take away the brutality and the disease,' he added, 'and the medieval period was a very stylish time.'

Michael did have Will, the Sancho Panza to his Don Juan, but apart from him it had proved hard to win poten-tial commune-dwellers over to his vision. Will had recently hired St John the Divine Church in Richmond for an early-music extravaganza. Eight people came.

'The real battle we have is to convince people of the glory of Britain's musical history,' said Michael, a little disconsolately. 'It's very odd. If you put on an early-music concert nobody goes, but pull out a cittern and a crumhorn on a train and everybody loves it. I think our next concert should be on the 5.42 to Huntington.'

I had brought Michael and Will over to Peckham with a goal in mind. A few miles away from our house is a place called One Tree Hill. There are more trees than one on the hill, but at its peak is an oak Elizabeth I is said to have planted. What better location to record The Princes In The

Tower than in the shade of this noble tree? NJ drove us up to the entrance of the park, Michael with his cittern, Will with his collection of medieval wind instruments and me with my Zoom, new batteries installed. It started to rain the moment we got out of the car.

'I found a Renaissance lute in a house clearance the other day,' said Michael as we traipsed up the hill. 'That was one of the best days of my life.'

At the top of the hill you could look down on South London, slabs of tower block breaking up the rows of little Victorian terraced houses that always struck me as somehow bleak; a reminder of the quiet desperation of the English that Pink Floyd wrote about in 'Time'. A large crow hopped across our path. A man walking his dog shot a surreptitious glance at Michael and Will, who were both wearing suede cloaks. We arrived at the oak, which was protected by a small iron railing. The tree turned out to be something of an impostor. An oak planted by Queen Elizabeth I did once stand in its spot, but the current one was planted in 1905 by Councillor H R Taylor (ex-mayor) and Councillor John Nisbett, chairman of the roads and public gardens committee of Camberwell Borough Council, which isn't quite the same. I wedged the Zoom between two branches of the tree, put on the headphones, and pressed record. Will and Michael ran through a rendition of 'Summer Is Icumen In', the ancient English round that goes back to the twelfth century and is the earliest surviving example of counter-point. As the virginal Sergeant Howie is roasted alive in the final scene of *The Wicker Man*, the islanders link arms and do a rousing rendition of this celebration of the outdoor season. The glories of Michael's cittern and Will's rauch pfeifer blasts were curtailed somewhat by the fact that we appeared to be under a busy flight path, and summer didn't appear to be icumen in at all, but they soldiered on with this piece of music so evocative of everyday joys in old England.

Michael suggested we search for a slightly less exposed spot since between the rain, the howling wind, the aeroplanes and the dog walkers, giving a spirited rendition of medieval and Elizabethan songs was proving difficult. We tried a church at the bottom of the hill but it was locked. We walked through some woods and found a place under another tree. It was silent save for birdsong and the wind's whistle through the branches. Michael and Will played an ancient piece called 'Grimstock' and we could have been in Sherwood Forest, the mischievous sprite Robin Goodfellow in our midst. Some children ran to the edge of the woods to see where the strange noise was coming from, took a look through the leaves, screamed, and ran away. We finished with an Elizabethan tune called 'Bring Me My Yellow Hose', in which a man laments the passing of his bachelor life – bachelors wore yellow hose back then – and the way in which his wife now controls his every move. 'If I but go to Islington my wife is watching there,' he moans. In seventeenth-century London Islington was famous for its prostitutes. He can't even go for an afternoon's whoring any more.

There are plenty of Elizabethan songs about the temptations of the whorehouse, and even more about the misery of marriage, but fewer from the woman's viewpoint. One notable exception is 'The Poor Whore's Complaint'.

Come listen a while and you shall hear,
How the poor whores fare in the winter,
They've hardly got any rags to hide their ware,
Indeed 'tis a despret thing Sir.
With their draggel tales that's nine inches deep,
And hardly a shoe or a stocking,
Yet if a cull* they by chance should meet,
At him they will be bobing.

[*man]

I asked Michael and Will to do a version of 'The Poor Whore's Complaint', feeling that in their reduced circumstances they might share her pain. But they didn't know it.

Michael and Will had resigned themselves to being impoverished and obscure. Even the folk and early-music crowd had little time for them. Michael's flamboyant dress sense and less than reverent attitude to tradition meant that those of a more orderly nature found him easy to dismiss. Will's frequent and lengthy monologues on Renaissance-era wind instruments had soporific qualities. After I made them undertake a half-hour walk to pick up Pearl from her ballet class, and then wondered if I had done the right thing in bringing two middle-aged men dressed as medieval minstrels into a hall full of five-year-olds in pink tutus and their vaguely alarmed mums in tracksuit trousers, I reflected on the fact that they had agreed to come all the way from Hampton Court to Peckham to make this preposterous recording under a fake Elizabethan tree. They really did belong to the troubadour tradition, travelling around the country and singing ancient songs for little more than their supper. I had found in Michael and Will the inheritors of the spirit of English music: downtrodden perhaps, and much mocked, yet still with their own peculiar dream intact.

Now it was time to meet that secretive community keeping the old songs of Britain alive that Sam Lee, that charismatic young man with the large teeth and wire-brush hair that I had met in Devon, had spoken of so fondly.

Chapter Five

By the Light of the Magical Moon: Gypsies in Sussex

THERE'S A THEORY THAT IF YOU WANT TO FIND THE roots and traditions of a culture, seek out the people at the bottom of the heap. Not influential, unlikely to be involved in the machinations of modernity and outside of the establishment, the communities with the lowest status frequently have an independence that maintains a strong, unchanging identity. About the ancient Scottish murder ballad 'The Twa Brothers', the great American song collector Francis James Child wrote in 1882: 'It is interesting to find the ballad still in the mouths of children in American cities – in the mouths of the poorest, whose heritage these old things are.'

The Scottish and English Travellers and Gypsies have been putting the wind up conservative Britain since their arrival in the mid-sixteenth century: too wild and unpredictable, untamed and unknown. Nobody wants them stopping at the bottom of their garden. The Kings and Queens of Egypt, as Gypsies were once known, have remained enigmatic and set apart. In 1540 Scotland's King James issued an edict ordering all Gypsies to 'pairt furth of this realme with their wifis, bairnis and companies' within thirty days or face execution. They have been brandished as a race of liars (in 1567 an Act was passed against the 'idel peopil calling themselves Egyptians') and thieves (in 1609 a new law allowed any of the king's subjects to 'take, apprehend, imprison and execute to death the said Egyptians, either men or women, as common, notorious and condemned thieffs'). The fiddler James MacPherson was hanged at Banff in 1700 for the crime of being an 'Egyptian', inspiring the ballad 'MacPherson's Rant'. The British, for the most part imbued with the Protestant work ethic, have always been suspicious of people that don't earn their living in a clear-cut way.

Like most people I had very little contact with Travellers. My brother and I liked to believe that our absent, alcoholic, maternal grandfather was a Romany, explaining our slightly werewolf-like appearance, but that's not grounded in any hard evidence. As a teenager searching for escape from the square life I took the occasional weekend break to a New Age travellers' festival before getting home in time for Mum to put tea on the table on Sunday evening, but these were tawdry, bleak affairs, filled with dreadlocked dropouts sitting around burning oil drums in an uncommunicative haze of cider fumes and dope smoke. Somebody would be walking around calling 'hash for cash' with all the enthusiasm of a plague caller telling survivors to bring out the dead. Occasionally one of the New Age travellers would stand up and flail about to incredibly loud electronic dance music before collapsing into the mud next to a dog named Giro, but on the whole the energy levels were low. For a people on the move, they seemed to be in a state of stasis and inertia.

The Romany Gypsies and the English, Scottish and Irish Travellers are an altogether different proposition. Isolation from the dominant culture was not a lifestyle choice. In the pull between the safety of cultivated land and the vitality of the wild the Gypsies fell into the latter camp; popular imagination has them in a dark wood at the edge of town. The seventeenth- and eighteenth-century peasant knew that ghosts and malevolent sprites dwelled at cross-roads, in rubbish heaps and forests; exactly the places Gypsies chose to stop at, partly because they were safer from persecution there.

The song that Sam Lee had sung with such melancholic clarity at the church in Devon, 'The Lakes of Shallin', was in the repertoire of Scottish Travellers, conjectured to have descended either from Romany Gypsies or from the ancient Celtic tinsmith caste, from where the term 'tinker' derives. It's also likely that Scottish Travellers come from a mix of displaced crofters, Scottish outlaws, deserting soldiers from the Battle of Culloden and Romanies, while the Travellers themselves push forward a belief that they are descended from the Royal family – but more of that later.

Sam suggested that if I really was interested in this world I should accompany him to a Romany step-dancing session he had heard about that was taking place in the Sussex countryside. Could I bring the eight-track and make a recording? 'I wouldn't advise it,' he said, cheerfully but cautiously. 'Gypsies have a lot of suspicion about losing their souls. They often don't like photographs or recordings for that reason.'

Centuries of prejudice have also meant that, while Gypsies and Travellers have inspired fear in settled populations, there's a much greater surge of fear going in the other direction. Folklore among the Scottish tinkers is filled with tales of 'burkers' (named after the notorious nineteenth-century body-snatchers Burke and Hare) hanging around the edges of towns, waiting to capture unsuspecting travelling folk and sell their bodies to medical schools. Tinkers even went so far as to demonise medical students, a group that generally don't get up to much more than wheeling each other around in shopping trolleys during Rag Week, as devilish, murderous ghouls.

This was the oral tradition, then. The concept of posterity in written or recorded form was irrelevant: it was the experience that counted. 'Storytelling creates a feeling of solidarity among those present,' wrote the folklorist Linda Williamson, who is married to a Traveller.

'The songs of the Travellers are all about telling stories,' confirmed Sam.

I was fascinated by this world I was about to enter, and the classifying, collecting side of me wanted to get a field recording to hold down an aspect of it. But this was a world that didn't want to be captured.

The day after recording Michael and Will up on One Tree Hill I drove up to Cecil Sharp House, where Sam works. He was finishing for the day and was trying to get twenty pounds out of a tiny birdlike lady who sat in a messy office filled with loose sheets of paper at the top of the building. She gave him short shrift. Apparently she was the accountant.

'She's one of the characters you get at a place like this,' said Sam, who was much younger and more fashionable than his colleagues. 'She used to do the accounts for the East End reclamation bus, which was run by Gypsies and went around buying and selling scrap metal. She knew the Krays. You don't mess with her.'

'Really?' I said, looking over at the little figure at her desk. 'She looks so sweet.'

'Sweet?' said Sam, wide-eyed. 'You should see her tattoos.'

Soon we were heading south towards Sussex. I asked Sam about his background. He didn't have a trace of Traveller blood in him, despite his surname being common among Gypsies. He was the child of well-to-do, liberal North London Jews and had been everything from an office clerk to a burlesque dancer before the old music of England and Scotland got under his skin. He didn't have much interest in the singers of the sixties folk revival. He preferred the old farmhands, fishermen and most of all Gypsies who had learned the songs from their mothers and fathers. 'I like the idea that music isn't a commodity, but something that tells the story of your life and is central to it,' he explained, driving in a way that could well have brought that story to a sudden end. 'When I was a kid I loved Michael Jackson and Prince – pop music that is totally universal and commercial. Now I've gone the other way.'

I had a feeling that music was going to become localised again. The twentieth century had been the age of globalisation. Cheap air travel made it possible for swathes of the population to go anywhere in the world and global food networks meant the idea of looking after yourself through growing vegetables and keeping livestock had gone for all but a tiny minority by the end of the century. But ecological and financial concerns were changing our attitudes. Flying everywhere was no longer attractive and the growth in farmers' markets and allotments proved there was a desire for greater self-sufficiency and provenance with our food.

It was the same with music. It had become a profession. If you turn on the television and see someone standing on a stage being paid millions of pounds to create a certain sound you're going to start believing that it's something they can do and you can't. But even from what I had seen in my recent travels through southern England, I felt we were returning to an age in which people were making music that is an extension and expression of their daily reality. Paradoxically the Travellers, the most traditional of all British groups, could just point the way forward towards a more self-contained, spontaneous relationship with music.

Sam and I discovered that we shared formative childhood experiences. We had both spent summers on a hippy holiday project called Forest School Camps. Inaugurated in the late 1950s by an idealistic group of former Boy Scouts, Forest School Camps take place deep in the British country-side – the ones I went on were in the Brecon Beacons of Wales – and involve sleeping in tents, going for long hikes, exploring caves and sitting around campfires in the evening singing songs. One of the goals of the camps is to make children independent and aware of the impact they have on the land. We had to build a trench that we then crapped in, washing our bottoms with water rather than toilet paper for minimum environmental damage. The camps foster a sense of community. Everyone has to help out with chores, from washing billycans to building fires, and they are proof that a group of people can be self-sufficient while still having fun in the form of group singing and disappearing into the bushes at night in pairs, although the latter was an experience I personally missed out on. Built on an Arcadian dream, Forest School Camps aimed for a rustic utopia.

I hated every moment of it. Apart from occasional snatches of revelation (the first time I ever saw a grown woman naked – an enormous ginger-pubed lesbian who hiked in the nude) memories of both holidays are filled with nothing but loneliness and suffering. My parents were getting separated (hence the reason I was sent there in the first place, looking back on it) and my insecurities must have shone through, as I got bullied for the first time in my life and there was no escape. Feral hippy children took one look at my suburban trainers and gelled hair and rooted me out as an easy target. I got into a fight and ended up having to accompany my tormenter in a version of 'Green Grow The Rushes, O' at the suggestion of a group leader in a Tibetan pillbox hat. And people were always juggling. Everywhere you looked: juggling. It may explain why to this day the sight of a juggler at rock festivals always makes me want to take one of those bowling-pin-shaped things they throw in the air and shove it up their arse.

Had I gone a year later I probably would have loved Forest School Camps. It's the closest the average city-dwelling child can get to real rural freedom, and the spirit in which the camps are set up is generous and optimistic. Sam had the opposite experience to me. He was getting bullied at school and it was at the camps he found acceptance. 'Everything significant happened to me there – my sexual awakening, the realisation that I was gay, and most of all my love of folk music,' said Sam, large teeth shining joyously at the memory. 'Singing around the campfire, I discovered that music is a shared experience and one that's best experienced actively.'

Forest School Camps offered a potted Gypsy experience: setting up camp and then moving on, learning to look after yourself without leaning on outside help, and sharing in the process of making music and dance that is relevant to you and your people. For the last few decades, however, few Gypsies and Travellers in Britain still live the itinerant life. 'Most are settled now,' said Sam. 'You do still get Gypsy caravans, but most live in flats or in trailers on the edges of towns. Many spend a few months of each year on the road before returning to a permanent base. But it's common for the communities to remain strong. Marrying "outside" is still an issue.'

We arrived at the step-dancing location. It was in a barn in some woods, not far from a pub on the outskirts of a tiny Sussex hamlet about ten miles from the town of Lewes – in the middle of nowhere, in other words. There were about ten people there; all of those dancing were women and all of the musicians – on fiddle, accordion and penny whistle – were men. The women were from the same family; the oldest was a tiny white-haired woman of 85 who didn't stop dancing for the entire time we were there, and the youngest was a shy-looking, black-haired teenager who sat on a chair with an uneasy smile. Sam had met them at a meeting outside the BBC's Broadcasting House in Central London to protest against the corporation's cessation of funding for a Gypsy community radio station and they had invited him down to the dance. They were friendly. They showed me how to step-dance (it's all about getting a clicking rhythm going by whacking your heels against the floor) and asked if I wanted a beer. They were slightly less friendly after I told them what my surname was – they had mistaken me for a Gypsy and assumed I was a Faa or a Penfold, not a Hodgkinson – but it didn't last long.

Night was approaching. The wood was a world of silvery light and shaded, shifting shapes. A full moon shone above us, and its suffused brilliance lit up everything close and nothing in the distance. One of the dancers, a very thin woman with jet-black hair and dark eyes, stood entirely still and sang a song called 'Once I Had A True Love', her head raised with formal dignity.

'It's fascinating,' whispered Sam, leaning towards me as we watched the woman sing. 'I asked her what songs she knew and she said she didn't know any, and in fact she knows loads without even realising. That's a real Romany thing – these songs are so integral to their life that they don't really have a concept of knowledge of them. They're just part of the language and fabric of everyday life and they come out unconsciously.'

The scene reminded me of an old children's book. The Gypsies really were deep in the woods, singing and dancing by the light of the magical moon. You could picture it as a silhouette, perhaps with a cat playing the fiddle and an owl on the accordion. The step-dancing started up again and they made me have another go. 'He's got the gear for it,' they said, pointing at the heels of my brown leather boots. 'There you go. You're getting it.'

After half an hour of joyful dancing the atmosphere changed. Word came to the women that one of their uncles was dying. 'He's on his way out,' the thin woman told me, unsentimental but warm. The five women, relatives all, duly said goodbye and left. The male musicians continued to play. Then I found out there was another reason for their sudden departure. There had been a nondescript-looking man sitting in one of the chairs who hadn't really been talking to anyone all night. The women had just found out that he was involved in an organisation that was reclaiming English traditional music as the true voice of the English patriot. With the contradictions that are at the heart of extreme thinking this man had come to check out the Romanies as the keepers of the tradition, perhaps not taking into account that in the history of the far right Gypsies have always been the first to have the finger pointed at them.

Step-dancing with the Gypsies was a moving, if short-lived, experience. There was a sense that this didn't need to go anywhere. It could have happened hundreds of years ago and yet it didn't feel like an exercise in nostalgia, or the re-creation of a period piece. These mostly middle-aged and elderly ladies were connecting with something that was deep inside them.

'My experience with the Gypsy community is that they keep alive all of these old songs that are thought to have been lost forever,' said Sam, as we drove under neon lights on empty roads towards London. 'If you talk to people in the folk world they'll tell you that the last of the great folk singers have died and the oral tradition has died with them. The songs have been collected on manuscript or tape and now what we are left with is essentially a revival. It's always going to be second-hand. But because the Travellers are still divorced from mainstream society they have held on to something.'

Sam believed that because most of us watch the same television programmes and hear the same pop songs, the experience of community music was dying out. I wasn't so sure. A lot of the music I heard in Peckham, typically made in teenagers' bedrooms on computers or even a PlayStation games console, frequently name-checked friends, local shops like the Beyonce Nail Parlour and the Mixed Blessings Bakery, even the 171 bus. I put it to Sam that a reflection of a modern reality is as valuable as something passed down, unchanging, through the generations.

'The sadness for me is not that people are singing something contemporary, but that they are replicating something outside of their own experience,' said Sam. 'I like the way ideas, language and memory are passed on with the Travellers. They still have an emotional relationship with these songs.'

I needed to get some field recordings of Travellers' songs, even if that did mean hammering another nail into the coffin of the oral tradition. And there were wonderful recordings of Gypsy singers out there. Hamish Henderson, the great champion of Scottish song, discovered Traveller singers like the regal Belle Stewart, a descendant of one of the dispossessed clans who supported the losing side in the Battle of Culloden in 1746, and, most significantly, Jeannie Robertson.

Known as the Queen of the Heather, Jeannie Robertson was a powerful figure. In 1953 Hamish tracked her down to a house in Gallowgate in Aberdeen, the heartland of the Scottish ballad tradition, following a tip-off from a travelling salesman. When she answered the door and he told her that he was collecting songs and would like to record her, she challenged him to sing the first line of the old Scottish ballad 'The Battle of Harlaw' before letting him in. He did it. Hamish wrote of discovering Jeannie as finding 'the inglorious mountain-track that is The Way'. This outsider, this tough, stately woman, was the essence of Scotland he had been searching for.

Jeannie subsequently became something of a

celebrity, appearing in David Attenborough's film *The Ballad Hunters* and generally being exalted among high society as the pure voice of the travelling people. But she remained a storyteller, never happier than when reciting long tales of supernatural escapades to her own kind around a campfire.

'Those that aren't alive now could tell ye a lot o' good stories,' Jeannie told Hamish. 'They could tell stories, and maybe tell it to ye afore ye went to bed at night, and then it was continued like a continued picture at the desperate bit, the bit ye were aye waitin' to hear. So ye were fair anxious for the first 'oor or twa after . . . and the story started again.'

Hamish praised Jeannie as one of the great exponents of storytelling, an art that continues to be an integral part of Traveller and Gypsy culture. 'Her physical presence is formidable,' he wrote. 'She turns her great black eyes on a member of the audience, and draws him willy-nilly into a sort of mute participation. And when she tells the "true" stories of ghosts and fairies . . . it is obvious that she belongs to a culture in which belief in the supernatural is still very much a fact of life, and for which the alien phantasmagoric world of scalpel-toting predators has a more than symbolic reality.'

Magic is the key to the travelling people of Britain. Others imbue them with magical properties, while the sacrosanct value of things impossible to define by science and economics has not been lost in the people themselves.

Jeannie died in 1975, but her nephew Stanley, to whom she had passed down many of the songs, was alive, well, living in Aberdeen and apparently only too happy to talk to a flattie (non-traveller) such as myself.

Travellers and Gypsies have actually seen their status go down over the last century. Their old trades of horse dealing and tinsmithing don't have much of a place in a post-industrial society, and twentieth-century legislation has criminalised the itinerant life. The Highways and Byways Act of 1959 made it illegal for families to stop at the side of the road, the Control of Development Act in 1960 meant that farmers could no longer allow Travellers to stay on their land without a licence, and the Criminal Justice Act of 1994 gave police the right to impound vehicles if more than six were travelling together. This was the real reason why most Travellers either lived in flats or in static caravans on vacant scraps of land on the edges of towns. And an event that happened in Italy two days before I met Stanley went some way to show how bad things had got. On a crowded beach in Naples the bodies of drowned Roma sisters, sixteen-year-old Cristina and fourteen-year-old Violetta, lay on the sand, their feet poking out of beach towels as if on mortuary slabs. This coincided with the Italian government's interior minister Roberto Marroni pushing to fingerprint every Roma, and camps were being attacked and torched. A photograph shows a middle-aged couple a few feet away, seemingly indifferent to the evidence of this tragedy before them. The image went around the world and became the latest chapter in the story of an ongoing persecution.

Scottish Travellers were once so terrified of medical students that they would steer clear of college buildings for fear of being cut up in the name of research. In the 21st century, on a beach in Italy, the unconcern of the settled to the fates of the nomadic makes the Scottish Travellers' fears seem reasonable.

Stanley Robertson was determined to break down these boundaries and prejudices by bringing the song and storytelling traditions of the Travellers into the wider world. It was working, too. After leaving school illiterate and with no qualifications, and after decades of filleting in Aberdeen fish houses, he was making the most of his retirement by travelling around the country telling stories and singing songs. He made open use of Cant, the cover-tongue Travellers use when they don't want to be understood. He was down in London for a few days, staying at Sam Lee's parents' house in North London, and it seemed that any friend of Sam's was a friend of Stanley's.

'Samuel is one of my special students,' said Stanley, a tall, dapper man in a flat cap and a tweed suit, when I turned up at the house two days after returning from the step-dancing session in Sussex, with the intention of making as many field recordings of Stanley as he would allow. 'When I first saw him I looked at him out of the corner of my eye and said: "That's a Lee". He's Nathan Lee, the Gypsy prince.'

As much as the occasionally flamboyant Sam Lee would have loved this romantic title for himself, I felt compelled to tell Stanley that Sam was in fact Jewish. 'Ah, but you see, I'm very pro-Jewish,' said Stanley, who had a lullaby rolling voice, like the wind at night. 'They live the same kind of lives as us.'

We sat at the large wooden table in the Lees's kitchen. It was warm and bright, and Sam's parents were in the garden, reading and occasionally poking their head around the door with a smile to see what was going on. Stanley arranged himself in a position suitable for storytelling, and he began.

'All of our ancient ballads have been handed down through the oral tradition and they're incredibly rare as none of my folk could read or write,' he said, arms crossed neatly on the table before him. 'My father was an excellent singer, my auntie was the inimitable Jeannie Robertson, and I heard these wonderful ballads all through my days. See, folk have forgotten the old-fashioned right to sing. Folk are stylised now. They use an instrument and music to time their times.'

I wasn't exactly sure what that meant, but I think he was saying that singing was now approached as an art form divorced from the daily expression of life. He was a living example of how it could be entwined with it. His speaking voice was so melodic, and his singing voice so conversational, that it was hard to say where one stopped and the other began. Halfway through describing how the old ballads were used to bring the news, and of how the minstrels that once carried them would turn them into dance tunes to increase their commercial potential, he fell into song without my even realising it. He fixed me with a powerful, benign stare, raised his arms outwards, and brought the song alive with exuberance.

The singing voice was clear, if a little wavering. It was only later that I learned Stanley had had a stroke two years earlier that had left him temporarily incapable of speech.

'We were given no history, no geography, no schooling,' he said as the song (about true love, I think) came to an end. Born in the poorest street in Aberdeen at the onset of World War II, part Romany and mostly Scottish Traveller, Stanley comes from a family of soldiers; his grandfather fought in the Boer War and his father and uncle fought in the Great War and World War II. It was through singing the ballads that Stanley kept not only their memory alive, but the memories of all that shared the ballad's experience.

'When you sing a ballad you're nay on your own,' he explained, leaning forward and speaking in an emphatic whisper. 'You're singing with a tribe. You're a villain, you're a wronged woman, you're a wee boy with a letter, you're everyone. And your voice changes. Sometimes it's hard for modern people to understand this. My people have sympathy and empathy for all those we sing aboot.'

He crossed his arms in a *fait accompli* manner. 'I tap the ballad oot,' he said, rapping a military beat on the old wooden table. 'See, we believe in a thing called the *mysie*. It's a Traveller's term. It's a corruption of the muse and you need to have it inside you. Jeannie used to have it and, oh my goodness, the shivers you got when she used to sing. The hair used to rise. I sing with an *ing* and an *ong*.'

I was going to ask him what an ing and an ong was, but it was hard to get a word in edgewise.

'The Travellers are elemental singers,' he bellowed, raising his arms. 'We're like the wind! The wind is nay a rush through the trees. The wind *sighs* through the trees.'

He began to sing. '"I am feeling good, I am feeling good, I am feeling good, going through the wood." There we have a sprightly wind, gently hopping along, like a wee imp coming to you. But now there's a gale force and the winds are shaking, nearly breaking! "I AM FEELING GOOD, I AM FEELING GOOD, I AM FEELING GOOD, GOING THROUGH THE WOOD,"' he roared, banging his fist on the table so hard that Sam Lee's mum rushed in from the garden to see if anything was the matter. 'It's a cry of the pipers,' he said to her, and she looked reassured. 'If we were in a big camp and wanted to find each other I would sing that and my friend would harmonise with it until we knew where the other was. Now you try that.'

'I'm not a very good singer,' I told him.

'Nonsense! Och, it's only words. You take a low note and I'll take a high note.'

We tried it. At first I was hopelessly out, but after a while Stanley showed me how to find the tune. 'The travelling folk inhabit the ballad,' he explained. 'You're in it, across it, above it, below it, front elevation, side elevation . . . you have to see every side of it.'

It did feel good. For most of us who have become divorced from this very natural act, it is hard not to sing without feeling self-conscious. But if you keep going, no matter how terrible you sound, you can get past that. Singing with Stanley had a refreshing power to it, like having an internal shower. I could completely understand why NJ's mother felt better equipped to deal with the trials of life after singing with her choir.

After getting poetic about the joys of burning a willow

broom ('it's the finest aromatic smell you ever found – get a wither broom, build a wee fire and burn the broom. It will open up your senses') and talking about how the world becomes a finer place when you know you are dying ('as you go up the scaffold you ken how beautiful the wee birdies' songs are'), he came to a subject that seemed to preoccupy the travelling people: persecution.

'Karl Marx said that you can tell about a people through their music, and the Travellers sing big, heavy ballads,' he said in a rhythmic tone. 'I've had prejudice all my life. People call us Tinkies, but we're not tinkers. Every day the local paper says something bad about Travellers. They never call us the tradition bearers or anything nice. My Auntie Jeannie got an MBE from the Queen and she spoke like royalty. We are royalty, anyway. We are the illegitimate Royal family of Scotland, descended from Bonnie Prince Charlie. My sister is the spitting image of the Queen. They could be sisters.'

I had heard this theory before: that the Travellers of Scotland were descended from Charles Edward Stuart, a.k.a. Bonny Prince Charlie, the leader of the Jacobite Uprising who was defeated by the English at the Battle of Culloden in 1746 and then fled to the Isle of Skye disguised as an Irish maid (he is said to have been as pretty as a girl, hence the 'Bonnie' tag). What followed were the Clearances, one of the bleakest episodes in Scotland's history, when crofters were forcibly cleared off their land and the English government broke up the old clans, even banning the wearing of tartan. Subsistence-level farmers were displaced as increasing demand in England for cattle and sheep inspired Scottish landlords to clear their lands of the people that lived off them.

It was an entrancing image, to think Britain's eternal outsiders are part of the family at the heart of its establishment, but I couldn't quite understand how Stanley's sister could be related to the present Queen. Bonny Prince Charlie was a Stuart and that line ended with his failed uprising. Elizabeth II descended from the Hanoverian line that began with George I. But I wasn't about to argue the finer details of royal succession with Stanley, particularly as he had already entered into a reverie about the Clearances. Tears glassed his eyes as he told the story of a song called 'Highland Widow's Lament'. 'It's a wealthy woman crying as she laments the end of her old life as she's forced into the low country. She's saying "sad am I" in Gallic at the end of each line.'

He began to sing. I knew the song. The words were written or at least collected by Robbie Burns and a version appears in *The Wicker Man*. Stanley sang with great passion and feeling, and he rejected the idea that Robbie Burns wrote the song; it was one of those held by the Gypsies. 'See, we're the gan-aboot folk,' he said in his melodic way. 'The Travellers were the reporters of their day and they brought the stories to the different areas.'

I wondered if this tradition would continue. The travelling people of Britain had steadfastly held on to the past for centuries. 'That sort of lad just lives from day to day,' a young Scottish Traveller once said to Hamish Henderson, referring to an Irish tramp frequently spotted wandering around Scotland. 'But we live entirely in the past.' Perhaps the modern age had finally won. Sam had told me that of Stanley's two sons, one was interested in the old songs and the other seemed embarrassed by them, treating his father's dedication to them as something of a joke. But I could see how much these songs meant to Stanley: by inhabiting them, they inhabited him. I reflected that in the oral tradition the song must change with every person that sang it. He rejected this notion.

'See, my folk are very particular about the way you do a song,' he replied. 'Jeannie had a song called "My Son

David" that's about one brother killing another and it goes back to the tenth century. She didnae like people messing around with the tune.'

I had heard about this. It was one of the Edward Ballads. I mentioned this to Stanley.

'Edward is revivalist rubbish!' he shouted, hammering a fist on the table again.

Anything to do with the revival – by which Stanley meant the resurgence of interest in folk music in the late fifties and sixties – appeared to be the enemy, presumably because people were reviving something that was not a part of them. But he was happily teaching Sam the songs. What was the difference? It seems that with aspects of the shared culture that are untutored and organic people feel such an ownership and, certainly in Stanley's case, an affection and affinity that only their version is right. It is similar to claiming that the flowers in your valley are more beautiful than any flowers anywhere else in the world.

I felt Stanley was wrong about the Edward Ballads, even though his approach to storytelling and balladry was so inspiring. In 1882 Francis Child's *The English And Scottish Popular Ballads* published 'Edward', a fragmented trio of tunes that feature a mother quizzing her son about the blood on his shirt and then discovering his crime of fratricide. There is nothing sterilised about them. The first is 'Son Davie', taken from the recitation of an old woman.

> What bluid's that on thy coat lap,
> Son Davie, son Davie?
> What bluid's that on thy coat lap?
> And the truth come tell to me.

Son Davie claims that it's the blood of his hawk, and then the blood of his greyhound, before admitting that it is the blood of his brother John, the result of an argument about the cutting of a willow wand. The mother asks how her son would like to die. 'I'll set foot in a bottomless ship,' he replies. To his wife, Davie promises to leave 'grief and sorrow all her life', to his son, 'the weary world to wander up and down'. But most devastating of all is what he will leave to his dear old mother, as promised in the final verse.

> What wilt thou leave to thy mother dear,
> Son Davie, son Davie?'
> A fire o' coals to burn her, wi' hearty cheer,
> And she'll never get mair o' me.

Another version, first written down by David Dalrymple in 1765, substitutes Davie for Edward and is no less psychopathic. This time the murderer says that his wife and children can go out and beg as far as he is concerned, and for his mother, 'The curse of hell frae me sall ye beir'. There are endless variations, and a similar story and tune are found in Norway, Denmark and Germany. The Gypsies and Travellers may be upholding the tradition, but the reality is that such dark and powerful songs live forever, in one form or another. If they are collected and written down they are not preserved in aspic: everyone brings something of themselves to them and as such they're forever in a state of flux.

I recorded Stanley singing 'The Clattering Of The Clyde Waters', a song of old Scotland for which he is famous, and 'The Highland Widow's Lament'. He stood up as he sang, head raised upwards, gesticulating dramatically as he acted out each line. Sam's mother listened in the corner of the room. We were in a smart house in North London, urbane and controlled, but Stanley was filling it with something wild and untamable.

Stanley had an appointment to keep. He asked Sam's father if he could use his aftershave since his own had been confiscated by security at Aberdeen Airport. He took this as proof of further persecution of the Travellers, but Sam's dad explained that no liquids were allowed as hand luggage on an airplane any more. 'Ah, but they're clever, y'see,' said Stanley, talking to Sam's father with the authority of one that had seen every trick in the book. 'That's what they *want* you to think. But they don't mind selling you aftershave on the plane, do they? As if I haven't seen that trick before. They steal it and sell it back to you!'

Few Gypsies were still on the road. But one evening at the cottage in Mabe in Cornwall, Tiffany and Jarvis had received a visit from three young men who had forsaken a settled existence for the itinerant life. Ed, Will and Ginger left their homes with no money and the barest of possessions and took off on journeys that lasted for months, singing old English folk songs to make enough money for cakes and ale and sleeping wherever they were when night fell, from church porches to forest floors. They didn't have mobile phones, or bank accounts, or even surnames, but they did have that value-range portal of 21st-century communication, the MySpace site. Eventually they got back to me. It turned out that Ed and Ginger were brothers, and all three were living in an apple orchard at the back of their parents' house in Selling, a village in Kent. They would be hanging around for a bit before heading off again in the autumn, this time for Scotland. If I could make it to Selling some time before they left they would be happy to sing a song or two.

It was time to visit Ed, Will and Ginger in Kent, before embarking on a much bigger journey northwards. Also in Kent, in the tough dock town of Chatham, was a strange young man called Pete Molinari, whose story told of another, less rosy side of the British experience.

Chapter Six

The Garden of England: Kent

THE ASTRA WAS GETTING EVER MORE DECREPIT. ALONG with the many bumps and scrapes that NJ inflicted on the car as punishment for its ugliness and general lack of chic, not to mention the black panel giving it a Frankenstein's monster aspect, it now demanded a complex manoeuvre for the most basic maintenance. The handle to open the bonnet had snapped off and the spring releasing it had rusted into paralysis, meaning the only way to open the bonnet was for one person to clamber down by the brake and clutch pedals and yank a cable with a pair of pliers while someone else gave the centre of the bonnet a hearty kick. The Astra had not discovered modern audio technology either. It only had a cassette deck by way of in-car entertainment, and we only had one tape: a compilation of British folk music made by a friend as an accompaniment to the field-recording adventure.

It was a warm summer Wednesday when NJ and I took the A2 that runs out of the bleakly expanding suburbs of southeast London towards an apple orchard at the back of a house down a watercolour-pretty country lane in Kent. The pure-voiced strains of Anne Briggs's version of the old seduce-them-and-leave-them tune 'Blackwaterside' leaked out of the speakers. Wastelands of dilapidated buildings and factories on the edge of the capital gave way to oast houses, those cylindrical grain-storing buildings so redolent of Kent, and muddy, uneven lanes and old men on bicycles. We passed village greens holding war memorials where may-poles once stood. We arrived at the apple orchard an hour after dropping the children off at their school in Peckham. I wondered how long London to Faversham would take by foot . . . about a week, I supposed.

A large willow tree was swaying in the breeze, as was a line of tall daisies. The apple blossom had budded towards fruit, too early yet to pick. There was a rust-red double-decker bus at the front of the orchard, and at the back were three old vans that had been transformed into homes, one each for Ed, Will and Ginger. Out of objects they had found the three young men had turned these stationary, former industrial-purpose automobiles into dingle-dell dwellings. One had a little round window cut into its side. Another had a prehistoric cast-iron stove with a zigzag chimney rising up out of the roof. All were furnished with chairs and stools made of driftwood, little stacks of greasy paperback cook-books, and frayed Moroccan rugs that might once have belonged to smart family homes. Nothing matched and everything worked towards a feeling of welcome and a certain Gypsy romance. Ed, Will and Ginger were sitting in the thick smoke of a fire, heating a kettle for tea. With their thin, young men's beards, layers of clothing in various shades of green, leaves in their hair and boots so heavily used they were moulded into the shape of their feet, they looked like a displaced sector of Robin Hood's merry men.

'We'd like to do "John Barleycorn",' said Will, the tallest of the three, when I asked them which song they would have to represent them. Telling the story of how barley is turned into beer and whisky, the song imagines John Barleycorn as a heroic little character who goes through all kinds of horrific events in his journey from cereal crop to alcoholic brew. It also has elements of sacrifice: John Barleycorn is the vegetable king that must die for the harvest. It was suitable for the land we were in, where hops and barley are the agricultural mainstays and beer takes on an almost sacred importance.

'We find "John Barleycorn" pertinent to Britain because it offers a seamless blend of the pagan myth of the recurring king with the single, resurrected Christ figure,' said Will with earnest politeness. 'It's usually taken as a pagan ale celebration, but the early Christians promoted the song too.'

I held the Zoom at chest height, put on the head-phones, and pressed record. The little digital lines jumped up and down. The three young men harmonised well, a result of spending the better part of three years on the road together, and the recording sounded good with the crackle of the fire and the occasional squawk of a goose that was wandering about rather busily nearby accompanying the voices. Then they sang a tune called 'Country Life' with lusty enthusiasm and rallying hand movements until Ginger collapsed into a coughing fit – an occupational hazard, I couldn't help but suspect, of the outdoor life. As we sat around by the fire and drank tea they told me about how they had ended up on this strange path.

'We did the old Pilgrim's Way walk from Winchester to Canterbury about three years ago, just to see if we could do it,' Will began. 'That was a bit of a stroll, only lasting for three weeks. We got hideously lost and wet and it all went wrong.'

'We wanted to visit Thomas Becket's tomb at Canter-bury Cathedral, but we got turned away because there was a concert going on,' said Ginger. 'Can you believe it? We were the only people there who had actually done the pilgrimage and they wouldn't let us in.'

Despite their sufferings, Ed, Will and Ginger got a taste for this slow-moving way of life. They worked out what was necessary: a good sleeping bag, walking boots, layers of clothing and a sheet of tarpaulin to string up among the trees they slept under. They lived off berries and mushrooms, learning how to forage dry wood for fires, steam clothes dry and keep warm in freezing conditions. They learned how to poo in the woods.

'People don't know how to take a crap outside any more,' said Ed. 'The first thing you see in a copse of woodland is a ring of hastily laid poos with bits of shitty paper everywhere.'

'It's an art that we have lost,' said Ginger solemnly, nodding reflectively into the fire. 'You dig a nice big hole with a stick, get some water, wash your bum, and use leaves. Any leaves will do once you get the hang of it.'

'Or moss,' added Ed in a wistful tone.

'Or best of all, sphagnum,' added Will, plaintively. 'Ooh, that's a treat . . .'

When it became evident that they had to find some way of making money for food and the occasional beer, the trio discovered that people seemed to respond well to the sight and sound of three strangely dressed young men heartily belting out traditional songs in a village square. They also discovered that, in Britain, singing in public is a legal issue.

'The best place to sing is in pubs,' said Will. 'Everyone loves it. But you actually need a licence to sing in a public space in Britain.'

'The laws are crazy,' said Ed. 'Legally, you can't sing "Happy Birthday" unless the pub has a licence, and yet you can shout and swear as much as you like and the television can be on top volume.'

They also discovered that there is no better way to break down social barriers than to sing. Busking led to offers to stay in strangers' homes, especially after explaining the nature of their mission to walk across Britain, and even pub landlords that had earlier in the evening told them they weren't allowed to sing would offer the trio the use of the garden or an upstairs room for the night.

'You get passed around,' said Will. 'Somebody offers you shelter and then they tell their friend in the next village to look out for you. We have found a far greater hospitality and openness than most people expect, but there's a lot of isolation too. You pass through a suburb and see a TV glowing out of every window, showing the same programme. Yet give people the opportunity to come together through singing and they do, and they love it.'

If three ragged men could bring out the latent generosity of the average person simply by walking and singing traditional songs, then surely these old ballads did still have power and relevance. And the songs were still a part of the travelling people I had met the week before. We said goodbye to these young lords of the woods. NJ had come with me because she wanted to visit a friend who lived in the next village along, so after dropping her off at a converted barn about three miles up the road, I made the drive to Chatham, where a world awaited that could not have been more different from the one I had just left.

Half an hour later the Astra spluttered to a halt in a car park next to the River Medway, into which a late sixteenth-century parish clerk once threw a body, according to local folklore. The body was that of an unknown man washed ashore at Chatham and buried in its churchyard. But Our Lady of Chatham, the town's very own Virgin Mary, objected, tapping on the parish clerk's window one night and telling him that the body belonged to a wicked man. According to William Lambarde's 1576 English county history *The Perambulation of Kent,* Our Lady couldn't bear 'this sinful person's ghastly grinning' so near her shrine in the churchyard, and demanded his removal. The clerk did her bidding and the body washed up in nearby Gillingham a few days later.

There was no bloated corpse of a wrongdoer to greet me at the bank of the Medway that afternoon, but a small, dark man with a black pompadour hairstyle, a shining leather jacket and an excess of gold jewellery. He was leaning against a pillar, looking nervous. This was Pete Molinari, and I knew what he was scared about. He had often told me how dangerous Chatham was. We were in one of the Medway towns, where, he claimed, little happened except fights on Saturday night and the occasional drunken fumble along the quayside. He remembered being caught by the aggrieved boyfriend of one of his conquests. The man took a swipe at him, but Pete ducked and the fist intended for his face went straight through a pub window. Pete ran away in his highly polished boots while the man screamed at him as he tried to extricate his arm from a mass of shattered glass.

Upon entering Chatham I had passed grey concrete walkways, boarded-up shop fronts and quivering muscles on leads that passed for dogs, but before that was the Kentish countryside: the land of cakes and ale, of hop farms and thatched cottages with roses around the door. This flat, oaken oasis of calm surrounding the town must surely have a pacifying effect. It couldn't be that bad. Could it?

Perhaps it was Pete that brought out this latent violence. The son of an Italian-Egyptian father and a Maltese mother, he grew up in a small modern house near the station alongside six brothers and three sisters. While his elder brothers played sport, hung out in gangs and graduated to jobs as builders and taxi drivers, Pete spent a lot of time in the art room at school, developing a fascination for the romantic America of Jack Kerouac and Woody Guthrie and resolving to never have any kind of normal nine-to-five career whatsoever. Discovering that he had an amazing falsetto pitched somewhere between Roy Orbison and Nina Simone, he set about learning to play the guitar. Before long he was in Greenwich Village in New York, living off hats passed round the crowd and the generosity of women.

I met Pete a few years before, just after he returned to England. Somehow I ended up being his manager (unpaid), not only organising his gigs but also giving him a place to crash (our sofa), providing life's essentials (hair pomade, Cuban-heeled boots) and introducing him to the kind of women he liked (if they were capable of picking him up and throwing him across the room, they were in).

It began to put a strain on my relationship with NJ. Pete was staying at our house two or three times a week, eating dinner with us and talking about his three favourite subjects: Woody Guthrie, the Chatham poet/painter/musician Billy Childish, and himself. Then there was the time he spent in the bathroom.

'Your bitch has been in there for an hour and a half,' said NJ one morning, late for a meeting, through tightened lips.

I marched upstairs and rapped a military beat on the bathroom door. 'Do you know how long you've been in there? Get a move on!'

'I can't find the conditioner,' came the muffled reply.

Eventually he emerged, molecules collapsing under the weight of a hitherto undiscovered formula of product, a glorious pompadour shining in the morning light, and said, 'Any chance of a coffee?'

Then I heard angry grunts from NJ as she spent five minutes putting the tops back on all of her skin and hair lotions.

Now I was on his turf, and Pete wanted to pay back all those hours spent in the bathroom by offering his services for a field recording and then inviting me to the family home for a traditional Molinari lunch. 'How about making a recording on the high street, as if you're a busker?' I asked him as I lurched out of the car and took the Zoom – still in an Asda carrier bag – out of the boot.

'I don't think that's a good idea,' he said. 'It's bad enough just walking down the street. You don't want to attract attention to yourself here –'

'Oh, nonsense,' I snapped. 'Come on, let's show these so-called chavs a thing or two.'

It was a clear sunny day. I had decided to wear cut-off denim jeans, a tight T-shirt bearing the legend California Singing Cowboys, a denim sailor's cap and large Ray-Ban sunglasses; an ideal outfit for a day in the provinces. Pete was relatively dressed down in his black tailored trousers, black Cuban-heeled boots, black shirt and leather jacket, as well as his usual accessories of gold chains, rings on all fingers and guitar. We set off for the high street. It looked much like any other high street in Britain, with its branch of WH Smith's, chain coffee shops with metal chairs clanking about on the pavement outside and cheap clothing stores, but I noticed that the people of Chatham were notable in liking to keep what they wore to a minimum. The women had tracksuit trousers and small pink tops that failed to contain their sometimes-ample frames and the men favoured shaven heads, acrylic shorts, Caterpillar work boots and nothing on top. There were a lot of tattoos about, often of the tribal variety: on the chests, arms and necks of the men and on the smalls of the backs of the women.

At first I thought it was just my imagination, but it did seem that we were getting some rather suspicious looks as we walked down the high street. 'It's all right for this bit, but it gets progressively worse as you go towards Tesco,' said

Pete as we strutted along. 'I don't know what it is about Chatham, but people love to fight. Maybe because it's always been a working town, fighting is the quickest way of letting off steam. OK, we should probably turn back now.'

'I'm sure you exaggerate,' I said as we crossed a grim pollution-soaked roundabout and came around the back end of a slablike building containing a branch of Tesco's. Then I felt something hard hit my back, accompanied by a clatter of metal. We darted round to see an enormous, snarling woman who appeared to have thrown a chair at us.

'Get out of our town, you fucking poofters,' she screamed, lank mud-blonde hair flapping against a red, round face.

'What did we do to deserve that?' I asked Pete as we quickened our pace in order to get away from the snarling, red-faced, pony-tailed behemoth.

'I think I made eye contact by mistake.'

'Maybe we should turn back the other way after all.'

We passed a theatre on the high street hosting a show featuring The Ladyboys Of Bangkok and headed for the refuge of a greasy spoon filled with old men and women sitting over racing forms and stained copies of *Chat* magazine. A sour-faced girl slapped two cups of tea down on the Formica table before us with spill-inducing ferocity and marched off.

'I have a complicated relationship with Chatham,' said Pete, his hand shaking slightly as he dropped a spoonful of sugar into what tea remained in his cup. 'I spend half of my time trying to get out of it, but I'm still here, perhaps because secretly I know that being in Chatham gives me an edge and a desire to write songs that might go if I moved to London. I mean, I've had people spit at me. The reason I involve myself with blues and folk is because it has a lot to do with the people, and living in Chatham means that it's impossible not to write about people – not to keep your feet on the ground.'

But Pete's music was as much about escapism and fantasy as it was about reality, with references to riding trains to Mississippi and coming out of the wilderness to step into the sun. 'When I was a kid I would see people falling out of the pub or getting into fights and I would hate it, so I lost myself in country and blues to create a world away from it all,' he said quietly. 'I used to stare at the records going round on my dad's old Dansette like they were magical portals into another world. I was outside of mainstream white culture already because my parents are foreign, and here I was in this redneck town where you're meant to constantly prove that you're tough. All of this is going to have an influence on what you write about.'

By the time he hit his teens Pete had for some reason developed an interest in the Hindu sacred text the *Bhagvad Gita*, enraging his staunchly Catholic father in the process and becoming ever more of a misfit in a town innately suspicious of anything it was not familiar with. He idolised distant figures like Marlon Brando and Johnny Cash, who appeared to achieve so much while being non-conformist and uncompromising. His one inspiration closer to home was Billy Childish, who has made staying in a provincial town while self-releasing his records and self-publishing his books something of a *raison d'être*.

'Billy was doing poetry readings in the back rooms of the roughest pubs in Chatham,' remembered Pete. 'He was accessible, and he made it seem possible to do things your own way. I would see this big tall guy with a handlebar moustache and an army coat stomping around town like he had just come out of World War Two, and he fascinated me. So I got to know him. He showed me that it wasn't impossible for someone from a place like this to do more than just work on the docks and get drunk. He showed me that you could be an artist, even if you came from a place like Chatham.'

Once again, I asked Pete if he would consider allowing me to record him as he played his guitar and sang on the high street. After a while he said, 'I'll give it a go, but I'm packing up at the first sign of trouble.'

It didn't take long. I had got the equipment out, and Pete had just started on a song called 'Indescribably Blue', when a clutch of shirtless teens in grey and white shell-suit trousers hanging limply around their lower halves crowded around us. A couple of girls were with them.

'Fuckin' Elvis,' shouted one pimple-strewn youth.

'Greasy-haired cunt,' shouted another.

I made the mistake of looking up from my vantage point of being crouched down on the pavement next to Pete, headphones over my ears as I tried to capture this authentic Chatham experience.

'What you lookin' at, ya fuckin' poofter?'

'You want some, do ya?'

'Perhaps this wasn't such a good idea,' I said, hurriedly putting away the eight-track as Pete took the guitar strap off his shoulders and fumbled it back into his case. The youths cackled.

'I'm beginning to see what you mean,' I said as we shuffled off at a lightning pace along the crowded high street, occasionally looking back to see if we were being followed (we weren't).

'It's always worse when there are girls around,' said Pete, breathlessly. 'That's when they feel the need to show off and prove themselves.'

A little further down the high street, just after I overheard an old lady say, 'Would you look at this pair,' as she jabbed a wrinkled finger in our direction, we saw a statuesque, smiling, extremely striking black girl sitting on a bench, eating a sandwich with an older lady. 'Wow, Chatham isn't so bad after all!' I said to Pete.

'That's Tendayi,' he replied. 'She's got an amazing

singing voice but she's generally too shy to let anyone know about it. She's one of those rare people that just sing for the sake of it – you meet people that say they love to sing and then they come out with something that sounds like Mariah Carey because they want to be on TV. She's the opposite. Let's ask her if she'll do a recording. You never know.'

Pete introduced us, and Tendayi introduced the older woman as her mother Florence. We told them about the hostility our very beings appeared to bring out in the people of Chatham.

'Chatham is interesting, isn't it?' said Tendayi with a sunny laugh, long legs stretching out in the midday sun. 'A girl punched me in the face when I was fifteen, but that's about all the trouble I've had. But then a moment ago a woman walked past and said to her dog, "Come on, Blackie, come on, Negro, oh, come on, you skranky old dog Nigger." I couldn't believe it. She was standing right next to us but I don't think it even occurred to her that we might be offended.' Florence started to laugh.

Pete told Tendayi of my field-recording project, and asked if she might consider singing us a song for it. 'Well,' she said, putting a finger to her mouth, 'I've got to go to the opticians' in a minute, and then this afternoon I'm setting off for a music festival, but I suppose I could fit something in before I leave.'

We arranged to go to Tendayi's house in an hour. In the meantime we would go back to Pete's and make a recording there – it seemed like trying to do something on the streets of Chatham was just too risky. As we walked past the railway station we approached a family carrying a pram up some steps. Mum and Dad had the pram in one hand and a can of beer in the other while two bare-chested, shaven-headed boys of about eight and ten tried to push each other over.

'Let's hold back a bit,' said Pete as we came up behind them. 'I've had enough trouble for one day . . .'

'Come on, Pete,' I said. 'What are they going to do? They're saddled with a pram.'

'I'd feel safer if they were nailed to it.'

We did manage to get to Pete's house, a clean if nondescript modern terrace, in one piece, although two small girls stopped playing with their hula-hoops as we passed and ran up to demand money for sweets, jumping up and attempting to punch us in the face when we told them to go away. We passed a tired-looking bar called O'Connell's, where red-faced men stood outside the door, smoking and staring at everyone that passed them.

'What would happen if we went in there?' I asked Pete.

'I've seen people flying through the window of O'Connell's,' he said. 'It's like *Gunfight At The OK Corral*. You get the entire pub throwing punches at each other. I can get away with going in because my brothers drink there, but I try and avoid it anyway. I got off the train the other day and these people I knew told me to come and have a pint with them in O'Connell's. I said I was tired and just wanted to go home, so then it's: "Oh, so you're too fucking famous to have a drink with your old mates now, then?" You can't win.'

This was an attitude redolent of 21st-century Britain. The worst thing you can do is to not be one of the gang. We are living in an age when the country abhors celebrity and yet is fascinated with it; when gossip magazines print poor-quality photographs of reality-television stars and draw rings around their slightly flabby thighs like the playground bully finding an imperfection about another child and mercilessly tormenting her for it. But in being 'just like us' (a favourite phrase of the gossip magazines) these people become blank canvases upon which the non-famous can project their dreams. In the absence of heroic figures we elevate mundane people into positions of fame. Pete Molinari, on the other hand, is a talented loner who needed a stage to escape from the pressure to be the same as everybody else. He is always going to be treated with suspicion by the people he left behind, despite never wanting to be in their gang in the first place. As his fame grew the situation could only get worse.

At least he was safe at home. We went into the kitchen, which was clean and plain, with some framed family photographs and icons of saints hanging on the walls. It had a hatch that went through to the living room and some newspaper cuttings about Pete were on the fridge. Various brothers and sisters, some of them with babies or small children in tow, came and went and said hello, seemingly on some kind of rotational basis. It was hard to tell how many still lived at home, but this house was the hub for a family that, one way or another, stayed close to one another. All were interested to meet Pete's friend, and welcoming. Pete's mother, a tiny Maltese woman with a thick thatch of curly hair and a broad, warm grin, had spent all morning cooking us lunch: aubergine and black olive salad, sea bass and red peppers stuffed with wild rice, sautéed onions and garlic, peas, thyme, raisins, parsley and feta. It was delicious.

'Most of the boys' friends,' she said, 'they don't like my cooking. It's nice to have someone that eats my Maltese food.'

'They don't know what they're missing,' I said. 'This is wonderful.'

'The average Chatham bloke won't eat anything foreign,' said Pete. 'My brothers' friends wouldn't touch this. It has to be fish and chips or a curry.'

'Curry is foreign, isn't it?'

'That's the funny thing,' he said as he skewered an olive. 'It's acceptable to them when nothing else is. One thing I would say in Chatham's favour is that you get to the root of the place very quickly. If you go to New York you find myth: you look for the spirit of Bob Dylan in Greenwich Village and you very quickly find a lot of people trading on that piece of history. That's not the case in Chatham. What you see is what you get, and there's no glamour. That's why Billy Childish has stayed here. It keeps him close to the earth.'

It was time to catch Tendayi before she went off to her festival. On the way to her house we walked across a park on a hill that looked down onto the Medway Delta. A huge industrial estate gave way to a skyline of cranes, and beyond that a flat expanse of land along the river with a timber warehouse and empty space that didn't look like it would stay empty for long. You could see the Medway towns of Rochester and Strood in the distance. We walked to the top of the grassy hill and looked down.

'When I was a kid I used to come up here all the time because my parents didn't have a garden,' Pete said. He pointed to a factory at the beginning of the grey industrial mass below us. 'That's the ropery, where my dad worked when he first came over from Egypt. And over there is New Road, where the prostitutes come out at night. You used to look down and just see river. Now it's all industrial.'

We walked down the hill and came upon a war memorial. The words 'Lest We Forget' were carved into the stone, which had inspired a song by Pete of the same name. We came to a bandstand that, with its faded chipped paint, graffiti and wooden boards strewn with crushed beer cans and burned plastic bottles, looked like the ghost of a jollier age.

'This is where brass bands used to play every Sunday,' said Pete as we walked up the wooden steps of the band-stand and kicked at the ash and charcoal at its burned centre. 'Now it's just thugs hanging out and spray-painting "Sharon is a whore" on the walls.'

We passed the Kent Institute of Art and Design, where Billy Childish, the artist Tracey Emin, Pete Molinari and pretty much every other Medway youth who didn't spend

Friday nights beating each other up found solace, and arrived at the tall Victorian house where Tendayi lived with her parents when she wasn't studying politics at the LSE in London. Her mother made us all a cup of tea and we went down some wooden steps at the back of the house that led to a small garden shaded by wisteria and clematis. As a little dog scampered up and down the steps and her mother hung out the washing, Tendayi told us how she learned to sing.

'I was born in Zambia, and lived there and in Kenya until coming to Chatham as a teenager,' she said, rolling a cigarette. 'Singing and dancing is second nature in Africa. One of the first things I noticed about coming to England is that people have to get drunk to dance here, whereas in Africa it's a part of daily life that you take for granted. I started singing in church, but very early on I discovered that I love jazz and blues. I love Nina Simone, Billie Holliday, and old songs like "Wade In The Water" and "God Bless The Child"; songs about the strength of the spirit.'

Tendayi said she had no intention of becoming a professional singer because she felt self-conscious when people looked at her. She had done some modelling, but didn't enjoy the experience of being objectified and assessed. I asked her if she would let me record her singing something. 'I could do "Amazing Grace",' she offered, with a slight smile.

After a few nervous giggles and false starts she was relaxed enough to sing, but every time she reached the high notes the little dog started barking. We tried 'Summertime' – it was a bright, warm day, and the song suited the mood of the afternoon in this pretty shaded garden. She sang with cool restraint, a jazz style so different and so much more elegant than the vocal gymnastics many jazz-inflected modern American R&B singers go for. She was enjoying the discipline of hitting the notes the melody demanded. I played along on guitar, and then when it became clear that I wasn't good enough Pete took over. It was what I had been searching for: a chance encounter leading to a field recording that captured a shade of British life.

Tendayi had her festival to get to, and I needed to pick up NJ in order that we got back to London in time to pick up the kids from their after-school clubs, and I still hadn't got a full song out of Pete yet. So we said goodbye and headed back to Pete's house. We were walking through a narrow, barren, litter-strewn alleyway around the back of a row of shops when a man ran up behind us. We tensed and turned round to face him. The man stopped by a row of dustbins, stared at us for a second or two, and passed by.

'What was that about?' I said.

'I think he thought about mugging us and then changed his mind,' said Pete, breathlessly. 'Honestly, the moment I leave my house it feels like I'm running the gauntlet in this town.'

We went back to the family kitchen to record Pete. I put the Zoom on the table and pressed record, then Pete sang a tune called 'Black Town', a lament for his life in Chatham. The tiled walls of the kitchen and the projecting timbre of Pete's voice produced acoustics perfectly suited to a field recording, and in terms of the quality of sound it was the best so far. 'It's too late, too late, to leave this place,' he sang in a haunting minor key, and I began to understand his situation, of fealty to a loving family combined with ambition to make it on his own, of an attachment to a town he hated but which made him what he is. There are sensitive, artistic people all over Britain like this, who don't fit in with the abiding culture of their place of birth but are reluctant to leave it lest something of themselves gets lost in the process. For a while in the mid-nineties every town had a Robert Smith clone; a young man with backcombed black hair, red lipstick and a big mohair jumper in tribute to the lead singer of the goth-pop band The Cure. Pete talked a lot about moving to London. Seeing him in Chatham, despite the abuse he got on a daily basis, it was hard to imagine him making that leap.

Pete's dad turned up, a stocky Mediterranean man with curly grey hair and a large gold crucifix hanging around his neck. He took my hand and gave it a firm, manly shake. He brought out a bottle and slammed it down on the table. It was Muscat, and it was an altar wine made in accordance with Canon 924 of the Code of Canon Law. He poured three small glasses despite my protestations that I was about to drive off through Kent and couldn't really have a drink.

'You be OK,' he said, knocking back his glass.

'He's driving, Dad,' said Pete. 'He can't drink it.'

'If he get stopped and arrest I feel awful,' said his mother. 'They stop people sometime.'

'He'll be fine! It's good for him!' shouted Pete's dad, thick eyebrows glistening with Catholic defiance.

'Leave him alone,' said Pete.

'You shut up!'

'I'll have a taste,' I said, taking a sip of the sweet wine. 'It's very nice.'

Pete's dad nodded approvingly. 'What about you?' he said, jabbing a finger at his son.

'I don't like it,' said Pete, glumly.

'What wrong with you?'

'Don't make him,' said Pete's mother, flapping her hands. 'You know he don't like to drink.'

'Ach!' And he picked up Pete's glass and sank it in one.

It was time to leave. The family came out to say goodbye, standing by the frosted glass of their front door as I put the Zoom and the headphones that went with it back in the boot of the Astra. Some children on bicycles came to watch this not particularly interesting scene.

'Are you a rock star?' one of them asked Pete.

'Not yet,' he replied.

Pete's family's house was in a row that all had the same style of front, give or take the addition of a stone lion here or a palm tree next to the drive there, and yet in each one were lives so dizzyingly various. Behind each door was a different story. To think you can make assumptions on how people live according to the kind of house they live in or the appearance they have is to be misguided. We can never really know.

The electric window of the Astra groaned downwards as I waved goodbye to the Molinaris and drove along the street, past the alleyway we almost got mugged in, past O'Connell's bar and its life-hardened clientele standing on the street corner outside, and out of Chatham's mean streets and into the surrounding Kentish pastures. Back up the small winding roads that passed thatched cottages, post-boxes built into uneven stone pillars and rows of gently swaying trees, I swerved the car into the drive of the converted barn that NJ's friend, a former model called Jan, lived in. They were by an old oak table, drinking wine, eating mushroom soup and talking fashion, and I wondered if it really was possible to capture in field recordings a sense of place when individual lives are so markedly different.

We headed back towards the capital, passing through the suburb of Plumstead, where middle-aged Indian women in salwar kameezes and anoraks pushed shopping trolleys along quiet streets, and talked about the next journey. This time I would keep going, through the North, Scotland and Wales, and hope that both the Astra and the Zoom lasted out before the journey was over. Perhaps then there would be a collection of recordings that would, with any luck, hold something of the spirit of this small island. But first it was time to get something from a city that has elements of the entire world within its sprawling limits, and yet its own binding character too.

As the Astra coughed its way past a row of halal butchers to Martin Carthy's rendition of 'Scarborough Fair', I thought about the kind of song I associated with London. It certainly wasn't 'Scarborough Fair'. It was the great songs by The Rolling Stones, The Kinks and The Who; songs that made you think of being young, and having fun, and strutting down Carnaby Street in your new pair of Chelsea boots, determined not to let it be known that they're pinching your toes. After the second or third beer in a pub or bar, the music that sounds the best is all a product of 1960s London. You can't help but sing along to the bits you know from 'Get Off Of My Cloud' by The Rolling Stones and 'Substitute' by The Who, and after one beer too many you might even find yourself busting a few Jaggeresque struts, much to your regret the following morning.

The hits from Swinging London have become the modern folk songs of Britain. What could be more of a folk experience than a coach-load of schoolchildren singing along to 'Yellow Submarine'? It was time to get back to London and explore what has become the soundtrack to modernity, to hope for the future, and to the consumer age: pop.

Chapter Seven

London, Part One: Pop in Suburbia

B EFORE THE EARLY TWENTIETH CENTURY, WHEN THE Berliner Gramophone Company dispatched adventurer salesmen across the world to not only flog their company's wares but also discover musicians to make records to play on them, music as a product existed on the page and in the concert hall. Sales of records remained a low-key affair until the 1950s when Britain discovered a way to market youth, hope and desirability to the world through the mass production of circular pieces of plastic: pop music.

I discovered the sixties through hearing 'Foxy Lady' by Jimi Hendrix on the radio one night, aged twelve, when I should have been asleep. It was the eighties, the charts were filled with future landfill like 'Living In A Box' by Living In A Box, and this sounded like nothing I had ever heard: fresh, exciting and raw. Hendrix led to a fascination with the sixties and later the seventies that continues to this day. Social, historical and economic forces in Britain conspired to leave a legacy of pop culture in that period that stands above everything that has come since, and the capital offered the ultimate haven for reinvention, for escaping from the places where little happened and entering into a new age of bright lights and synthetic fabrics.

Looking at old copies of the *New Musical Express* reveals that the sixties charts did have their fair share of forgettable, shallow products from The Searchers and Helen

Shapiro, but at the same time The Beatles, The Who, The Kinks and The Rolling Stones were using the formula of the pop song to capture everything from art-school theorising to English satire to experiments in spirituality. Somehow this small island got it right, and in what amounted to a very successful exercise in cultural colonialism Britain – or rather, London – was sold to the world through the three-minute pop song.

A few months earlier I had met Pete Townshend, guitarist in The Who and one of my favourite songwriters of all time. It had been for an interview with Pete and his girlfriend Rachel Fuller, a classically trained pianist who once did a stint as an organist in a crematorium, about a project they were embarking on that involved doing impromptu jam sessions with whichever famous pop stars they happened to bump into. At the same time Pete was launching an incredibly complex project called The Method, a computer program that created musical portraits of a person based on the personal information they gave it, although for some reason the ensuing pieces all ended up sounding like something the American minimalist composer Terry Riley might have come up with. With two interviews in quick succession I felt that I had broken the ice with Pete enough to ask him if he would talk to me about Britain's musical legacy from his viewpoint as one of the people that fashioned it. To my surprise he agreed. On receipt of this happy news I didn't feel that I could also ask him if he would mind laying down an acoustic rendition for me to record on the eight-track – so I didn't.

When we were boys my brother and I believed that all of The Who lived together in a big house on the top of Richmond Hill, which was exciting since we lived in a not-so-big semi at the bottom of the hill. We knew that Keith Moon lived in the basement, playing drums in a bamboo cage, while John Entwistle did the gardening, Roger Daltrey fished for trout in the nearby River Thames and Pete Townshend composed rock operas in a psychedelic bolthole in the attic. It wasn't true – Ronnie Wood of The Rolling Stones lived there – but strangely enough it was now Pete and Rachel's home.

On a yellow-bright morning I took the train to Richmond, now one of London's wealthiest suburbs and apparently ideal for rich rock stars with its mix of flash and gentility, Turneresque river views, smart antiques shops and mum-friendly cafés. Pete opened the door and made a pot of coffee himself, which doesn't seem significant until you discover that rock stars with forty years of fame behind them get to the point where they don't expect to have to press the 'up' button on the elevator. We went into a conservatory where there was a grand piano, Peter Blake's *Babe Rainbow*, and a soaring view of the river below. We sat at a long table and Pete reflected on his part in the creation of the pop dream as he straightened cups and coffee pots before him.

Pete Townshend was a product of the chaos and slump that came in the wake of World War II. His parents were big-band musicians playing to the troops in Europe, and for them the war was a glamorous, exciting time when being in a band meant being in the best gang in the world; the one that everybody welcomed. Music served as entertainment, a very necessary diversion at a time when nobody knew if they would be alive or dead by the morning. Then the war ended, Pete's mother fell pregnant, and the dour reality of life in post-war Britain took hold.

'The war was over,' said Pete. 'My dad was still out in Germany, entertaining the troops. My mum was still trying to paint nylons on the back of her skirt. She's in her early twenties, she's drop-dead gorgeous, her husband's somewhere else, and she's lumbered with a snotty little brat – me – in the West London suburb of Acton. She joined the air force at the age of sixteen. Now that peace has finally arrived she wants the glamour to continue, and she wants valediction of this time she's been promised. What's actually going on is that we're in the dourest time in the history of the twentieth century. When TV finally comes along it's *Muffin the Mule* for the children and *Omnibus* for the grown-ups and it's so fucking boring beyond belief. But then something happened . . .'

A new generation discovered that the seemingly barren landscape of post-war Britain was filled with gold; a little tarnished and buried, perhaps, but there. Children born around the time the war ended, brought up on rations and resentment, were finding that all that was needed to build a kaleidoscopic new world was right under their noses, in the shadows and hidden corners of the world they inhabited.

'It was gold that nobody could see,' said Pete. 'I've always had a big mouth and I couldn't stop talking about it, and the more I talked the more I was told to shut up. I would run in and say to my dad, "I've just heard the most amazing banjo music on the radio!" And my dad would reply, "The piccaninnie music?" And then: "I've heard some wonderful choral music by Byrd." "Oh, nonsense." This wasn't just my dad. This was the attitude of the musicians of the time. They were lads with trumpets who got drunk and got the Royal Air Force through the war, and they had a very clear idea of their role and function. They certainly weren't interested in discovery. Music went with smoking and dancing and being silly and glamorous, but for my generation music was cathartic and profound. It released people and expressed what they couldn't express. I think Roger [Daltrey] was quite disappointed by that. He wanted to be a pop star. He wanted to be Elvis Presley. But by the time we came along that was no longer enough.'

By his teens Pete was discovering London's hidden world of exotic music. Jazz, blues and rock'n'roll records from America were coming over for the first time, but it was also possible to walk into a pub in Finsbury Park in North London and hear the most powerfully authentic Irish music outside of Dublin.

'I would go into these pubs and see some old guy, completely fucking paralytic with drink, pick up a violin and play the same incredibly complicated and beautiful melody that another drunk guy was playing on the accordion. Elsewhere in London you could hear Spanish music, Scottish music, even Scandinavian music. It was all happening right here, and yet I would tell my parents or my teachers about this and they were not only uninterested; they were downright hostile.'

That was the mix of excitement, antagonism and conflict that created sixties London. And when the revolution came it happened in the suburbs, those stretches of in-between land built on the post-war dream of happiness through material security and physical safety that are the spiritual home of the lower-middle classes; the section of society that understands pop music better than anyone. Soho was a dangerous place then, carved up between the Vice Squad and porn barons like Paul Raymond, and in the late fifties and early sixties only the artistic bohemian elite led by painters such as Francis Bacon and Frank Auerbach laid claim to its creative soul. For The Kinks up in Muswell Hill, The Rolling Stones in Dartford and then Richmond, David Bowie in Bromley and The Who in Acton and Shepherd's Bush, London was a place of margins.

'It really did happen in the suburbs,' said Pete of the birth of pop in London. 'In the early days of The Who it was clear that an artistic renaissance could not take place in Soho. You had the Two I's coffee bar where you could find Tommy Steele with a guitar, but that was finishing at about the time we started. The suburbs were like standing on a hillside and seeing where the church and the park was and having a view on the whole town. They were a filter; a place of distillation. I woke up one day after my parents had moved from Acton to Wood Grange Avenue in Ealing, which is right out in West London, and thought, I'm at the centre of the universe. When The Who did their first gigs at The Marquee I would dress up in my mod gear, put a Rickenbacker under my arm, and take the tube to Piccadilly Circus. And when I came up to the street I had the feeling that I had found the Holy Grail. When I talk to Mick [Jagger] about it, or Ray Davies or David Bowie, I realise that we came from a time and a place when all these things were just out there, waiting to be found. I didn't go out and actively seek out records by Big Bill Broonzy or Leadbelly. I allowed things to rain on me.'

There was a network of bands playing in venues throughout North, South and West London – nothing was happening in East London until midget mods The Small Faces came along – and they spied on one another. 'There was The Kinks up in Muswell Hill, who looked completely ridiculous with their long bouffant hair and ruffled shirts. I remember saying to Roger, "Why are they wearing seventeenth-century outfits?" Then you had The Stones and The Yardbirds getting fucking huge in Richmond. The Yardbirds had this gimmick based on a rumour that their singer Keith Relf was dying. Eric [Clapton, The Yardbirds' guitarist] would play faster and faster and Keith, who was asthmatic, would try to keep up on the harmonica, and then Eric would go faster, and Keith would try to keep up and start wheezing, so it looked like Keith was really going to die and it would be Eric that killed him. The point is that we were all constantly upbraided for failing to rise to the example set by our parents, who had thrown themselves so unflinchingly against the German war machine and come out victorious, so we were looking for new ways to express ourselves, to forge our own identity.'

The mod phenomenon was a product of all this, of a new age in consumerism coinciding with a widening of world-views. There's a national tendency to think of immigration as a recent thing, but on the street Pete grew up on there were Polish, Japanese, Irish and Jamaican families, and their influences filtered into what became pop culture. At the same time there was a post-war generation with no interest in wearing uniforms. Pete was an art student with plans of making installation sculptures when a visionary young proto-mod called Pete Meaden saw the possibilities of The Detours, the straightforward R&B group Pete was playing in at the time, for transformation. Meaden became The Who's first manager, believing that the band could act as a mirror for the smart young faces hanging around Shepherds Bush and Soho.

'The mod thing was weird,' said Pete, when I asked him about how The Detours morphed into a pop-mod phenomenon called The Who. 'Originally you had people like Marc Bolan, who was a mod at twelve. He went to Paris and saw boys on the Left Bank smoking Gauloises and listening to Charlie Parker, wearing elegantly cut suits and riding scooters, and he imported it back to North London. That was an elitist thing that only a very few could relate to – I mean, Charlie Parker is great but he's inaccessible to most people, so the music shifted to something everyone could dance to, which was R&B. That happened at about the time Pete Meaden found us.'

There's an element of the British character that is terrified of sex, and the ritualised behaviour of the mods typified that. Very, very few mod boys are gay, but they accentuate effeminacy through sharp clothes, make-up and delicate hairstyles. Speed is the mod drug of choice and that reduces the sex drive. The old courtship rituals of the Saturday night dance are upturned at mod clubs: boys dance on their own, peacocks lost in narcissistic dreams, while mod girls typically don't dress too sexily – they may be wearing miniskirts, but just as common are boyish hairstyles, shapeless leather coats, thick tights and acrylic polo-necks. While their adversaries the rockers celebrated old-fashioned masculinity and in doing so remained steadfastly traditional, the mods paved the way for a new androgyny that has been the benchmark of British youth culture, far more so than in any other culture, ever since. In many ways the mods are the perfect pop phenomenon. They turn themselves into a product.

'When I first met Marc Bolan, Rod Stewart and David Bowie there was no doubt about it: they were gay,' said Pete. 'The Scene Club, which was a mod favourite, kept getting raided by the Vice Squad because they thought rent boys were operating out of it. It was assumed that a lot of us were gay, actually. When Kit [Lambert, The Who's second manager alongside Chris Stamp, brother of actor Terence] took me to a gay restaurant on the King's Road everyone assumed I was Kit's funny-looking boy. When I finally got my slinky, cutout-model girlfriend and turned up at the same restaurant everyone was thinking: she's with him because he's a pop star and he's with her because she looks like Jean Shrimpton. *But we know the truth.*'

Very quickly The Who achieved Pete Meaden's dream of mirroring this new breed of young suburban Briton, and by the time Kit Lambert and Chris Stamp came along Pete Townshend was writing songs according to the demands of the audience. '"Substitute" and "I'm A Boy" were little stories that came out of seeing what the fans wanted, and trying to write about their lives,' he said. 'The rest of the guys had no interest in the fans – well, they were interested in the girls, but I had my eyes on the boys because I could see they were the ones that really understood what we were doing. In a way I was bullied by the fans, which were very different from those of The Beatles and The

Rolling Stones in that they weren't just screaming girls. If you went to a theatre after The Beatles played there all the seats would be wet, and it might be polite to say that these girls had peed themselves but that wasn't the case. That was not our situation. I would see a particular piece of clothing worn by someone in the audience and like it, wear it the next week, and then come down the following week to see everyone wearing it. I thought The Who was an art installation that would last a couple of years. I didn't really like the fact that I had ended up in a band with three builders, and would have preferred it if The Who didn't sound the way it did, but the audience decided on the course the band took.'

The Who's songs were telling stories and painting vignettes of everyday life from the perspective of being young in London in the sixties. And this was not a time when prime ministers kept electric guitars in the halls of power. Pete was inspired to write The Who's famous song 'My Generation' after he left his first car, an old hearse, overnight on a street in Belgravia. The Queen Mother happened to drive past in the morning and, offended by the ugliness of the enormous vehicle, commanded to her driver: 'Have it removed!' Such was the power of the establishment then (and perhaps that power still exists) that her wishes were carried out. Townshend was left hearse-less.

'Nothing has really changed,' said Pete, when I suggested that pop music lost its power when it became co-opted by the establishment – there was a time, after all, when The Rolling Stones were considered enough of a threat for the establishment to attempt to break them through phoney drug busts and constant harassment. Now Mick Jagger has a knighthood. 'The world still revolves around an axis of economic and political power. It's no surprise that the most successful period in The Who's career was when Keith Moon was prepared to be a self-destructive clown, the lovable Moon The Loon, George Best meets Max Wall. It was a desolate, devastating thing to watch. Keith was part of an artistic installation in the shape of The Who, and what was so difficult to bear was that he was one of the few people to really understand it, yet he was prepared to destroy it.'

There's a song by The Who that captures the mood of the times: 'I Can See For Miles'. Pete was operating when the clouds over Britain were clearing for the first time; when all of a sudden it was possible to hear Bach and Bo Diddley, for men to wear eyeliner and for women to enjoy sex on their own terms, and to explore what it means to be alive through the previously dismissed medium of pop music.

In the forty years since that has happened pop has reached its zenith and come crashing down again. The Internet, something Pete's old art school tutor Roy Ascott predicted decades before its arrival, has universalised pop but also made it less important. Suburban London produced bands like The Rolling Stones and The Who that left behind hundreds of future songs owned by everyone, literally if not legally, to be sung in bars, school playgrounds and coaches the world over. They made millionaires of the people that played in them and they mirrored the lives of their audiences. It was hard to see how that could happen again.

'When we started out it felt like you were putting your head through a curtain and saying, "There's Jimmy Reed, and there's Thomas Tallis," and there was a perfect view. The problem now is that the Internet delivers music and information in an inert way. The ability to see things clearly simply by standing still is what's missing. You are alone at a computer, feeling you have the world at your fingertips when in fact you are running around this huge library like a chicken with its head cut off. But there are periodic revisits to that polar centre, that place we were all trying to get to. The function of music is still the same. The dancing, the public spectacle, the fame and the live gigs are less important than they appear. What is important is the straight line, uncomplicated, uncluttered, between the artist and the listener. It's a pure line of communication and therefore affirmation of: are you where I am? That was all The Who were ever really trying to achieve.'

I said goodbye to Pete and Rachel and walked down Richmond Hill along Queens Road, where our family had its brief period of normality complete with Victorian-style home décor and a Volvo in the drive, and took the train from Richmond to Waterloo and then Queens Road, Peckham, and wondered if The Who still upheld that pure line of communication. Pete Townshend's gift was that he was a restless, unsatisfied soul. He may have been very rich indeed, but he was too bright and too complicated to use that wealth to divorce himself from everybody else in the way that lesser talents have – Rod Stewart, for example. I didn't have much interest in going to The Who's latest concert, but the legacy Pete had left behind, from the manic early hits like 'Can't Explain' and 'My Generation' to the grey melancholy of his mod opera *Quadrophenia* to the depravity of *Tommy*, his distorted semi-autobiography of a deaf, dumb and blind boy becoming a false messiah through the preposterous medium of pinball – surely a metaphor for the equally preposterous medium of pop – captured the British imagination. The Who is an example of what pop, as exciting, amoral, fantastical and realistic as it is, can achieve.

Over the next few weeks I made various attempts to understand modern pop music in London. I went with a Japanese friend to a karaoke bar in Soho and discovered that the cheesier and camper the song was, the more fun it was to sing: 'Stayin' Alive' by The Bee Gees and 'Thank You For

The Music' by ABBA made sense in this environment while 'She's Lost Control' by Joy Division didn't. I listened out to what the girls on the back of the top deck of the 171 from Peckham sang along to. It was all R&B by American super-stars like Mary J Blige and Beyonce Knowles. British music rarely got a look-in.

I took note of what the children liked. Otto, who was seven, appeared to have a real hatred of pure pop. He presented me with a drawing of a boy covering his ears and sticking out his tongue as broken notes danced about his head. Underneath the picture he had written: 'Gary Barlow is RUBISH'.

'Why don't you like Gary Barlow?' I asked him, surprised that he had even heard of the leader of nineties boy-band sensation Take That.

'Because he's rubbish,' he replied. For Otto, pop was terrible and rock was great. He loved 'Smoke On The Water' by Deep Purple and 'The Ace Of Spades' by Motorhead. Keith Moon was his hero. Girls Aloud were as bad as it got.

'I like the classic guys,' said Otto on his musical tastes, answering the question from the vantage point of lying down on the living-room floor, creating mythical beasts with a selection of coloured pencils. 'The Beatles, Mick Dagger, Sky Saxon . . .' Sky Saxon was the lead singer of The Seeds and not quite on the same classic level as Mick Dagger, although of a similar vintage. 'Girls at my school like the modern stuff, the fashion music, like Rihanna. I hate it.'

Pearl, who was five, took a more sympathetic view of pop. But what she and her best friend Rosa really connected with were songs from the musicals. They loved *The Sound Of Music* and sang 'Do-Re-Mi', surely one of the most brilliantly simple pieces of music ever written, all the time. They loved *Bugsy Malone*, *High School Musical* and perhaps surprisingly the sixties flop *Camelot* and the French fantasy *Peau d'Ane*, in which a king threatens to marry his daughter (she *is*

Catherine Deneuve, although this is not really an excuse) and a donkey shits gold coins. I made a recording of Pearl giving a spirited performance of 'Do-Re-Mi' in our living room, her Peckham twang more apparent on the playback than it was in daily life, in an attempt to capture an authentic voice of our nation's musical youth.

Rosa and Pearl had plans for the future. They were forming a singing ballet troupe with Rosa on lead vocals and Pearl providing the dancing. I asked them what kind of material they would be doing. 'High School Musical,' they replied, absently. Rosa, the more theatrical of the two, took little persuasion to do a version of the *Bugsy Malone* song 'My Name Is Tallulah', originally performed by 12-going-on-25 Jodie Foster, complete with rolling eyes and shimmering jazz hands. Pearl was more reticent, but both of these girls had discovered for themselves the joy of theatricality, of music as glamour and escapism.

I was thinking about all of this when, tired and uninspired one evening, I turned on the television to watch the Brit Awards, the annual pop industry showcase that is about as far from the elemental traditions of Britain it is possible to find. I was ready to dismiss the whole thing as a pointless sham when The Arctic Monkeys, the clever and successful Sheffield group that have been one of the few modern bands to capture aspects of Britain in an honest and recognisable way, came onto the stage drunk and sarcastic. They were making fun of the Brit School, the southeast London comprehensive that is part-funded by the British music industry and which concentrates on the performing arts so much that it keeps pumping out massively successful pop stars: Katie Melua, Leona Lewis, Adele, Amy Winehouse and The Kooks were a few of the stars of the day that claimed the Brit as their alma mater.

Half of the audience was made up of children from the Brit School, excited to be there, and all of a sudden The

Arctic Monkeys seemed like the cool kids taking the piss out of the classroom swots. I thought of Pearl and Rosa, a few years on, working hard on their first performance, and it made me want to go up to The Arctics and kick their little monkey butts. But I decided to go the other way and investigate the Brit School. It's in the suburbs, of course – in Selhurst in Croydon, which isn't so far from where we live, so should Pearl go full throttle down the jazz-hands road she might want to apply for the Brit as her secondary school. I contacted the administrator, Arthur Boulton, and explained what I was doing. He wrote back to say that he would happily arrange for a day trip and a guided tour of the school.

Selhurst is not a glamorous place. It has the dour practicality of an average down-to-heel London suburb: a grey concrete train station, small greasy cafés with immovable plastic seats, Poundstretcher shops, industrial estates and rows of terraced pre-war houses with St George's cross flags and little front gardens that have an occasional nod to exoticism in the form of a palm tree or a yucca. The Brit is a few streets away from the station and looks like a fairly typical comprehensive: playing fields surround a central modern building and a handful of nondescript pre-fabricated blocks.

I arrived at a quarter to nine. There was a lot of hugging going on. The school foyer was like a cross between an institution hall, the green room at London Palladium and a junior fashion show. 'Oh my God, hat hair!' screamed one girl in a red cape and yellow drainpipes, clutching her head theatrically. In the background you could hear a band running through Bob Dylan's 'Mr Tambourine Man'. Lank-haired youths with bodies like angle-poise lamps and guitars on their backs shuffled past. A group of girls in leotards with tight ponytails marched up the stairs. You half-expected a miniature Marcel Marceau to walk in, miming an excuse about how the dog ate his homework, before getting shoved out of the way by half the cast of *Chicago*.

Arthur met me at the entrance hall. A light-voiced man with a large grey moustache, Arthur taught final-year students the business end of the pop world; a tough call at a time when much of it was going through a huge period of uncertainty and change due to the revolutionising power of the Internet. 'We hold auditions in the evening for the industry, but the students are warned not to give out anything more than their name,' he explained. 'Most are under eighteen and they can't sign contracts, so if any of them get offers from agents or managers they can come in with their parents to explain the contract to them. If they want to take it further I'll put them in touch with a series of entertainment lawyers.' As extracurricular activities go, it made a change from judo.

There was no bell to announce it – the teachers reason that when the kids have left school there will be nobody to tell them to get to rehearsals on time so they had to learn self-discipline – but it was time for the first lesson of the day, which took the form of a trip with a group of Year 10 (fourteen- and fifteen-year-old) music students performing a concert at a primary school for autistic children. Arthur had told me that the students regularly stage concerts and plays at everything from hospices to prisons 'to give something back to the community, and to remind them how lucky they are'. As the kids crammed into a back room to run through their numbers I cornered a few to ask how the Brit differs from a normal school.

'There's no bullying or racism or anything because we've all got something in common,' said a tall, pretty fifteen-year-old from Peckham called Coco, who applied for the Brit on the advice of her singing teacher. 'There are no physical fights. But everyone from my old school thinks I've changed because it's all gone to my head.'

'They treat you more like adults here, as individuals rather than children,' added her friend Christina, who was playing piano in the concert. Christina got up at a quarter to six to make the ninety-minute journey from her home in East London to the school, and had wanted to go to the Brit since she was ten. 'There are lots of us that live far away, and that just shows how much we want to come to this school. They're very strict about punctuality and attendance so that when we're older we know we should be on time and have that discipline.'

Coco was initially sceptical about the Brit. 'I didn't want to go to a performing arts school with people doing jazz hands everywhere,' she said. 'I was totally against the idea of being surrounded by emotionally needy teenagers. But then I went to Pimlico Comprehensive and someone tried to cut my hair off. So here I am.'

I asked the girls what they would like to do when they're older. Coco said she wanted to write film soundtracks, be a singer, and 'do some fashion label stuff', although not necessarily in that order. Christina plumped for the simpler answer of being a musician, and she would settle for being a music teacher. Then it was time to perform the show. It was not the easiest of audiences – some of the autistic children were hiding under the benches and covering their ears while others were threatening to start a stage invasion – but the performers took it in their stride.

An abiding memory of school mornings for me is being beaten around the head with a pillow by my mother until I finally got out of bed to make it in time for the school bell. Imagining what made fourteen-year-old Christina leap up before dawn to skip off to the first lesson of the day was hard, but as Arthur said, 'It's all about commitment. We have a very low absenteeism level and there are always kids staying on for rehearsals at the end of the school day. The biggest problem we have is chucking them out so we can close up.'

On the journey back from the autism school a stereo-typically grumpy coach driver snapped at the kids for not putting their bags into the luggage hold. It was a reminder that this was still a school like any other. And this journey might be worse than most: the kids shrieked every time the coach hit a speed bump. 'They can be quite dramatic,' said the music teacher, a woman named Liz, 'but they're more grounded than you think. Fame is not a word that comes up on a daily basis.'

The school had an uneasy relationship with fame. While proud of former students who are now household names – bland pop favourite Katie Melua is remembered fondly as a kind, popular girl who worked hard – it was emphasised to me again and again that the school encour-aged creativity and artistic endeavour, not stardom or diva-like behaviour.

'I'm always amazed at how nice the kids are,' said Liz. 'It's because they learn to work together here, and a lot of them would have struggled to fit in elsewhere. There's a girl in Year 10 who comes to school in her pyjamas. There's a boy on the arts strand who dresses as a girl. You meet some of these kids and you think: thank *God* they found this place.'

It's common for famous Brit alumni to distance them-selves from the school. 'Once you've left it might not be very cool to say you went to the Brit, although it's very cool for the kids now,' said Liz. 'It's much more rock'n'roll to say you dropped out of school and never had a music lesson in your life than admitting you studied for years and had a really good education.'

After lunch it was time for Arthur's lesson with senior music students: on contracts. 'The American R&B group TLC made $175 million in record sales and ended up bank-rupt,' he told the class of eighteen-year-olds. 'The reason for that was a bad contract that gave them only two per cent of royalties. You need to understand the implications of your business arrangement with a manager or a record company.'

'Can my mum manage me?'

'What experience has she got, Nathan?'

'I think she might have a degree.'

'This is a bit random,' asked a girl, 'but can you send managers a bottle of vodka?'

The class told me about their experiences at the Brit. 'I came here because my previous school was rubbish and wanting to be a musician was frowned on there,' said the potentially mum-managed Nathan, who had his future career mapped out: be in a band, get signed by a record company, and become a producer when the band split up. 'You leave here believing it's possible to make it as a musician, while also knowing how the business works.'

'On my first day here some musical-theatre students were doing an African dance in the corridor,' said a boy called Ollie. 'Musical theatre may be our sworn enemies, but I have to admit they add to the unique energy of the place.'

This wasn't the first time I had heard mutterings about musical theatre. The Brit may not be the English equivalent of the eighties American TV series *Fame*, but if you do walk into the canteen to see a group of teenagers standing on the tables, hoofing their way through a number from *Bugsy Malone* and doing the dreaded jazz hands, the chances are they're musical-theatre students.

'They tend to be the most vocal,' explained Arthur. 'Music students are a bit cooler. Dance students are perfectly turned out and always on time. Production students, who do all the backstage work for everyone else, are the most grown-up.'

It was time to meet these musical-theatre students, older versions of Pearl and Rosa for whom the magic of song and dance had never faded. The problems faced by these boys and girls were different, if no less significant, from those of the average flamboyant teen. 'People see musical-theatre students and say, "They're fine, they're happy, they're dancing on the tables," but we constantly need to address their emotional welfare,' whispered the course director, a boxer's son called Adrian, as we sat in on a class in which students were tackling issues of racism and nationality. 'We won't have a boy of sixteen being picked on because he's gay, but that boy might be worried about dealing with four auditions in two weeks, performing eight shows, getting his band together, getting into drama school, exposing his feelings on a daily basis – and just being a teenager.'

A girl called Charnele was pointing out the offensiveness of the term black-on-black crime while a boy called Declan stated it is almost impossible to decide who is British and who isn't, concluding, 'You can't have a ten-year warranty on being British.' These teenagers were talking about belonging when the majority were the odd ones out in their own communities.

'The nicest thing about coming here,' said Charnele, 'is being around people that are normal.' Mass hysteria from the 'normal' people ensued.

Out of all the students I had met, Charnele and Declan were the most animated, vocal and, for want of a better term, showbiz. Both were dedicated to their cause: Charnele made an hour-and-a-half trip from North London to the Brit every weekday while Declan had moved out of his family home in Luton to lodge near to the school. 'I've been in musicals since I was five and there's nothing else in the world I've ever wanted to do,' he said. 'Coming here has made me think practically about money and career, but also encouraged me to believe that following my dream is possible.'

'The weekend comes and I can't wait to get back to school on Monday,' claimed Charnele. 'When I said earlier that people are normal here, I meant they're more open-minded. Everyone at my old school was black and it was like us and them. Here, nobody cares about your background because everyone is different. Everyone has a talent.'

This is the great equalising power of pop. Its blandness is its strength. One's background or ethnicity is irrelevant; it all falls into the great melting pot, smoothing out strong flavours to form a mass that is never too much of one thing or another but has a universal appeal, like tomato ketchup. In one sense, pop is the real folk music of Britain. One could argue that since it depends on fame and glamour it is the opposite of the people's music, but you could hardly say that crowding around a karaoke machine and belting out 'Burning Love' by Leona Lewis is less of an authentic folk experience than standing up in a remote pub in the Scottish Highlands and giving a pure-voice rendition of an ancient ballad like 'Andrew Lammie', a finger in the ear and a pint of bitter on the gnarled wooden table before you.

The journey into pop was odd, though. Much of my travelling around Britain had so far involved seeing how communities involved themselves in music, and how people could have a relationship with singing without worrying about taking it up as a profession. Pop was all about professionalism. In a few years' time many of the kids I had met at the Brit would be dealing with the insecurities and realities of being a performer, at a time when the old model of making money through flogging records to the public is collapsing. Living her adult life through the prism of fame was at least partly to blame for the unravelling of former Brit School musical-theatre student Amy Winehouse, and while most of the Brit alumni seemed better equipped, you did have to wonder how much any school should be encouraging young people to live their lives in public. Before I left, there was a chance to ask Arthur about the ethical issue of the Brit's role in providing talent for the British entertainment industry.

'The one part of this job that makes me pause for thought is the way the mass media treats people,' said Arthur, sitting in an office filled with all the usual papers on exam results and timetables that you would expect to see in any school in the country. 'Do I want to encourage that? We can't possibly prepare someone for the strange experience of fame. But we can develop people as whole people, rather than just the part of the brain that learns music or acting. And the reality is that fame and fortune will only be an issue for a small percentage of our students.'

It was the end of the school day. Before leaving I spotted Declan and Charnele practising co-ordinated dance moves in a corridor, and for these lively teenagers, whose hugely different backgrounds meant they would have been unlikely to have encountered one another away from the Brit, schooldays might really be the happiest of their lives. Who knows what the harsh world of pop, musical theatre and show business would have in store for them? It would take strength of character to deal with the sneering from more credible performers, not to mention the endless insecurities that trying to make a living in this world would throw at them.

Now it was time to look into the other side of the capital's musical life: the unregulated, anarchic world of the underground.

Chapter Eight

London, Part Two: The Underground

WE WERE IN THE VAUXHALL ASTRA, SPLUTTERING along Evelina Road in Nunhead in southeast London, a few streets away from our house. Along what passes for a high street there are boarded-up shop façades, 'Ayres the Bakers', where the same silent, cross-legged tramp always sits outside, and a decent fish-monger's that anyone living in the area clings to desperately as a symbol of hope for things to come. The children go to a school up the hill and at the end of the road was Peckham Rye, the flat expanse of land where William Blake once saw angels. This was our neighbourhood, a little downtrodden, perhaps, but not without its own character.

'Look at those dudes,' said NJ, pointing to two men, one with longish blond hair and the other with a quivering Afro, riding bicycles that looked like pedal-powered versions of Hell's Angels choppers, low-slung and laid-back. They wore leather jackets and faded denims, had guitar cases strapped to their backs and were weaving in and out of traffic, appearing so much more liberated than all of us in our motor-powered cages.

'That's Tim and Lewis,' I said, and lowered the window in an attempt to catch them, but it was too late. They cut across Nunhead Lane and were off-roading through Peckham Rye, cut-price free-birds on a pedestrian walkway to nowhere.

Tim and Lewis were a part of the bohemian underground that London, for all its high costs, is capable of supporting. Tim wrote surreal, observational songs inspired by Peckham and the forthcoming end of the world, performing them under the moniker The Boycott Coca-Cola Experience. Lewis was one of the best guitarists I had ever heard, a latter-day Jimi Hendrix with the looks to match. Both had kids, and both got by through busking – Lewis in particular was in thrall to the romantic idea of travelling around with his guitar and playing to whoever turned up, wherever he might be.

They also performed regularly at a night called The Easycome, which had been running in various pub back rooms in Nunhead, southeast London for the last fifteen years, organised – if that's the word – by a man called Andy Hank Dog who had long dreadlocks and a cowboy hat under which was a rarely seen, ultra-shiny dome of dazzling baldness. Some of the people that got up to perform at The Easycome were awful, a very few were brilliant, and most were just OK. On the first night I went there a middle-aged woman in thigh-high leather boots and a bizarre sparkly mini-dress handed out percussion instruments from an Asda carrier bag before getting up on stage and howling while a silent man, presumably her boyfriend or husband, played guitar with the kind of stoic discipline someone in his position would need. The woman was leaping about, doing the splits – not advisable unless you think carefully about your underwear beforehand – and shrieking.

It was awful. But what made it particularly disturbing was that she looked rather a lot like my mother.

I had known Tim for years. A tall, handsome Lancastrian with a face that doesn't move much and an upper lip that is entirely static, he had tried out various day jobs and been unhappy in all of them when, in his mid-thirties and with three young daughters, he decided to pack it all in and take the seemingly unstable career move of writing and performing songs about Peckham while moving towards a self-sufficient lifestyle. Convinced that the energy sources the twentieth-century Western world had taken for granted so far would soon come to an end, Tim was building his own: the amplifier he played with was bicycle-powered, and he even had a solar-powered oven to bake his Eccles cakes in.

It was a gamble that paid off. Tim's new path came at a time when London councils, desperate to prove their green credentials, were handing out grants to anything that made a visible display of ecological awareness. Tim's bicycle-run miniature rock concerts fitted the bill perfectly. He was self-contained and content.

One evening Tim came over to the house to record a song about Ayres the Bakers, which he had performed that afternoon with Lewis at a free local festival called I Love Peckham. He and Lewis had set up their bicycle-powered equipment in a vacant space just behind Peckham Library, an area generally reserved for crack-dealing and mugging, and during their performance they had been surrounded by about thirty teenage boys, hoodies pulled over their heads like junior Grim Reapers. 'It really felt like they were going to beat us up,' said Tim. 'There was Lewis, playing his acoustic guitar and looking like Jimi Hendrix, and all these kids were jostling around us. But suddenly the atmosphere changed and they got into it.'

Tim sang a song called 'Café Spice', named after a cheap restaurant on Rye Lane. One verse describes a Chinese man coming in to the café to hawk counterfeit DVDs from a plastic bag. 'I said, "Where did you get those DVDs from?" He said, "Four for ten pound".' It was reminiscent of the scenes the country blues singers of the American South conjured up in the thirties and forties, and also of something Mark E Smith of The Fall, the great master of the mystical everyday, might write. It was proof that you didn't have to dream of distant worlds to create material. The most fascinating aspects of life are right there on your doorstep.

'Ever since I was a kid I've been a fan of music,' said Tim, when I asked him why he decided to jack it all in and become an ecologically friendly cycling minstrel. 'I was going to the Easycome every Wednesday night and was enjoying watching all these people get up and do something, however good or bad they were, and it started to change my view of music. When you watch someone really bad get up on stage and perform with confidence, it's inspiring. So what really inspired me was when *you* picked up the guitar and started doing gigs. At that point I thought: if he can do it, there's really no excuse.'

I'm not entirely sure that this was complimentary. But it was true that I had picked up the guitar not so long ago, at the age of 34, and had even been foolhardy enough to perform a number at the Easycome. The guitar has been a close companion ever since, but Tim took it much further than I ever did. 'In the past, I always obsessed over bands,' he said. 'For years I listened to nothing but The Fall. Now I hardly listen to music at all. It was like I spent twenty years soaking up music and finally it's ready to come out of me. But what's really fascinated me is how I've always been a shy person, and yet I can get up on stage and do these ridiculous songs when I certainly can't sing and can't even play guitar very well. It's a myth that only special people can perform. You have a go and realise that anyone can do it.'

I had always thought that Tim was on a mission to lecture the world on the importance of ecological self-sufficiency. It seemed that I was wrong. 'The bicycle-powered thing was a cynical ploy to get gigs,' he said. 'And it worked. Councils have budgets for anything you can legitimately call green and I get as many pedal-powered gigs as I can cope with. At first I thought all my songs had to be about the destruction of the planet. Now my attitude is: sod the educational crap. I'm just going to travel around and have fun.'

Tim's shows had been transformed by meeting Lewis. 'He's the most musical person I've ever met. He rides his bike playing guitar and goes to bed with it. He's a kid, really. He's a total inspiration because as long as he's playing music, he's happy. Most people think there's a set way of making it, like you're only someone if you're on the front page of the tabloids, falling out of a nightclub after winning *Britain's Got Talent*. But Lewis and I can go anywhere and do gigs, and whether people like what we do or not doesn't matter. People either call us hippies, or cunts, or they love it. And I've noticed that none of it, the abuse and hostility or the glory, really affects me that much. It's the doing it in the first place that makes the difference. Honestly, I've never felt so alive.'

I needed to make a field recording of Lewis. While Tim was consciously making a decision to ditch the straight world and become a street musician, Lewis had never known any other life. Now in his early thirties, he had managed to avoid conventional employment in favour of playing guitar, performing wherever he could, and driving around in an enormous, dilapidated green van that he sometimes slept in. He suggested we make a recording in Greenwich Foot Tunnel, which stretches from one side of the River Thames to the other and is accessible only by lift. Buskers are strictly forbidden.

A few days later I met Tim and Lewis outside what remains of the *Cutty Sark* in Greenwich. Lewis was emulating his hero, the thirties Mississippi country blues legend Robert Johnson: fedora tilted at a jaunty angle, grey jacket, black shirt and tie with tie clip, ironed black cotton trousers and black leather shoes. He had a one-man-band set-up strapped to a shopping trolley, complete with a guitar and amplifier, two kick drums and a cymbal, a harmonica, a microphone and a microphone stand. 'We're going to last about a minute,' said Tim, nervously, as we called for the lift down to the foot tunnel. 'There's a guy who's employed to chuck you out at the first sign of busking.'

'You've got to try though, haven't you?' said Lewis, breaking into a wide, wild grin reminiscent of Phil Lynott, the hard-living, late lead singer of the Irish seventies rock band Thin Lizzy. 'You're bound to get great acoustics in a tunnel.'

The middle-aged man operating the lift stared at his copy of the *Sun* in silence as we piled in with Lewis's musical trolley and my recording equipment. We walked into the middle of the tunnel and Lewis set up. A Japanese girl stopped to watch him. He started playing a blues with a heavy beat and an incessant riff called 'Fresh Air'. He got through about a minute of it before the lift operator marched towards us holding a battered laminated card before us. 'If you don't stop playing immediately I have no choice but to call the police,' he announced, sounding more scared than scary. 'You ain't allowed to do that here.'

Lewis didn't stop. The man thrust the card an inch away from his face. 'Them cameras are filming everything wot you do,' he said. 'If you continue you'll be banned from using this tunnel for a year.' He sounded like he was reciting the words, like he had used them many times before.

The Japanese girl took a photograph.

'We're doing one track,' said Lewis moodily, unapologetically, like someone aware of his higher status. 'We're recording.'

'I'm doing a project,' I told him. 'He's a living legend of the blues.'

'It don't matter what you're doing or who you are. It don't matter if you're students – although you look a bit long in the tooth for that – or professionals. You've got to get written permission from the council before you can come down here and make your record or what have you. You can't do nuffink without it.'

Lewis shook his head as he started packing up. 'I hate being moved on, man,' he muttered, more to himself than the (rather unconvincing) figure of authority currently spoiling our plans. I suggested we record a track in his van. 'Maybe you're right,' he said. 'Maybe this wasn't the place to do "Fresh Air". There isn't enough of it down here.'

We walked to the semi-derelict street the van was parked on, where two boys were kicking a football between a wire fence and the side of the van and lines of washing were draped across the walls of the tenement block that shadowed us. 'I reckon we can drive up to where my mum lives in Blackheath,' said Lewis, loading the equipment into the back of the van as the boys stopped to crowd around and ask him what he was doing with his guitar-amplifier-drum-shopping-trolley arrangement. 'With any luck there won't be anyone to move us on there.'

It was a grey day, and cold. We drove through empty streets lined with estates, the old van creaking up the hill until Lewis parked it next to the flat expanse of the heath itself. The small council house he grew up in was a couple of streets away. As Tim and I sat in the front of the van Lewis crouched in the back, his miniature drum kit and micro-phone stand taking up the space between a small sink and a gas heater. Above him was a tangle of electrical cables, metal fibres poking out of them with threatening irregularity. He started on a song with a folk-blues tinge called 'Wilderness'. 'It's about letting the wilderness grow,' he said quietly, with a placid smile. 'Some day it will take over the city and cover all the buildings and we'll start all over again. I want to embrace the wilderness. I'll keep walking until I leave the city and reach the countryside.'

'Have you been to the countryside recently?' I asked him.

He looked upwards in thought. 'I did get out, not so long ago,' he said. 'It was really nice. I watched a tractor pulling a plough. It was like an oil painting . . . groovy stuff, man.'

I started to record Lewis doing 'Fresh Air' once more. This time we got through about two minutes before there was a knock on the side of the van. Tim opened it to reveal a smiling, lank-haired, middle-aged woman holding a clutch of canvas safari hats.

'Any of you fellows want to buy a hat?' said the woman in a cheerful croak. She held up her wares. 'Boys like you might need them for protection.'

'I'm all right, and he's already got a nice hat,' I said, pointing to Lewis.

Lewis craned his neck round and looked at the woman, rather irritably. 'Can't you see we're recording, Mum?' he said. 'Right, Tim. From now on, you guard the door. No mums allowed.'

'I just came to tell you to watch out,' she said with a smile, eyes sliding sideways. 'There's a couple of community coppers prowling around.'

Lewis tried to get through 'Fresh Air' for the third time. It was all going well – I think we might have got through two and a half minutes of the song – when he stopped suddenly and said, 'Hey, there's my nan! Bang on the window, will you, Tim?'

A tiny old lady with white hair and a broad grin appeared at the side door this time. ''Ello, Lew,' she said. 'Do you and your friends want a cup of tea?'

'We're all right, Nan,' he replied, smiling back at her. 'We're recording a song.'

Her eyes widened. 'Ooh! Don't let me stop you. Cheerio.' She tottered off.

All of Lewis's current songs were about nature, and the countryside, and escape, at a time when he was thinking of giving up the itinerant musician's life to train as a para-medic. 'I've got to be a family man, man,' he said, shaking his head. 'I can't go on like this forever. But then have you seen Hank Dog's new girlfriend? Oh my gosh!'

Andy Hank Dog was of indefinite age, but we had worked out that he could not be less than fifty. He claimed to have once been in The Sex Pistols. He had never, as far as any of us knew, had a job.

'She's beautiful,' said Lewis, excitedly. 'At first I thought it was just Hank Dog's lucky night, but she really is his girlfriend. It's amazing! She gives all of mankind a ray of hope. When I saw her with Andy I thought: maybe it's not time to settle down just yet. Maybe there is still time to see things, to play guitar, to be a musician without any money or prospects and still manage to get a nice girl . . .'

It took three or four more attempts, but he did finally nail a take of 'Fresh Air'. Lewis was an incredible musician. His timing was perfect, he could play three instruments at once, and he created a totally committed sound on his guitar that was as much a product of growing up without much money in southeast London as it was of learning to play the blues like Robert Johnson. He was one of the most charismatic and talented people I had met on the journey so far, and you knew that his character was such that he could never be a professional musician in the conventional sense. He was too anarchic – and uncalculating.

This was London's musical underground. Pop depended on a well-established industry to support it, but just below the surface were thousands of people making music on guitars or computers, finding little places like The Easycome to perform it, and getting it out through Internet sites such as MySpace. Most did it alongside some other way of making a living. The strange sub-genre of British hip-hop known as grime was a case in point. With the minimum of a musical backing, typically made on a computer program that comes with the games console PlayStation or with one called Frooty Loops, young Londoners were making aural commentaries on their lives and aspirations. It was multi-racial, although it was primarily a product of second or third generation Black British kids finding their own voice, and it had little to do with the mainstream.

Grime was just one strand in the ever-changing creative underground of the capital. British urban music shifted constantly, had some relation to hip-hop and dance, and very rarely got beyond a certain level. American hip-hop stars like 50 Cent and Puff Daddy made great shows of their wealth, put a huge emphasis on expensive production values and went on about God. Rappers from London insulted each other and wrote songs about the Number 38 bus to Hackney. Very few achieved any kind of real fame outside of their immediate field; that summer the West London-born singer Estelle had successfully made the transition from hip-hop local heroine to proper US-style R&B superstar, but she was an anomaly. Americans are not afraid of success. The British are. Grime's great hope and talent, a tiny north London teenager called Louise Harman who performed under the name of Lady Sovereign, sabotaged her career at the point when it was all about to happen.

Attempts to contact Lady Sovereign came to nothing. She was the funniest and best-known rapper to come out of the grime world and nobody seemed to know what had happened to her. I tried to contact various other grime people through the music-sharing social network site MySpace, but nobody got back to me. Eventually, at around the point I was about to give up on London and take off on another road trip, I got a call from someone called Medasyn. A friend of a friend had told him about what I was doing, and since he was Lady Sovereign's producer alongside a host of lesser-known MCs he might be a good person to talk to. He was happy to meet up.

The following day I cycled over to a dilapidated, graffiti-covered warehouse on Bethnal Green Road in East London, where a dark, desolate entrance led to a urine-soaked stairwell. 'Is this the fifth floor?' I asked a middle-aged Indian woman who passed me on the stairs. She looked scared and quickened her pace. Finally I found huge iron double doors that, with a hefty shove, opened up onto a network of units occupied by urban-music producers, artists and record-label owners. Within this concrete labyrinth was the person who could best tell me why the stars of London's urban-music underground always seem to end up shooting themselves in the foot.

Medasyn, a fresh-faced man of about thirty known to his mum and dad as Gabriel Olegavich, took me into his studio, a cramped space filled with computers, keyboards, cables and musical instruments. The walls were covered in stickers and posters for club nights. There would have been a magnificent view of London if you could see through the, for want of a better word, grime.

'I really need to clean those windows,' he said cheerfully as I tried to look out of them. 'It's one of those jobs that I've been meaning to get around to for the last . . .' he counted out numbers on his fingers, '. . . seven years.'

It was Gabriel who had discovered Lady Sovereign in the first place. I asked him what had happened to her.

'She took the whole putting yourself down thing so far,' said Gabriel, 'that she fucked up her entire career.'

Gabriel, who grew up in Greenwich in southeast London, met Lady Sovereign through a community theatre project at the Albany Theatre in nearby Deptford in 2002. 'I started working with these boys doing MCing, but all the lyrics were about violence and I could see that the whole thing was going to collapse if it didn't develop,' he said. 'So I asked around to see if there were any female rappers. Everyone said that the best one was a fifteen-year-old midget from Kilburn called Lady Sovereign.'

Back then Lady Sovereign was a fresh and very funny rapper who was a star of a small scene that centred on raves and pirate radio stations in Hackney and Kilburn. The daughter of punks, she became a self-deprecating stereotype of the London council-estate girl: hair scraped back to facelift-giving proportions, fingers laden with gold rings that could have been worth thousands or might have fallen off a market stall at Peckham Rye, and wearing the kind of androgynous tracksuit-type 'leisurewear' that has become the uniform for urban working-class Britain. She had the talent and intelligence to do for England what the rapper Eminem did for America: capture a side of modern life with wit and accuracy, and create scenarios that were authentic and relatable. While her British male counterparts were rapping about how many guns they had, Sovereign was writing songs about friends that put on so much fake tan they ended up a similar shade to the popular soft drink Tango.

As her confidence grew, Lady Sovereign's vocal style developed from a fake Jamaican patois into the cockney she actually spoke in. Her rapping became frenetic, reflecting the fact that she wasn't stoned on a Jamaican beach but living in one of the fastest-moving cities in the world. And she took on the punk influence that she had grown up with. She developed to the point where the music she made was no longer a pastiche, but a true expression of her environment and her daily reality.

Word got out about Lady Sovereign. Before long the record industry had high hopes for her. She was signed to Def Jam, the hugely influential American hip-hop label, and put on a seven-week tour of the US supporting the superstar singer Gwen Stefani. This is how English acts break in

America: they get a prestigious support slot and do as much local radio, television, newspaper and magazine promotion as time will allow. Each day spent in a new town is dedicated to interviews while the evening is given over to the concert. Jay-Z held her up as a great new talent. Def Jam pumped money into her based on the belief that she would sell at least a million records in the US alone.

Lady Sovereign didn't do a single interview throughout the whole seven-week tour. She refused to leave her hotel room until it was time to do the gig.

'Def Jam are used to artists imbued with the American work ethic, and Sov is lazy,' said Gabriel. 'But the real problem was that she started to doubt herself. All of a sudden nothing was good enough. Every time she came here to record a new track she would find fault with whatever she did. The worst time was when she was meant to headline a festival in Germany and she wouldn't come out of her flat. The rest of the band was outside, pleading with her. It was awful.'

What was it about local music in London that made its artists commit career hari-kari the moment it looked like it was all going to happen? The So Solid Crew was another example – a group of friends from an estate in Wandsworth brimming over with ideas and energy, who descended into paranoia and in-fighting not long after having a breakthrough hit with 2001's '21 Seconds'. Perhaps Lady Sovereign simply went as far as she could go. She wrote songs that insulted starlets hardly anyone knew. A north London singer called Jentina had a rather unsophisticated track called 'Badass Stripper'. Sovereign responded with a song called 'Sadass Stripper', which upset Jentina so much that she effectively gave up on a career in music. Lady Sovereign was a very British star: clever, funny, small-minded and incapable of dealing with the world on a grand scale.

Grime itself is a product of a makeshift, small-scale mentality. On the computer program Frooty Loops the factory setting for the rhythm is 140 beats per minute. That became the tempo the majority of grime was set to, partly because the people making it couldn't be bothered to explore the program any further. The music got simpler and simpler until it consisted of nothing more than a long bass note, some handclaps and a beat, over which people rapped. Pirate radio shows were the medium for this to get out to some sort of audience. 'The music became rough and uncommercial and sooner or later someone said, "That sounds grimy, man",' explained Gabriel. 'At the same time there was a shop in Croydon called Big Apple Records that was fostering a local black music scene. It all came from there.'

Many of the people producing grime were the children of West African immigrants, and it had a memory of Ghanaian and Nigerian music in its complex stop-start rhythms. The songs changed so fast it was almost impossible to catch a hold of them. Musicians made dub plates – pieces of vinyl that can only be played two or three times before wearing out – that were then given to DJs to spin in clubs and raves where MCs would rap over them, generally coming up with something on the spot. In this ever-shifting world the moment was all. I told Gabriel about my problems in getting hold of any grime artists.

'This is why the whole British MC thing never gets anywhere,' said Gabriel, leaning back in his chair with the air of a man who had dealt with broken expectations more than once. 'You contact them, you set something up, they're excited and keen, and then they don't turn up. It happens all the time.'

A uniquely British style that thrived away from the mainstream was bhangra, that high-energy mix of Punjabi folk and disco that came out of Southall, Birmingham and Wolverhampton in the seventies and eighties. I knew someone that could give me something of an insight into this world. Tjinder Singh, born in Wolverhampton to Punjabi parents, led a band called Cornershop that had a number-one hit in 1997 with 'Brimful Of Asha', a joyful ode to the Bollywood playback singer Asha Bhosle. Bhangra was a big influence on Tjinder, and he was happy to meet up and explain how it developed.

'Punjabi folk songs are parochial,' said Tjinder, a broad-faced man with a strong Midlands accent, despite having lived in the capital for close on half his life. 'They tend to be made up on the spot and they might have a go at someone in the village, or talk about the wedding that's happening that day. There are loads of ones about sex. You get lines like: "Your parents are away and we could meet in the sugar cane fields. How about it?" That tradition, which has now gone, is where bhangra has its roots.'

When Tjinder was growing up the Punjabi wedding song – typically risqué and usually specific to the couple getting married – was at the heart of the culture. Groups would play in the temples, however naughty their lyrics might be, since the temples were for the community as much as they were places of worship. But as tensions between Sikhs and Hindus in India grew and the concept of *Khalistan* – Sikh independence of mind and state, demanding Punjab's status as a separate sovereign state – took hold in the late seventies, the fun-loving wedding singers found themselves kicked out onto the street, as Sikh temples in Britain became centres of increasingly dogmatic religious power.

'As Khalistan got bigger the religion got stricter, and although everyone is deemed equal in the temple, to represent the temple through performing there is another matter,' explained Tjinder. 'So the musicians that used to play there for weddings and so on went straight to the local hall and started up their own thing. The halls got bigger, someone bought some disco lights, a few white chaps were roped in to play guitar and keyboards, and then you had bhangra.'

Bhangra became an expression of freedom for British Sikhs not interested in being wholly consumed by the ideologies of Khalistan, which became increasingly militant, culminating in the bombing of Air India Flight 182 in 1985 that resulted in the death of 329 passengers. Bhangra was born of nostalgia for a more innocent India – the dances mimicked the movements of labourers cutting sugar cane – as well as the simple joy of going to the disco and having fun. It hit a boom in the early nineties when huge swathes of Punjabi teenagers would bunk off school and go to daytime raves their parents never knew about, and it is still around today, supported by radio stations like Sunrise and Radio Asia. When he formed Cornershop, initially a noisy punk-rock group that discovered their poppier side later on, Tjinder sought to perform gigs in the spiritual homes of bhangra: Midlands working men's clubs.

'How did it go down?' I asked.

He thought about that for a while, and said, 'Like a lead balloon.'

———————◆————————

There was a time when it seemed London's urban underground music scene was going to break out of its self-imposed ghetto. On starting university in London I had a girlfriend that lived in Sunderland. On the rare occasions she came down south the only thing she wanted to do was go to the club run by the musical collective Soul II Soul at the Africa Centre in Covent Garden. She had read about it, and heard songs by Soul II Soul on the radio, and to her it symbolised all that was fashionable and exciting about the capital. This was the early nineties and, being a typical narrow-minded student, I dismissed Soul II Soul as commercial and uninteresting, but we went to the club anyway, and it was clear that something special was going on. It had the atmosphere of a place that inspired people, that made things happen, and that represented the multi-faceted reality of London. David Bowie's 'Young Americans' would be played alongside a James Brown track, and you felt the people there were taking everything they had grown up with and turning it into something of their own; something that looked to the future.

Soul II Soul was the brainchild of Jazzie B, a north London-born son of Antiguan parents, who started out running Caribbean-style sound systems and slowly expanded Soul II Soul as a brand complete with a shop, a club, a record label, a band and even a philosophy. Perhaps unsurprisingly he grew up in an open-minded household: his parents listened to everything from country and western to The Beatles and American soul singers like Donny Hathaway, while his elder brothers discovered Jamaican ska and reggae, calypso, and a lot of R&B from the labels Stax and Motown. We met for peppermint tea in a hotel bar in central London, and he told me about his theory on how the great curse and strength of British music is the fact that it is always local.

'There's something about British music that never takes itself too seriously, while at the same time knowing that it is the most important thing in the world,' he said, dread-locks turning to grey stacked high on his head. 'We understand that you can be deeply passionate about music and message without overloading it with emotion – nobody in Britain would come up with such a sentimental tune as R

Kelly's "I Believe I Can Fly", for example, unless they were taking the piss.'

R Kelly was an American R&B superstar of dubious moral fibre who really did appear to suffer some sort of messianic self-delusion.

'Grime is a case in point,' Jazzie B continued. 'However much they try and sound like they're from the Bronx they end up being extremely local, suburban even, and through that representing their lives. With a big American artist like Madonna she has to be so far out of your reach that her very appeal is her distance. But look at Amy Winehouse – she seems like one of us. Her music is raw and it's not trying to be anything other than what it is. American music is so often super-slick, well produced, and predictable. Even rap is in the mainstream now, and it's rarely about anything more than the American Dream. There's an element of British music that is always on the margins, always from the underground, and the kids making music on PlayStations could only get away with it here because in America you would have to have a big, grandiose sound to get anywhere. With Soul II Soul we were arrogant enough to call our first album *Club Classics Volume One*, as if there were going to be another ten to follow, but we still knew that we were basically operating out of a little club in Covent Garden.'

Soul II Soul captured an aspirational but positive moment in early nineties London. The democratising power of rave had influenced the capital's culture profoundly and music no longer had to be drawn up on racial or tribal lines. At the same time people were ready to dress up again, to make the most of everything that keeps London alive and to bring a touch of glamour to the reality of their lives. 'It has a lot to do with the class system, and with the remnants of colonialism,' said Jazzie B, when I asked him what Soul II Soul was inspired by. 'You have to remember that Bob

Marley was from the colonies – I think his dad was Scottish – and he talked about natural truths we could all relate to. The whole tradition of the sound system, which is more like having a team than being a musician, was a product of the colonial islands, and the British class system means that you always have people trying to prove themselves while knowing that whatever they will do will only go so far.'

Club Classics Volume One remained the first in a series of one.

———————— ·◆· ————————

Later that day, returning to Peckham and thinking about the trip north that lay ahead, I realised that what could be seen as underground London's great weakness was actually its strength. If you walk along Peckham's Rye Lane there is always somebody you haven't seen before trying to sell something you possibly didn't know existed. Alongside the rows of long-established butchers and fishmongers you might see a man flogging votive candles out of a crate set up on a bollard, or a woman selling hair extensions from a shop space that a week before was boarded up. Nail parlours and hairdressers pop up for a year and go away again. Things change and static does not set in. The music that comes from this world is a reflection of it: unregulated and ever-shifting, it does not stay still. To control it is to negate it.

Now it was time to prepare for my major journey north, out of this world in flux and into the heart of Britain's unchanging landscape, to find out if there was such a thing as an ancient line that ran through the heart of British life.

Chapter Nine

The Ancient Spirit, Part One: Robin Hood's Bay, Yorkshire

THE OLD SONGS OF THE ISLAND OF ENGLAND, SCOTLAND and Wales were still alive. The travelling people I had met had shown me that. Somehow these songs, fashioned hundreds of years ago and articulating the eternal dramas of existence – love, longing, rejection, abandon, rape, war, drunkenness – were not mere museum pieces but fragments of communal memories.

'But the old folk songs are dead,' said a father of one of my son's friends, when I told him what I was doing over the summer. We were standing in the playground on a bright summer morning, dropping our children off at school. 'I don't know them and neither do most people, so how can they still be alive?'

A few feet away Pearl was singing 'Baa Baa Black Sheep' as she skipped about the playground. It was only afterwards that I realised the significance of my five-year-old daughter's unconscious evocation of this ancient tune, and through it, the ancient spirit itself.

The next leg of the journey would be dedicated to discovering if the old songs of England did have relevance and life in the modern age, or whether Charles Hazlewood was right and the people's music was really whatever happened to be hitting the nation's collective consciousness at the time. I had contacted Jon and Fiona, the couple that ran the Sheffield label Singing Knives, which Cornwall's Jarvis and Tiffany had told me about. Jon and Fiona had in turn sent a record by a Bradford girl called Stephanie Hladowski. It had a lovely cover featuring embroidery of a house and a garden, and I noticed that all the songs were traditional.

I put it on. Stephanie Hladowski, who I had never heard of before, sang old Gypsy ballads like 'Andrew Lammie' and 'The Month Of January' with such tender but elemental beauty that she sounded disconnected from an earthly body; a spectral being hanging over the land. She sounded rather like a little girl, but also a very old woman. It was as if she was singing these songs to herself, unaware that anyone was listening. It was gentle music – she either sang unaccompanied, or backed by a bouzouki – but not without power.

I looked on Stephanie's MySpace site, but it didn't reveal much beyond that she liked dub reggae and Eastern European devotional music. I sent her a message and didn't get a response. I contacted Jon and Fiona and got a couple of numbers for her. There was no answer for either, but a day or so later I received a call from Stephanie's mother. Stephanie had been in France with her boyfriend, and now she had a kidney infection, but she was sure that her daughter would be happy to meet as soon as she got better.

I had to make a field recording of Stephanie. There was something in her voice that captured mysterious, historical forces of Britain in an unfettered, natural way, as if she was the medium for the ghosts inhabiting these old ballads. I wondered what she looked like. I imagined a dark-eyed beauty in Gypsy skirt and heavy jewellery and looked forward to meeting her. In the meantime I needed to plan some more stops on the journey northwards, since I couldn't exactly put all the eggs in one basket and assume that the answer lay with a girl I had never met in a city I had never visited.

That evening NJ and I watched a documentary from the mid-sixties called 'Travelling For A Living'. It's about a trio of singing siblings from Hull called The Watersons who, orphaned as children and brought up by their Gypsy grand-mother, formed a band with their friend John and went around the pubs singing traditional English and Scottish songs. There was Lal, the quiet, poetic younger sister, Mike, the Peter Pan-like brother, and sensible, no-nonsense Norma who, as the eldest, took on the role of family matriarch. In the film the siblings are living together alongside Mike's wife and young daughter in a house in the centre of Hull where the curtains are always drawn and nobody goes to bed until the dawn is approaching. There are all kinds of folk legends dropping by, such as the Newcastle singer Louis Killen who juggled a singing career with working on the shipyards, and Anne Briggs, a striking black-haired free spirit, also orphaned, famously in love with the travelling life and shy of recording studios, who eschewed any kind of professional career for freewheeling adventure.

The film is evocative of a time when most of Great Britain was resolutely not swinging and what fun there was happened in the pubs: packed, noisy, smoke-thick and ale-sodden rooms where age was not an issue and most of the community was represented in one way or another. Made in 1964, when The Watersons were becoming stars of the burgeoning revival in folk music, 'Travelling For A Living' paints an attractive picture of this unusual family as they argue about money, get lost driving up and down England in their battered Transit van, and sing to young crowds in Hull pubs. 'The Watersons get up when they want, avoid conventional employment, and are happy,' says the plummy voiceover. 'This is unacceptable to the people of Hull.'

Lal Waterson died in 1998 at the age of 55, but in her curtailed life she sang traditional ballads and wrote intimate songs filled with sadness and mystery that go to the heart of the English character. Her style of singing is so barren it's almost tuneless, and reminiscent of the slate-grey stone of a Yorkshire church, or the chill wind that cuts into your face on a dale in winter. She wrote a lot of her songs in Robin Hood's Bay in Yorkshire, a seaside town where most of The Watersons have been based since leaving Hull in the 1970s. 'Sleeping in my bed, strange thoughts running through my head,' she sings on 'Fine Horseman', a paean to an imaginary lover. 'Dreaming that you were playing with my hair . . . fine flying sparrow, and a fine horseman.' The personal becomes universally resonant.

Norma Waterson married the folk singer and guitarist Martin Carthy, the kind of man nobody can find anything bad to say about. Martin, a former choirboy from Hampstead in north London, fell in love with the old songs of Britain as a teenager and set about working out ways to accompany them on guitar, famously authoring an arrangement for the traditional song 'Scarborough Fair' that he then showed to the visiting American Paul Simon. Simon & Garfunkel's subsequent version of the tune became very famous indeed.

Norma and Martin still lived in Robin Hood's Bay, as did Lal's children Olly and Marry. If I could make it up there they would be happy to meet me. I decided to wait until I got there to ask if I could make a field recording of them.

Then there was Scotland. If I were to drive as far as North Yorkshire it would surely make sense to keep going. I knew of a village called Anstruther in Fife that had got the songwriting bug bad: everyone from the girl working in the fishing museum to the postman was penning Bob Dylan-like three-minute masterpieces.

Glasgow would be worth visiting, too. A friend had recommended I talk to a Glaswegian singer called Alasdair Roberts, who has an ability to write songs that sound like they have been around for about a thousand years – he wasn't the most extroverted person, apparently, but he knew how to carry the past into modern times. And he was a friend of Alex Neilson, a young drummer and singer that Jon and Fiona of Singing Knives claimed had a stronger understanding of the mysticism in ancient British music than anyone.

I realised that I had met Alex Neilson. The summer previously in Cornwall NJ, Otto, Pearl and I had gone for a ride on *Rosemarie*, the boat that Jarvis and Tiffany of Thistletown and latterly The Rosemarie Band lived on, with a strange young ginger-haired man with an impish face and his quiet, alabaster-skinned, blonde English rose of a girlfriend. Tiffany introduced them as Alex and Lavinia and told us they performed as a duo called Directing Hand. They didn't say much at first. But when we moored on Flushing Beach to explore the rocky coastline and the sandy coves within it Otto and Alex constructed an elaborate fantasy about dragons living at the bottom of chasms and sea serpents slithering through the rock pools. That evening Jarvis and Tiffany staged a mini-festival in the garden of the cottage at Mabe, where I was later to make a field recording of The Rosemarie Band. As the orange sun melted into the highest branches of the trees a torch of bright red hair glowed at the centre of the stage (actually a slightly raised section of the garden). With his hands behind his back and his head tilted upwards Alex sang an old ballad called 'Death And The Lady' in a high, reedy voice. He didn't appear to belong to the modern age. He was like a young troubadour, singing for his supper in the encampments outside the castle.

Then he sat behind the drums and set about hammering them maniacally as Lavinia sang the old Irish tune 'My Lagan Love' with such delicacy, such perfect, cut-glass, soprano precision, that it was transcendent. She didn't sound human – she sounded like a fairy. Under the shadows of the trees and the falling sun you could be forgiven for mistaking her as a nature sprite, escaped from the pages of a children's book illustrated by Arthur Rackham. Then she began the most terrifying caterwauling I have ever heard. Whatever power Lavinia and Alex had harnessed moments before was now unleashed upon the forces of chaos. It turned out that Lavinia was classically trained, and the purge-like screams were an attempt to escape from the bonds of her rigorous education. People looked nervous. Otto and Pearl covered their ears. A goat impaled itself on a barbed-wire fence.

Alex would be the perfect person to speak to about the ancient spirit, since he didn't appear to be too concerned with the external, curatorial aspects of British music. He seemed to be in search of something deeper, more unfathomable. Robin Hood's Bay, Fife, Glasgow and Bradford formed a rectangle across England and Scotland, a standing stone of a map of British musical traditions. Sheffield wasn't too far from Bradford, either. From there I would head west – to Manchester, perhaps, or Liverpool; industrial towns with music that had penetrated the entire world.

I said goodbye to the children, employed NJ as a bonnet kicker in order to fill the Astra's radiator with water, went so far as to check the oil, kissed NJ and reversed the car out of the drive, knocking over a brown wheelie bin intended for garden refuse in the process and setting off a particularly neurotic car alarm as the back of the Astra gently massaged the bumper of a car parked on the street outside.

It was a long drive, at least seven hours. The car's single tape of old British folk songs went around several times. Shirley Collins's voice – sounding like a tasty potato grown in a flinty field in Sussex, and that's meant as a compliment – singing the ballad 'The Plains Of Waterloo' was the soundtrack to the just-add-people instant construction that is a motorway service station on the M1 past Birmingham. As her sister Dolly played ancient, difficult-to-tune instruments like the sackbut and the virginal, Shirley evoked the spirit of a woman seeking news of her lost love Billy Smith, last heard fighting valiantly against Napoleon Bonaparte on the plains of Waterloo.

The Suffolk singer John Goodluck sang the Hammer Horror-like mystery fable 'The Suffolk Miracle' – father separates his daughter from her lover and sends her to live with her uncle, her lover dies of a broken heart and then turns up as a zombie at the uncle's house, takes her on horseback to her father and then melts after getting too close to the fire, after which the daughter dies of a broken heart – as the car sat in non-moving traffic caused by an overturned mobile home. The middle-aged owners of the stranded colossus stood on the hard shoulder, mobile phones at their ears, as lights flashed around them.

Hours later, after driving down a seemingly ever-narrowing road that cut through expanses of marshy moorland, the Astra finally dropped into Robin Hood's Bay, a hill-based town that leads steeply into a rocky bay where lobster cages line a pebbled path, fishermen sit in meditative silence along the jetty and bits of cliff fall into the sea at alarmingly close intervals. A row of bed and breakfasts with busy shrub-filled front gardens line the steep street that heads down to the bay. A boulder thundered down into the waves as soon as I arrived. There was a notice about a Save Robin's Hood Bay campaign, but what could really be done? Natural erosion was eating away at the rock face.

To one side of the bay is the lower part of the town, where tiny frosted windows reveal trays of gingerbread men and teacakes, little stone alleys shadowed by houses leaning inwards lead to miniature bridges across streams, and stone steps run alongside the river that cuts through the village like a main artery. You could imagine *The Wicker Man*'s

Sergeant Howie being led a deadly dance through the narrow lanes by giggling villagers. And you could imagine Robin Hood, whether a historical figure or a mythical outcrop of the god of fertility the Green Man, finding shelter from King John, the phoney king of England, and his thuggish retinue in one of the bay's dark caves. Everywhere the emphasis is on the small and cosy: little shops sell hand-embroidered cushions and short Victorian-style streetlights occupy raised stone corners. But in the eighteenth century this was the busiest smuggling village on the Yorkshire coast. Apparently the wives of smugglers would lean out of the tiny sash windows of the houses to pour boiling water on excise men hoping to locate contraband goods in the narrow alleyways below.

My B&B was in the street that looks down onto the bay. The B&B is an institution that reflects the British character: well meaning, but stiff and unable to cope. The summer before Otto was born NJ and I had stayed in quite a few, and they seemed to all be run by people that *wanted* to be friendly and welcoming to these paying guests invading their houses but couldn't quite bring themselves to do it. The rooms revealed a pathological fear of dirt coupled with an absolute refusal to have any taste whatsoever. Glasses and cups came with protective sheets of clingfilm, booking a double meant two single beds (sex or even physical intimacy not being activities the British really approve of) and decoration came in the form of a plastic-framed etching of a clutter of doe-eyed puppies above the legend, written in italics, 'Heaven is a place on earth'.

Then there is the B&B breakfast ritual. This involves filling out a form, to be 'popped' (to use the term popular with B&B landladies) into a little wooden box at the foot of the stairs by 9 p.m. at the latest, to denote what you would like to have. You can have one sausage plus bacon plus a fried egg OR two sausages but no bacon OR two fried eggs and fried bread but no bacon or sausage OR a continental breakfast in the classier joints, which involves a croissant from Marks & Spencer's, a glass of orange juice and a Nescafé.

The following morning you arrive at breakfast (served between 8.30 and 9 a.m.) to share a table with your fellow guests. One memorable B&B experience in Oxfordshire involved a very young couple from Prestwich who were employed in local government and wore matching glasses, two builders from Stirling working off last night's session with the fullest English breakfast sausages OR bacon would allow, and a vicar and his wife from Oxford who dominated the conversation by documenting in detail every single motorway, A road, B road and dirt track that led to them to our present location. Then I mistakenly wandered into a part of the house guests weren't meant to go in during a search for a downstairs toilet and got snarled at by the prim proprietress's husband and barked at by a labrador called Boy. Then the bill came for £100 and the order to clear out by eleven.

This time I had lucked out. Perhaps it was because the season hadn't started, or perhaps she was just an unusually nice B&B owner, but the woman that ran the place I stayed in couldn't have been more welcoming. The room was cheap – only £40 – and rather like a children's bedroom with added tea-making facilities. Breakfast was served any time before ten and you didn't have to choose between a fried egg OR hash browns but could have pretty much anything you wanted, including the kippers for which Robin Hood's Bay is famous. I put my luggage – one leather holdall, one reusable Asda plastic bag containing a Zoom portable recording studio – onto the bed, turned the television on for about a minute to be amazed Harold was still in *Neighbours* after all these years, and prepared to make the journey, all 200 metres of it, to the Watersons' house up the hill.

Outside a group of German schoolchildren huddled towards their coach, fluoro-rubber keychains glinting in the afternoon sun. An old lady barked at her dough-faced son, oversized and lumbering, as he held an Ordnance Survey map upside down and flapped about in the wind. Four builder-types in shorts with bald or shaved heads that were sitting around a B&Q table in the front garden of a cheap hotel pointed at me and started laughing – this happens with alarming regularity as soon as I leave London and I have no idea why, since as far as I can tell I have a very nondescript and unremarkable appearance. Hearty couples in matching red and white sensible all-weather gear marched up the steep hill from the bay carrying Thermos flasks. There was a group of seagulls huddled on a rooftop. A few tons of cliff crashed into the sea.

Martin Carthy and Norma Waterson live in a tall terraced house on a quiet, wide street just up from the bay. Martin answered the door. He was slight, and wore a Hawaiian shirt and an earring in each ear. 'Norma's baking scones in the back. She'll be out in a minute,' he said in a sandpaper voice. The first thing I saw, sitting on a hall shelf filled with unopened letters, was Stephanie Hladowski's embroidered album cover. I told him that I had just heard it and thought it was wonderful. 'How funny! I must confess I haven't listened to it yet,' he said. 'Somebody came up to me at a concert and gave it to me. It might have been her. I can't honestly remember. Anyway, come in.'

I was interrupting Martin's enjoyment of a mid-afternoon Wimbledon tennis match. An Eastern European giant was playing a Scottish local hero. He managed to turn the television off after much hesitation. Apart from the television, the room was like the parlour of a busy, lived-in and happy Edwardian home. Everything was old and bright and with a handcrafted, hand-painted look. The walls were covered with framed photographs and etchings of The

Watersons and their friends and all else was floral motifs, chintz, ornaments and wallpaper. It was elegant in its warmth and welcoming in its busy variety.

Both Martin Carthy and The Watersons were on the Astra's sole cassette tape. Martin Carthy sang his famous version of 'Scarborough Fair' and The Watersons sang 'Brave Wolfe', the story of Major General James Wolfe who died aged 32 at the moment of victory in the Battle of Quebec, thus ensuring eternal status as a folk hero. The Watersons approached folk songs in a lusty, wild way while Martin Carthy was more reverential to the tune. This made sense. Martin was a middle-class Londoner who discovered folk music as a teenager and has viewed it as a kind of exotic gold ever since, while The Watersons were taught a lot of the old songs by their Gypsy granny. For them it was the music they knew, not a rare, sacred artefact.

'When I was a boy, English folk songs were not common currency,' Martin began, as we sat in the living room next to a fireplace. 'They were under the radar, and I certainly had no idea if they existed in London, but in the countryside you did still have these old boys keeping the songs alive. There were men like Harry Cox – pretty old, but still singing – and Phil Tanner, singers with beautifully musical voices and a clear idea of what constituted a song and how it should go. They sang for their friends, and occasionally at small events, and they were wonderful performers. The music industry has always been pretty good at keeping out anything that doesn't conform, but slowly there emerged ways of discovering the rural music of old England.'

Growing up in the late 1950s, Martin did hear aspects of old English music on BBC radio, then called the Home Service, in programmes like *As I Roved Out*. Then in 1959, while still a schoolboy, Martin chanced upon a pub session by the Suffolk singer Sam Larner. He was transfixed.

'At the time I was in the school choir and we were doing Elizabethan music which, beautiful though it was, was very much of a period,' said Martin, still enthusiastic at the memory. 'What I realised when I heard Sam Larner singing a song that was written maybe five hundred years ago was that it was modern music. He wasn't singing it like a five-hundred-year-old man. He was singing it to you *now*, as a person living *now* and putting his experiences into the song. I was astonished, and puzzled. Here was this music that had always been there, at the heart of English life, and yet I had never heard it before. I had discovered Ravi Shankar at the same time, going to see him play sitar at the Royal Albert Hall alongside about a hundred Indian people eating picnics in the stalls, and Sam Larner was as exotic – and as foreign, in a way – as Ravi Shankar. I was a seventeen-year-old boy when I heard a man with no teeth singing songs that he had known all his life, and the music got its hooks into me. He had an absolute commitment to what he was doing. He had a confidence that said, "There you go, what do you think of that?"'

Martin had picked up the guitar two years earlier, as a fifteen-year-old excited by the British skiffle pioneer Lonnie Donegan's version of the American country-blues tune 'Rock Island Line'. By the time he discovered English traditional music he could play guitar well enough to work out ways to accompany the old tunes, thereby setting the pattern for the folk revival: songs that would have originally been sung unaccompanied were sung with guitar, and by the late sixties with full amplified bands.

'What excited me about the songs was their fluidity,' he continued. 'A lot of the songs started life as broadsides from the seventeenth and eighteenth centuries, sold for a penny in marketplaces and telling the latest news in song form. But then they get sung around the place and people mishear the words, change the melodies according to their voices, and change the names and places in them to make them relevant to their situation. "The Oxford Girl" is a case in point: it tells the story of the murder of a young woman by her lover. But you get similar stories, often with similar tunes, all across the country.'

Norma came in. She was slow-moving and somewhat regal, wrapped up in a long flowing printed dress and carrying a tray of the scones she had just finished baking. You could see the Gypsy in her. She looked like the type of woman who would flourish kindness on those she loved and be a formidable force against those that crossed her.

Had Norma and her siblings not been orphaned, it is unlikely they would have become England's foremost bastions of folk music. 'Two big wars killed off a lot of our traditions,' she said as she settled into what I imagine was her chair and her chair only. 'It's a miracle that this thing we have has survived at all. In the forties my father, for example, only wanted to hear jazz and swing because the Americans came over towards the end of the war and seemed impossibly glamorous to a generation of English people. But because we were orphaned we missed out on the New Orleans jazz and so on that everyone was listening to, as our grandmother taught us the songs that her family, who were all Gypsies, had been singing for generations.'

Martin and Norma liked Gypsies. They liked Stanley Robertson and they liked Sam Lee, however non-Gypsy he was. They talked fondly of Hamish Henderson. He had founded the School of Scottish Studies, which was devoted to the celebration of the country's oral history and folk traditions.

'He was an incredible man,' said Norma, a wistful smile washing over her face. 'He was lovely. Only died quite recently.'

'He was a poet and a songwriter,' added Martin, raising his eyebrows.

'He was a human being. What you call a human being.'

'He loved people. He had been in the 51st Highland Division in the North Africa campaign. He wrote "The Banks Of Sicily".'

Norma began to sing. 'The banks of Sicily, dee, deed-a-dum . . .' She waved her hands from side to side.

'Last time I saw him,' said Martin, pointing an index finger in my direction, 'he was trying to raise money for the grave of a woman called Belle Stewart, another Gypsy singer. He discovered Jeannie Robertson, Jane Turriff . . . all the great Scottish Traveller singers. The Gypsy singers carry all the big ballads, you know. There's a man up in Fife called Pete Shepherd who sat in a pub with a couple of Gypsies who sang him *an entire Robin Hood Ballad* . . .'

'You never get a full Robin Hood Ballad!' said Norma, wide-eyed. 'Never!'

'They haven't been orally collected since the sixteenth century,' added Martin, a little more casually, legs crossed as he sank back into an armchair. 'Cecil Sharp collected one or two but they're not very interesting.'

The Robin Hood Ballads, play-length epics that tell of the heroic deeds of this people's outlaw, were once known throughout England and Scotland. Evidence comes from place names alone: alongside Robin Hood's Bay there is Robin Hood's Tor near Matlock, Robin Hood's Cross in Lincolnshire and a chasm in Chatsworth in Derbyshire called Robin Hood's Leap. Francis Child collected a handful of the ballads, including the fragmented, 456-verse collection *The Gest Of Robyn Hode*, which has probably been around since the fourteenth century. The earliest mentions of Robin Hood being in ballad form rather than in text, it seems that he was not a historical figure but the greatest folk hero of them all: an everyman with regal dignity protecting the poor from the exploitative self-interest of the rich, to be reinvented according to the needs of the age and the community. Sometimes he was a magical nature spirit; at other times he was a stout yeoman with a good aim, as down-to-earth as they come. And to the Travellers of Britain Robin Hood was something of a Jesus figure.

Norma was a great believer in the idea of music as a necessary component of the fabric of daily life, and admirably, given that she was a professional singer, she denounced the fact that people became rich from doing this thing that should be a part of all of us. 'We have a strange relationship with music in this country,' she said in a close to stern tone. 'I refuse to believe that anyone is tone deaf, and it seems that if you're told enough times that you're rubbish at singing when you're at school, you believe that you can't do it at all. That's really sad. Music is not only a joyous thing; it's a fucking healthy thing too. You come off stage after singing all night and your blood is zinging and your head is going and you feel so much better than going to the gym for an hour. Our people are being deprived of that and I think it's a sad thing.'

Norma asked me what exactly I was doing. I told her that I was travelling around the island making field recordings in an attempt to capture the spirit of Britain. She leaned forward in her armchair and fixed me with a gimlet-eyed stare. 'Do you mean Britain, or England?'

I thought about the fact that I was on my way to Scotland, and hoped to go to Wales, and had only thought of exploring the geography of this island we happened to live on. Political considerations on the nature of sovereignty had not come into it.

'I hate the idea of Britain,' said Norma with a pout. 'I think the Scottish should be Scottish and proud of it, and the Irish should be Irish and the Welsh should be Welsh. England should have its own parliament and we should be proud of what we are. The union came about for reasons that are long gone. It was all about keeping one king or other on the throne.'

She went on to explain how the English practised on their own before embarking on the Highland Clearances. 'I have a feeling that all the urban troubles we are facing now are part of a direct line that go back to the English clearances,' she said, raising her eyebrows. 'Princess Diana's family, for example, razed eleven villages in 1496 to build their stately home of Althorp in 1509, and Henry VII fined the Earl Spencer £5,000 for it. Before then the common people had an acre of land to raise geese and sheep on and common land to grow vegetables on. They were self-sufficient. Then, after the clearances, all these people who had learned how to grow vegetables and so on were out on the road with nowhere to live. What are they supposed to do? The cottages they built have been burned down so that somebody could put sheep on their land. That's how the Spencers made their money.'

'It continued through the seventeenth and eighteenth centuries, so the English were having their land stolen by the people going to war against Napoleon,' added Martin. 'That's why there are so many songs from around that time about what a great guy Napoleon was. The ordinary people were in such dire straits that they thought of Napoleon as the man that would bring them bread and honey.'

'In France they called him the Corsican Idiot,' said Norma, nodding her head sagely. 'But in England they loved him. So you have a song like "Brave Wolfe", which is about this 32-year-old hero, but there are no songs about Wellington because he wasn't a sympathetic character for ordinary people.'

For Martin and Norma the traditional music of England wasn't just something to be enjoyed; it was a vital component of the identity of the people. It was an art shared, not bought; it was not a commodity that anyone could lay claim to. But singing was how they, and their daughter Eliza, made their money. I thought about 'Travelling For A Living', and asked Norma if she set out to be a professional singer.

'See, I still don't think of myself as professional,' she said, laughing. 'What happened to us was never a plan. Back when we were all in Hull I was a nurse, Michael was a builder, and our Lolly designed shields and coats of arms and things like that. Singing was what we had done since we were children and it was never our plan to seek fame and fortune. This guy owned a coffee bar in the centre of Hull and he said that if we sang in there for two nights a week he would give us five shillings. It all grew from there.'

By the early sixties folk clubs were sprouting up all over Britain, typically in the back rooms of pubs. The Watersons had one of their own, at The Bluebell in Hull every Sunday night. 'Going to the folk club weren't an unusual thing,' said Norma. 'It were like going to the pictures – just part of life. And you had your own set of songs that you knew and sang. It was all about an expression of your reality.'

What killed it, according to Martin, was the introduction of all kinds of rules about what you could and couldn't do in an attempt to create some sense of purity and authenticity, despite the fact that there clearly is no such thing in an ever-changing oral history tradition. I suggested that Ewan MacColl was the worst culprit for this, but Martin and Norma were quick to defend this Salford-born hard-line communist who insisted people sing songs from the place they were from in his club.

'He was a bugger in many ways, but he was a remarkable man,' said Martin. 'George Bernard Shaw said: "Beside myself, there is only one man of genius working in the theatre today and that is Ewan MacColl." He wrote beautiful songs like "Dirty Old Town", he was a great actor and playwright, and he was a pain in the arse.'

'Men of genius are often very difficult, and Ewan was a genius,' added Norma with a reflective smile. 'And his kids are fantastic so he couldn't have been that bad.'

As much as I liked the way Norma and Martin interpreted the old ballads of England, I was also fascinated by the way Lal Waterson had captured Yorkshire in her own songs. There's a track called 'The Bird', of which the Scottish singer Alasdair Roberts does a version, that is one of the saddest and yet strangely hopeful pieces of music I have ever heard. It describes waking up full of regret, and cursing the bird singing outside the window that pulls you out of your sleep, but then reflects on how beautiful the bird's song can be, and the suggestion of freedom it offers: 'But the bird, love, flies over the ocean . . . the bird, the bird flies over the sea.' I asked them about Lal.

'She was the artistic one,' said Norma. 'You couldn't say anything around her because it would always end up in a song. I remember her writing "The Bird". That was in Hull, in the house we lived in together in Park Avenue.'

About ten minutes later Lal's grown-up children, Olly and Marry, turned up. Olly had a round, open face, bright brown eyes, and the demeanour of a man who did not equate music with fame. Marry looked strikingly like Lal, with long fringed black hair, handsome and with a touch of the witch about her – although not in an evil way. It was only later that it occurred to me I might have been insensitive asking all these questions about their late mother, but they didn't show any signs of being bothered.

'You take it all for granted, don't you?' said Olly, when I asked him what it was like to have a mother writing songs all the time and a family in which everyone sings. 'It's what you know and it's nothing unusual.'

'Except when your mates come round,' said Marry.

They reminisced about the music the house was filled with – and it wasn't traditional English folk. They remembered hearing The Band, Van Morrison, Kate Bush and The Rolling Stones. 'A lot of traditional music is actually quite painful,' said Marry. 'It's pretty tuneless. To this day I hardly listen to the old songs, even though I like to sing them. They're a part of my life because I'm one of The Watersons.'

'I rebelled against it,' said Olly. 'We got dragged around folk clubs our entire childhood and it got to the point where I couldn't face listening to traditional music any more. I really enjoyed *not* going with the family to the folk clubs.'

Olly couldn't escape his destiny, though. After his wild years discovering, for all I know, Madonna and Michael Jackson he ended up back in Robin Hood's Bay, writing songs with his mother that ended up on an album they made together shortly before her death. As for the old songs of Britain, he has made his peace with them. 'The songs are like old friends to me now,' he said. 'They're the soundtrack to our lives because they've always been around us.'

'Folk music is perceived as being rather dowdy,' said Marry with a shrug. 'You know, old men in a pub with fingers in their ears.'

'But we take the piss out of it ourselves all the time,' added Olly. 'If you see our Norma getting excited as she comes down the stairs singing "He came over the lowlands" first thing in the morning, you can't take it that seriously. We're certainly not precious about it. The Watersons say that they never sing a song the same way twice. And our Michael [their uncle] always forgets the words and makes his own up. Everyone expects it of him.'

'Our Michael changes the tune and all,' said Marry. 'That's because he can't remember how it goes.'

In 'Travelling For A Living', the gap-toothed Mike Waterson comes across as the dreamer of the pack. It seems that nothing had changed. But he had managed to sire three daughters, and along with Marry's two young children there was a new generation of Watersons forming, ready to take on the mantle of the old. 'They're always popping out,' as Marry eloquently put it.

It was interesting that Marry and Olly had none of the zeal of some of the English folk musicians I had met. They weren't particularly interested in being true to the tradition or searching for an authentic voice. It sounded like they didn't even particularly *like* folk songs; they just happened to sing them. They were as much a part of their life as going to the pub and arguing about whose turn it was to do the dishes. I asked them if they thought of the old ballads as something intrinsic to Britain.

'The thought of British music conjures up a contemporary image,' said Olly, brown eyes reflecting on the idea. 'It makes me think of The Stone Roses and Oasis and that.'

'I've never really thought about it,' added Marry, after a while. 'But then, my children sing songs that wouldn't be in existence if it weren't for my family. They would have died out by now. But as much as this family is a product of Britain, it's a product of Hull, and Whitby, and Robin Hood's Bay. What we do is completely tied up with the place we live in. I suppose that's the same for most people.'

Norma was feeling too ill to sing. Every time I asked Martin he appeared to dash off without giving me an answer, but eventually Olly managed to convince him to do a saucy Elizabethan song called 'The Bedmaking', in which a young serving girl is seduced by the master of the house – bedmaking being a euphemism for something far more distracting. By the third verse she is caught and thrown out by the mistress of the house, and then returns with a child nine months later, which she duly presents to the master and tells him to face up to his fatherly duties. He played with a great drama, hitting the strings percussively in a stop-start style I had never heard before, and sang in a hearty, storytelling way, rather like one's dad might if he could hold a tune and had been making a dent in the real-ale cellar.

'I base everything I do on guitar on the skiffle of Lonnie Donegan and the playing style of Elizabeth Cotten,' he said. Lonnie Donegan introduced blues and country to the youth of 1950s England via kazoos and washboards, thereby giving birth to what became known as skiffle, and Elizabeth Cotten was a North Carolina-born woman who, having no conventional knowledge of how a guitar is played, invented her own rhythmic style of hitting alternating bass notes with her thumb and playing a melody with her fingers. Now it is used all over the world as the basis for folk and blues guitar playing. Cotten wrote a song aged eleven called 'Freight Train' that went on to become something of a standard, and as is befitting from an eleven-year-old black girl from North Carolina in 1906, it sounds like a very innocent, very gentle blues. Elizabeth Cotten worked in department stores and as a maid, and never seriously entertained the idea of making a living from music, but she became one of the most influential guitarists of the twentieth century.

Martin's version of 'The Bedmaking' was a fertile illustration of the ever-shifting nature of music. An old English tune, probably written to be sold as a broadside and no doubt a pop song of its day to be sung in bawdy taverns everywhere, was accompanied by a guitar style gleaned from the blues of the American South. It was alive as a result. The Zoom picked it up well: I put the eight-track on a small wooden table in the centre of the living room, put on my headphones, pressed record, then sat still and attempted not to make any noise. At one point you could hear a clatter coming from the kitchen – Norma putting away the tray of scones, presumably. Martin sang the song with gusto – once he remembered the words.

Marry then sang Lal's 'Fine Horseman' while Olly accompanied her on guitar. Marry didn't only look like her

mother, she sounded just like her too. It was uncanny. The
dark erotic mystery of the eerie, strangely emotionless song
filled the room and the late Lal Waterson was a spirit among
us. If this was strange for me I couldn't imagine what it must
have been like for Marry and Olly. Perhaps it was just
another way of laying flowers on their mother's grave.

Somehow it affected me. I couldn't help but think of
an ancient horseman, clad from head to toe in black and
with a horse similarly bedecked, riding across the rain-
soaked moors around Robin Hood's Bay. I thought of
Gawain, the brave knight of King Arthur's table who
chopped the head off a mysterious green visitor to Elsinore
only for the visitor to pick up his head and start laughing
and tell Gawain to visit him at his castle and await his doom.
I said goodbye to The Watersons and wandered around the
little bay, the people looking like puppets playing out a
drama that would never end. I drove the Astra – increasingly filled with oversized empty packets of Walker's
salt-and-vinegar crisps, plastic bottles of Diet Coke and
packets for the kind of motorway service station cheese sand-
wiches you can throw at a wall and expect to have bounce
straight back at your face – to Whitby.

Whitby is something of a stronghold for that strange
style subculture known as goth. I've always liked goths for
the fact that they stand for absolutely nothing whatsoever
beyond being pale and misunderstood. They wear black
clothes and make-up, have D H Lawrence novels sticking
out of their back pockets, and jobs in information technology. Around the corner from the flat we used to rent in
north London was an all-night goth club called The Slime-
light, and from ten on a Sunday morning you would see
them sitting cross-legged on Islington Green, doing each
other's hair. You can't imagine being punched by a goth.

Bram Stoker's most famous fictional creation, Count
Dracula, arrived in Britain via a boat that docked in Whitby.

The story goes that Bram Stoker was walking through the bleak ruins of the town's abbey, which was built in 650, when he had the idea for the most famous horror novel of them all in 1890. For this reason annual goth conventions have been held at the town for the past decade.

But the abbey already had mythical qualities. The seventh-century poet Caedmon was a cowherd there until one night he saw a man in a dream that told him to sing. The next day he recited to the Abbess Hilda what is now known as Caedmon's Hymn, which still exists in old English Northumbrian dialect, and became a monk devoted to composing inspirational religious poetry.

The provincial, northern goth appears to approve of Whitby, with its working docks and sticks of rock. I only went there to get fish and chips, and everywhere was closed by eight o'clock. Spotting a few goths hanging around the harbour, crimped black hair blowing in the sea breeze, was the one highlight of the trip. So I returned to Robin Hood's Bay and wandered through the tiny alleyways until I saw, through tiny thick glass windows embedded into a white stone wall, scenes of merriment inside a pub somewhere in the midst of the labyrinthine old town. There was a good-looking, statuesque barmaid serving a smiling old man. Behind them was a man playing a fiddle and another playing a drum. It looked like a warm, dry, beer-rich heaven.

The door creaked open. Just as it did for Sergeant Howie in *The Wicker Man* when he entered The Green Man pub on the island of Summerisle, the room fell quiet. Lined faces stared, mute and immovable. The barmaid raised her eyebrows. I walked towards the bar.

I was tired and hungry and fed up with the English side of pub life that considers every single person that walks into the place a potential threat or victim. This doesn't happen in restaurants or cafés. Why does it have to happen in pubs? If they had nothing better to do than stare at me, that was their problem. I was going to march up to the bar and order a pint and a sandwich – it didn't look like the sort of place that did much in the way of food but surely they could muster up a couple of slices of bread with some cheese in the middle – and sit in a corner and not bother anyone.

I did indeed march forward – and felt a massive crash against my forehead. So it had happened. They had brained me, and now intended to turn me into tomorrow's lunchtime menu. If I tasted horrible as a result of my service-station diet and carbon monoxide lungs that would serve them right. But when I came to, it was with a shock to discover I was sitting by a table, the barmaid pressing a cold flannel against my forehead.

'You all right, luv?' she said. 'You've been out cold.'

'Flamin' beam's going to do someone in for good before we know it,' said one of the old men. 'Get the lad a pint. Looks like he needs one.'

The beam in question was a huge, gnarled piece of black-painted wood that separated the entrance corner from the main bar. People bashed their heads on it on a weekly basis, apparently.

Five minutes later, the music started.

Chapter Ten

A Town of Bob Dylans: Anstruther in Fife, Scotland

THE FOLLOWING MORNING, WITH A SLIGHTLY SORE HEAD for more reasons than one, I set off on the eighthour drive to the village of Anstruther in Fife, where I was to meet some of the locals who had apparently been caught by the songwriting bug. But there was one more person to see in Robin Hood's Bay, someone who had been doing what I was doing for a summer – going around Britain and collecting songs – his entire life.

Doc Rowe is a pleasant if unusual man. A lean, good-looking fifty-something with a moustache and a checked shirt, he looks like he might be the bass player in a reasonably successful country-rock band. But he's dedicated his adult life to travelling up and down the country making field recordings, meeting old singers and filming traditional British events like summer fêtes, maypole dances and dangerous races after rolling balls of cheese (this happens in Gloucestershire). Nobody pays him for this, but the contribution that he's making to Britain's unofficial heritage is huge. The house he lives in a few miles into deep countryside up from Robin Hood's Bay, which is low-ceilinged and crammed with books, records and piles of manuscripts, is owned by his girlfriend Gill. He's got a small council flat in Clerkenwell in London, and what he does for money is a mystery. He's just honestly, naturally, helplessly obsessed with the folk traditions of Britain.

'It all started when I listened to the radio in the fifties as a little kid,' he said as we settled into broken armchairs with cups of tea. 'There used to be programmes on the BBC like *As I Roved Out*, in which a frightfully well-spoken presenter would introduce these singing farmers with incredibly broad regional accents. I grew up in a village in Devon and it was the first time I realised that there *was* such a thing as accents. It fascinated me, that all over Britain you could have people that spoke the same language in such different ways.'

The early BBC recordings of traditional singers were made on Shellac, which degenerates quickly and can only store up to two and a half minutes of sound. For this reason the men that sang and told the tales of their life (and they usually were men, mostly being found in pubs, although Alan Lomax was good at finding women singers) were told what to say for the recording so there was little that was natural about them. As Cecil Sharp had done when he collected songs from mostly old men and women, the BBC programmes of the 1950s presented the singers as the last of their kind. The recordings were made – the suggestion was – because without them the songs would die forever.

'That *really* confused me,' said Doc. 'Because I would hear a song on the radio presented as being on the point of extinction, and it would be one I knew from hearing the farmhands at the top of the hill singing it.' So he became a part of the generation that created the folk revival, going to play songs in folk clubs, attending CND marches, and embracing American culture on the one hand – everyone wanted a pair of Levi's – and rejecting it on the other. It was a time when communists such as Bert Lloyd and Ewan MacColl were reclaiming English traditional music as the voice of the people, much as Billy Bragg is doing today, although it never quite works to use music as a vehicle for an agenda because as soon as you think you've got it pinned down it slips through your hands like mercury.

'MacColl used traditional music as a weapon against the bourgeoisie,' said Doc. 'Bert Lloyd would set out to find old industrial songs from the northeast and then sing them in imitation Geordie. But the reality of the old songs is that they give people a sense of belonging. They become something owned by the community.'

Gill, a gentle woman with more than a slight erring towards the hippy, used 'The Padstow May Song' as an example. Around 1 May in Padstow in Cornwall a man dressed as a rather frightening wooden horse, like the one NJ and I had seen at Cecil Sharp House, snaps his way around the town. 'The Padstow May Song' is the accompanying tune of choice. 'We have a Padstow lad working in the harbour at Whitby,' she said. 'He goes home each year to see the Padstow May Day processions. It's about sharing in something that's a part of you. The point of this kind of music is that it gives you a sense of belonging because it remains independent and uncorrupted.'

Doc and Gill's great hero was Fred Jordan, the farm labourer from Shropshire who became something of a star after he was recorded by the BBC in the 1940s. He lived in a tiny cottage without running water or a television, made his singing debut aged six after singing 'The Gypsy's Warning' at a competition at Ludlow Town Hall, for which he won a pound, and brought out the emotion of old ballads like 'The Outlandish Knight', a tale of a rake first notated in 1776, through subtle touches of vibrato and a clear melodic timbre, singing with a fixed stare that headed towards somewhere over the horizon of his audience.

This was the kind of untutored, unspoiled singer held up by earnest, left-leaning folk fans as the font of traditional culture. But Jordan sounds like he was just as vulnerable to the temptations of fame as anyone else. Charismatic and sociable, he was astute enough to realise that his farm labourer's clothes and heavy accent were good things to wear for performances in front of the young, duffle-clad folk fans of the 1960s. He claimed to have learned his repertoire either from his mother or from Gypsies passing through Ludlow, although according to Doc he had a conflicting attitude to the latter.

'He didn't like Gypsies and Travellers,' said Doc. 'He didn't like the fact that they were being seen as the bearers of the tradition. I asked him once if he liked Norma Waterson. "Oh no," he said, looking alarmed. "There's too much of the Gypsy in her."'

It was time to get moving again. I cranked the putrid Astra into action, its lower half now brown from the mud it had gone through to get to Doc and Gill's house, which was at the end of a lane beyond a farm. I pulled it out from a yard filled with vehicles in various states of disrepair and waved goodbye to this couple so deeply entrenched in the culture of British rural life, and so welcoming to someone intrigued by their preoccupations. The car wobbled and bounced over stone and mud and passed the desolate farm, a cluster of trees, an old-fashioned red telephone box and a postbox built into a stone wall. Then it reached the road.

The car went up the hills and down the hills of the Pennines, where vast expanses of limestone-jutted land stretch out before a house breaks up their indifferent beauty. Silent lakes sink into the rising and falling hills of brown and green. The ruins of a stone farmhouse sat glumly in a wilderness of blanket bog. A small hill of loose stones was all that remained of a prehistoric hotspot. Every now and then a bleak town came and went. A few pasty faces stood around bus stops, smoking cigarettes and pushing prams. In one town some tracksuit-wearing, borderline-threatening youths hung around a drab building emblazoned with the legend

'YOUTHA – putting people *first!*' On a long up and down stretch of road in the Pennines there was the sign: '52 killed last year on this road. 54% improvement on last year. Well done!'

On the car's solitary tape a man called John Carter sang about a small bird in a cage – it was the song of a girl, 'not fifteen years of age' who, naïve to the ways of men because her parents had protected her so, falls prey to the advances of a handsome lad. He leaves her pregnant and disgraced, as is the way in so many of these songs. The car rumbled on through the Pennines and into Northumberland, where there were more trees and fewer towns. Shirley Collins's version of 'The Plains Of Waterloo' came and went, and came and went.

On the advice of one of the men in the pub with the low beam in Robin Hood's Bay I made a detour to visit a castle called Bellister, a fourteenth-century grey stone tower with a three-storey family home added on in the seventeenth century, now partly in ruins. It sits on a mound next to a twisted sycamore tree in Tynedale near Hadrian's Wall. Local folklore has it that Bellister is one of the most haunted buildings in Northumberland. In the seventeenth century, when a family called the Blenkinsops owned the castle, the Lord of Bellister allowed a white-haired wandering minstrel to spend the night there. But the Lord harboured suspicions that the minstrel was really a spy for a neighbouring baron, and asked one of his men to bring the old man before him. When he could not be found it seemed the Lord was correct. So he told his men to send out the bloodhounds. They found the minstrel later that night, near the River Tyne – and tore him to pieces. Intermittently ever since, the Grey Man of Bellister has appeared on the broken road leading up to the castle in the gloom of the evening, his tattered grey cloak flying in the wind.

It was still light when I arrived at the castle and the

Grey Man wasn't due to make an appearance for a few hours, but between the lamenting dirge of the nearby river, the bluster of the wind and the desolation of the surrounding hills waxing and waning into the far landscape, I could see that this would make a suitable home for a wronged, poverty-stricken balladeer such as he.

Soon after getting back into the car, it dawned on me that I was hungry and needed to take a leak. The road passed alongside a thick pine forest. A sign claimed that there was a woodland café within it, but after the car bounced along a stony track that cut through the forest for a few miles I gave up, pissed against a tree, and turned back to get onto the main road. There was nobody around.

Just when Anne Briggs sang 'Blackwaterside' for the fourth time that day the red light to designate low petrol clipped on. I hadn't seen too many petrol stations – only a lot of hills and trees, moorland stretching out onto an orange horizon and signs warning of blind summits. Then I came to it – the Last Café in England. It had a petrol station.

The Last Café appeared to have given up much hope of doing its country proud. Only one of the petrol pumps was working and that was filled with diesel. The café itself was a bleak pre-fabricated box with a stench of cooking fat and a few peeling posters of unappetising burgers on the walls. There was a woman sitting behind a counter, wearing large pink plastic-framed glasses and staring at the flickering strip light above her, her head resting on the short fingers of a soft, sullen hand. There was no sound and no movement in the café beyond a fly buzzing around the counter. Without turning away from the strip light the woman picked up a dog-eared copy of *Take A Break*, rolled it up, and brought it crashing down on the fly. Then she said: 'What can I get you, love?'

It was a bit of a pointless question since the café didn't have anything that she could get, at least not in the way of food. But she could stretch to a cup of tea, and there were a few chocolate bars that had only just passed their sell-by date. The tea urn wheezed and fizzed and something liquid came out amongst all the steam. 'Islands In The Stream' by Kenny Rogers and Dolly Parton was playing faintly in the background.

The Astra, a KitKat wrapper now added to the refuse collection around the passenger seat, sped into Scotland on an open road and went through some of the most glorious countryside I have ever seen. Hills of gorse and heather raised and dipped and the narrow road cut along its sides, twisting like a snake. Clusters of trees came and went. Occasionally a house broke up the expanse. There was a grandeur to the way the land went on forever, untouched and unchanging, and it felt distinct from the country I had just driven out of: a landscape that had more in common with the Wild West than the English countryside.

I cursed every unspoiled mile of it. A lack of built-up areas meant a lack of petrol. The car was juddering. Finally I came to a petrol station on the outskirts of Edinburgh and was safe to continue my ongoing journey. The car went around the city and over the Forth Bridge, which is being eternally painted by juvenile delinquents as part of an ongoing rehabilitation scheme, and into the long stretch of eastern Scotland known as Fife.

I took the slow route along the stretch of Scottish coastland known as the East Neuk. The road was interspersed with ominous industrial mini-centres and ultra-quaint fishing villages, and it twisted through narrow sections and endless sets of traffic lights. The car was beginning to smell. My bottom was seizing up. The tape of the songs went round and round, and some of them began to grate, particularly 'The Black Leg Miner' by Newcastle's Louis Killen. Killen is one of the most loved figures on the folk scene, a warm-hearted, principled man who is, legend has it, always up for drinking

into the early hours and making everyone around him laugh.
But on this early recording he sings about going 'doon the
pit of hell' in the thickest Geordie I have ever heard, and it all
began to seem forced: the political agenda of the song, the
worn-on-the-sleeve locality, sitting in a smoky folk club
listening to some old git moan on about joining the unions,
everything about it. What's more, through lack of food, poor
diet or endless driving, I was feeling sick.

I hated Britain and I hated folk music. It was all so
dreary and depressing. The towns I was passing were either
brutally functional or clinging on to some sort of Caledonian
Robbie Burns-approved tartan fantasy. Where was the life?
Who cared about keeping these old dirges alive? Let them
go the way of the dodo. They had had their chance.

It may well have been the endless driving and the lack
of anything decent to eat for the last twelve hours that put
these thoughts into my head, but arriving in Anstruther put
paid to such unhelpful flights of the mind. Anstruther is a
town with large grey stone buildings that are elegant but not
excessively so, a fish-and-chip shop voted the second-best in
Britain (it used to be the first, and the town has never recovered from its falling from pole position), a small working
harbour and views of the sea that, in the residue of the day,
have an orange Buddha-like peace to them. It also has a
strong Masonic presence and, until recently, Scotland's oldest
learner driver (he had just passed his test aged 84). There
are many tourists here, which means that nobody feels a
need to chase strangers out of town with clubs and pitch-
forks, but not so many that every other shop sells sticks of
rock and postcards of a pair of knockers painted to resemble
mice. This was the place where everyone wrote songs.

It would be impossible to know how many people in
this little village spent their evenings penning masterpieces,
but I had already come across a fair few. At the centre of
Anstruther's fertility was The Fence Collective, a DIY label

that had turned the town into a cultural hub with not much more than a CD burner and the back room of a seafront pub called The Ship's Tavern. A few years earlier I had visited Anstruther to go to a festival put on by Fence. In the church-like Erskine Hall, where end-of-term art projects by primary school children decorated the high stone walls and a leaflet on the notice board gave details of mother-and-baby yoga classes, a young woman called Jenny Gordon, performing under the name HMS Ginafore, was on stage, nervously strumming a guitar.

'Sorry, I got that one wrong,' she said to a crowd of around three hundred people. There was something about her perfectly formed songs and her complete lack of confidence that was captivating. After the gig Domino, the record label that was home to successful alternative-rock bands like The Arctic Monkeys and Franz Ferdinand, offered her a deal. She turned it down. Just before the gig started she was giving visitors a historical tour of Anstruther in her capacity as curator of the town's fishing museum.

Later on a man called UNPOC was due to do a set. UNPOC can sell out 3,000-seater stadiums in Sweden, but his performance that night was delayed by the sound engineer's late shift at the Co-op supermarket. HMS Ginafore's mother served home-made soup to the audience at the back of the hall. The concert was rounded off by a triumphant performance by The Fence Collective's founder Kenny Anderson. After the applause died down and the audience filtered through the old wooden doors of Erskine Hall, Kenny got a dustpan and brush and swept up the cigarette butts in the courtyard outside.

Kenny wrote and performed heartbreaking songs under the name King Creosote. He had younger twin brothers. There was Ian, who liked country rock, was reputed to be the best pedal-steel guitarist this side of Nashville and performed as Pip Dylan; and Gordon, who had suffered something of a breakdown some years back and had given up a promising musical career – he was the founder of a group called The Beta Band, who went on to be quite famous – to make increasingly odd, fragmented music as The Lone Pigeon that few ever heard. He was offered a deal by Domino, but couldn't decide whether he should make it as a pop star or follow in the footsteps of Jesus and travel to the Holy Land. He opted for the latter. He ended up in a Jerusalem psychiatric unit, having got so badly dehydrated and burned by the sun that he almost died. Eventually he was flown back to his parents' house in Scotland and he has remained in the East Neuk ever since, forming a group with other ex-members of The Beta Band called The Aliens. On the weekend I had gone up for the Fence festival he had made a rare appearance at The Ship Tavern, getting up on stage to sing rousing numbers the entire pub was harmonising to – even the tough old fisherman at the bar. You could have been mistaken for thinking that the songs were international hits, such was the affection and respect the town had for him, but they were Gordon's own.

There were others. Johnny Lynch ran the day-to-day operations of Fence Records as Kenny Anderson's one employee and released albums as The Pictish Trail. A bald man with a large beard called Gummi Bako worked as a delivery driver. Somebody called Super Shitbox did the odd gig and hung around the town, and perhaps unsurprisingly he was currently unemployed.

The closest the town had to a bona fide star was James Yorkston, a hearty, red-faced Scot who had returned to Anstruther after unhappy spells in London and Edinburgh trying to make it in the music industry. And there were various other policemen, postmen, butchers and bakers scattered about the place writing songs, few of them likely to be heard by anyone beyond the confines of The Ship Tavern.

I had contacted Johnny Lynch to make the most of this concentration of creative effort from such a distant outpost. Johnny offered his spare room/recording studio by way of accommodation, and would round up the cream of Anstruther's musical talent to represent the community with a field recording. Finally the car spluttered down the town's narrow cobbled streets. It didn't exactly look like a hive of activity. An old man walked past, bent into the rain. A mum dragged her daughter along, both of them buried under huge yellow mackintoshes.

I parked the car down a street shadowed by tall, narrow terraced houses painted white. The Astra's bonnet was steaming, but I decided that it must be condensation from the heavy rain – the temperature gauge was in the red, but only just. Johnny Lynch's house was through a tiny stone alleyway: you had to knock on what looked like a wooden garden door and then go through a courtyard filled with washing lines to get into the flat. Johnny was inside with his girlfriend. He had just finished making an entire album as The Pictish Trail in the bedroom I would be sleeping in, on a digital eight-track recorder exactly the same as the one I was making the field recordings on. He had written the songs in the kitchen, recorded them upstairs in the spare bedroom, and was preparing to promote, distribute and sell the finished copies from a tiny study downstairs where Fence Records was run.

After a takeaway at the second-best fish-and-chip shop in Britain we went back to the house to meet up with James Yorkston and Kenny Anderson, who turned up with his ten-year-old daughter Beth. James is a burly Viking type with thinning red hair, freckles and a rugby player's build; Kenny is a sad-eyed Scot with a beard. When he smiles, he looks rather like Muttley, the canine half of the popular man/dog cartoon villains Dastardly and Muttley. Jenny was meant to be coming, but the last anyone heard of her she was wavering between making a field recording and attending her weekly Jazzercise class. Gordon's mental health was better than it had been, but he was still erratic and nobody could be sure that he would turn up (he didn't). As Beth and Johnny's girlfriend played a computer game in the corner of the living room the three men told the story of Anstruther's musical renaissance.

'It began about ten years ago,' said James, leaning forward in a small, Ikea-like armchair. 'I had split up from my band and my long-term girlfriend and was living in Edinburgh, looking for something to do. I had heard that Kenny was doing shows in St Andrews, which is the nearest town to here, and at the time there really was nothing going on beyond bands in pubs playing "Brown Eyed Girl" and "In The Midnight Hour" to a dozen fishermen. So I went to see Kenny's gig and it was about as far from "Brown Eyed Girl" as you could get – it was chaotic and fun. Before you knew it there was a little scene being built around this guy making interesting music.'

Kenny had landed a Wednesday night residency at a wine bar in nearby St Andrews – the wealthy, rather elegant town where Prince William went to university – called Aikman's. He would play three- or four-hour sets consisting of mostly his own songs, something of a novelty at the time. Johnny Lynch had recently returned from America and gravitated to Kenny's performances too. Slowly and without planning, a community was forming.

'I had been busking around Britain with my brother Ian,' explained Kenny. 'Our other brother Gordon had formed The Beta Band at art college, but then he had his breakdown and left the rest of the band to go to London to make it. James had moved to Edinburgh and Ian and I were at something of a loose end. Then the daughter of the woman that owned Aikman's developed a crush on Ian and asked us to play her twenty-first birthday party. The woman had just revamped the wine bar and scared away the clientele by going upmarket so she was desperate, basically. When she saw that our performance brought a few people down she asked us back.'

'It wasn't like anything St Andrews had seen,' said James, his freckled, wide-eyed face glistening with excitement at the memory. 'Kenny would be screaming his head off in this smart, respectable wine bar and Gordon would come along and do jaw-droppingly good songs, even though he was going mad at the time. I was in a band that would rehearse and rehearse until you were totally sick of it, and here was Kenny doing something so much more interesting without any rehearsals whatsoever. Slowly, more and more of us got up on stage with him and joined in.'

Around the time of the wine bar concerts, Kenny made the perhaps not financially astute decision to buy the lease on a record shop that was about to go bankrupt. Sure enough, the record shop went bust again, but his time running it had made Kenny aware that the East Neuk was filled with talented, introverted people who were frustrated at not being able to find an outlet for their creative efforts. He released albums of his own and others' material that he multiplied on a CD burner and sold locally for £10 – again, not a great business decision since recordable CDs cost £12 at the time – and The Fence Collective was born.

'We made a very conscious decision *not* to move away,' said Kenny, who made his first solo albums in between picking up Beth from school and performing at weddings for cash on the weekends. 'There's a pace of life and an attitude here that we like, and we decided that if we lived frugally we could be self-sufficient. Now we write our own songs, we release our own records and we stage our own gigs. The alternative is to sign to a record label and before you know it, find yourself owing a debt you can never pay off.'

It was the experience of his friend Steve Mason, the former lead singer of The Beta Band, which warned Anderson of the perils of the mainstream record industry. On the weekend I had gone to Anstruther for the Fence festival Steve Mason turned up to play drums for UNPOC. A few months earlier The Beta Band had split up because they owed more than a million pounds to their record company, despite selling thousands of records, and they had no hope of ever paying it back. The Fence mentality, of doing something small and doing it on your own, was beginning to make sense.

Johnny Lynch was one of the many who were inspired by Kenny to hang around Fife instead of heading for the big city. A young St Andrews woman called KT Tunstall went the other way. She lived with Ian and Gordon in a cottage in Anstruther and performed regularly around the town before deciding that a life of isolation and poverty wasn't for her, so she moved down to London to make it. She did, spectacularly – KT Tunstall is a huge worldwide star. But the alternative offered by the people in Anstruther is not unattractive. James Yorkston looks like a builder. Kenny Anderson looks like a fisherman. They are making expressive music on their own terms in a place that, I had to admit, was a whole lot prettier than Peckham.

'There's a freedom here that's rare,' said James. 'After the wine bar gigs came to an end Kenny and Ian would play accordions and mandolins on Sunday nights in The Ship Tavern and invite anyone in the audience to get up on stage with them. The experience of spending my twenties playing in terrible bands took away my hair, it took away my pretty-boy good looks. What these guys were doing gave me hope.'

Slowly the following grew and the word got out, which helps explain why so many of the fishermen in The Ship Tavern knew the strange, altered-consciousness words to songs by The Lone Pigeon and King Creosote; songs that told stories about aliens landing on Earth and having surreal encounters in launderettes. I wondered if the locals that weren't involved in making music took offence at the raucous sing-alongs and the flux of incomers that Fence's increasing fame was creating.

'People realised that they would sell more rolls and beer if we put on an event,' Kenny replied. 'But on a day-to-day basis we're not really visible. We practise at home and put out the records from this house and keep ourselves to ourselves. The reality is that most of us are quite shy people who happen to like making music.'

This appeared to be the case with HMS Ginafore. I couldn't help but suspect that she was using Jazzercise as an excuse not to turn up to the recording session. Domino Records had used James Yorkston as a diplomatic middleman when attempting to sign her. 'They really offered her the best deal imaginable,' he remembered. 'I told her that she could make the album whenever she wanted, that she could record it with Kenny, and that she would get money for it. Her reply was: "How would you feel if I asked you to become a TV chef?"'

It was time for everyone to do the recording. Kenny wheezed his accordion into action and James and Johnny played guitars. I put the Zoom on the small, low coffee table in the middle of the room, fiddled with a few knobs and buttons in an attempt to look professional (all I ever really did was press record and make sure the recording level was high enough to pick up the sound), and put on the head-phones. 'Will you sing backing vocals?' Kenny asked Beth, but she made an embarrassed little grunt by way of answer and continued to play the computer game. James sang one of his songs called 'There She Blows', and Kenny sang one of Gordon's called 'Blue Mantle', which had the line, 'but the people, they were evil . . . some were good, but most of them were evil'. It was haunting, simple, and paranoid: the unfettered outpouring of a troubled mind.

'It's about Gordon's first visit to Earth,' explained Kenny with a slight, sad smile. 'He wrote when he first got ill. It was a hellish time, but it coincided with his best music. The Andersons have a tendency to jinx their lives in order to write better songs, and we're all a bit damaged, whether that's through depression or something more serious in the case of Gordon.'

They finished off with another moving song called 'Harper's Dough', which was written by Kenny. There was an Anstruther sound: acoustic, melancholic but rousing, and uncomplicated. Most of the songs were based around three or four chords, and the idea was that people could sing along to them or even learn to play them on guitar and have some sense of ownership over them. They were songs that were meant to be shared. It was incredibly refreshing to meet these people, living rather conventional lives, who found ways of making music without viewing that process through the disorientating lens of fame.

We went to The Ship Tavern, all low ceilings, nautical memorabilia and horseshoes hanging from the walls, and stayed until closing time. My head was in danger of hitting the table, and it was still driving through the quiet stretching roads of the Pennines and Northumberland. But before I fell asleep I asked Kenny what he felt he had achieved through Fence, given that he had, through example, inspired so many of the people of Anstruther to pick up a guitar or sit down at a piano and pen their own songs.

'If Fence is about anything,' he said with a look of bleary-eyed wisdom, 'it's that you don't have to be a star to make music. And that you can do it yourself.'

Chapter Eleven

The Ancient Spirit, Part Two: Edinburgh to Bradford

I N MEDIEVAL BRITAIN A FAVOURITE SUBJECT OF MORALITY plays was the contest between Death and a beautiful young lady or a feckless young man. In the sixteenth-century ballad 'Death And The Lady', which probably has its origins in the plays but turns up as a late-nineteenth-century broadside, one such woman walks along a country lane one morning in May as 'the birds did sing and the lambs did play', when she meets an old man with a bald head, a grey beard and a coat of myrtle grey. She asks the man which strange place he comes from. He introduces himself as Death. She offers gold and jewels, all her wealth, if he will let her live. He won't. Death, who has no use for such things, wants her and her alone. 'No longer glory in your pride,' he tells her. 'Your time has come and you must away.'

This is one of the ancient, anonymous songs that remind us the landscape of Britain is as exotic and as mysterious as the most labyrinthine souk or incense-sodden temple. It is reminiscent of the Ingmar Bergman film *The Seventh Seal*, in which a knight plays chess with Death in an attempt to outwit him. It has a moral purpose too: the woman has led an extravagant lifestyle, and now Death has caught her before she has time to repent and follow Christian virtues. Like so many of the old songs, 'Death And The

Lady' is a phantasmagorical story with no rational explanation, a little like a fairy tale, and it is an illustration of how humanity forms conclusions on the mysteries of life and death in the absence of science. The conclusions are no less profound for that.

Alex Neilson, who had sung 'Death And The Lady' that magical night in the garden of Mabe in Cornwall, was a Leeds-born musician transplanted to Glasgow whose interest was in all that harnessed something in front of us and yet out of reach, from free jazz to folk music to, perhaps surprisingly, the great chronicler of American blue-collar life Bruce Springsteen. Alex had just returned from a tour drumming for the American singer Will Oldham and he was back in Glasgow, kicking his heels until the next project presented itself. He invited me to stay.

Alex told me to drive to a Glasgow suburb called Govan, where he had been living for the last five years. 'Just call me when you get there and I'll come and find you,' he said lightly. The car dropped down a few more notches in status on the journey from Anstruther: another packet of a Ginster's cheese ploughman on the passenger seat, another oversized salt-and-vinegar crisp packet stuffed into the door, another couple of revolutions for the cassette tape of English folk songs, and the temperature gauge again hovering into the red. Somehow I ended up in Govan at midday, pulled the car up in a tiny side street, called Alex who was out shopping and would be over shortly, and took a stroll to take in the ambience of the place.

It was spitting rain. There were a lot of boarded-up houses. Charity shops and Chinese takeaways that doubled up as pizza bars and in some cases tripled up as kebab shops swamped the streets. On the corner of one street was a place called Brechin Bar (est. 1798), which had no windows of any sort whatsoever. Only an open door revealed the darkness inside. I could make out a handful of men standing around with pint glasses, looking glum. The dress code for Govan appeared to consist of loose-fitting shell suits, trainers and dangling cigarettes (for men and women), accessorised by prams and pregnant bellies (women between twelve and twenty-five), shopping trolleys (women aged thirty and upwards) and a can of Kestrel Super (essential for men, optional for women). There were a lot of people wandering about slowly, something you don't see much of in London. The unemployment office (rebranded as Jobcentre Plus) appeared to be the main focus of activity. There were quite a few old ladies walking around with heavy, younger men in tow, who were presumably – hopefully – their sons.

I scanned the sparse collection of wanted ads at Jobcentre Plus. I wandered into the British Heart Foundation shop and picked up a copy of *My Son* by Ted Beckham. Some teenage girls in matching white shell suits pointed at me and cackled. Alex Neilson arrived, looking impish with his short, bright ginger hair and mischievous glint; a young lord of misrule. We drove to his house a few streets away, where there was a collection of broken glass on the ground, a burned-out Ford Focus and a boarded-up hall on the corner. The long, wide street was empty save for a few people standing under an empty-framed bus shelter.

I asked Alex if Govan was famous for anything.

'Have you seen that TV programme *Rab C Nesbitt*, about an alcoholic tramp?' he replied lightly, kicking a half-burned plastic bottle away from his front door as he stuck the key in and shook it furiously until it opened. 'That was filmed here.'

Alex's flat was in a high-ceilinged Victorian house with large bay windows. There were walls of books and records, framed posters for concerts by the American jazz heroes Albert Ayler and John Coltrane on the walls, and a small room filled with a drum kit and dozens of hanging bells of various shapes and materials. There was also a young woman with flat, dark hair falling over her shoulders in waves and heavy eye make-up wandering around, wrapped in shawls. She told me in a heavy French accent that she lived in a commune on the outskirts of Paris. She had some sort of a dark beauty to her, like a doomed heroine of a Pre-Raphaelite painting. I never did find out what her name was.

I offered to go out and buy a bottle of wine, which Alex was grateful for since he was banned from the local shop, a semi-derelict collection of concrete breeze blocks with half-empty shelves and a large refrigerator well stocked with six-packs of Kestrel Super Strength beer. What crime had he committed to bring about such an injunction, I asked on my return? 'I went there the other day only to come home and discover that the milk I bought was off and the paper was missing the TV supplement,' he explained. 'So I went back to complain, and they told me to get out and never come back again.' This was unfortunate, since the shop was the only thing Alex's particular section of Govan offered in the way of convenience.

Alex made a curry, opened the bottle of wine and confirmed that he had convinced his friend Alasdair Roberts to come over for the field-recording session. This was exciting news. Alasdair is one of the best folk singers in Britain. I had seen him perform at a tribute to Lal Waterson and had been captivated enough by his singing voice, which is gentle but with a strong, deep Glasgow accent, to buy whatever albums by him I could find. He sang a lot of old folk songs but wrote his own too, and it was hard to tell where one began and the other stopped, such was his talent for writing stories in the spirit of the old ballads. I was also struck by the fact that Alasdair is unbelievably thin. His body is shaped like a T: broad shoulders top what is essentially a long straight line. I had been warned that he was extremely shy.

After the curry, as Alex called Alasdair and French
Mystery Girl wandered around the flat adjusting her shawl
and staring mysteriously into slightly tragic worlds located
somewhere in the middle distance, I had a look at a few of
the book titles on the shelves of the living room. There was
The White Goddess by Robert Graves, one of the most
powerful investigations into the pagan practices of Britain
ever written, a biography of Bruce Springsteen and a book
called *Where Is Saint George? Pagan Imagery In English Folk
Song* by Bob Stewart. When he came off the phone I asked
Alex, who couldn't have been more than 24, how he got into
the old music of Britain.

'It was when I was eighteen,' he began, standing
politely before me – he appeared to be an extremely well-
behaved, well-brought-up young man, but there was
something about the way he looked at you that suggested
the possibility of insurgency. 'I was in a charity shop in my
home town of Leeds and I picked up a record called *Sea
Songs And Sea Shanties*. I was reading *Moby Dick* at the time
and this world of seafaring and whaling became very interesting to me. There was something romantic about it –
treacherous as well. The music was so different from what I
was used to, but then there was something familiar about it,
like it stirred something deep within my memory.'

Through the album of sea shanties Alex heard the
music of The Watersons, and the sense of homecoming was
even stronger this time. The Watersons' home town of Hull
is not far from Leeds, and they were singing songs about
everyday people and everyday dramas that were rooted in
the locality of the place. 'They really revolutionised the way
I thought about music,' he said. 'All of a sudden I realised
that music wasn't this professional choice; it was an extension of your daily reality and the community you may or
may not have been a part of. At the time I was listening to
free jazz, which is improvisational and uses a lot of drone,

and here were these old songs that also used drone and could also be improvised, since nobody really knew what the tunes were so everybody approached them in a different way. The way The Watersons approached the old songs in particular was primal and rooted to the earth. It sounded like nothing else I had ever heard. Maybe it was the accents they sang in that got to me, but there was something about them that told of the secret history of Britain. It was like I was hearing these songs for the first time and yet I had concurrently known them all my life. I have never been the slightest bit patriotic, but the songs of The Watersons awakened a sense of national identity in me.'

Alex went deep into a discovery of traditional British music from then on. He sought out recordings by the Gypsy singers Margaret Barry and Jeannie Robertson, made pilgrimages to the library at Cecil Sharp House in London, and travelled around the country to sing at folk clubs wherever he could, usually to an audience made up of people at least forty years older than him. He discovered that the folk scene was full of self-appointed custodians of traditional music, and he believed that these people somehow missed the point of what they believed they were preserving: that the elemental cannot be preserved in aspic.

'The whole idea of authenticity is a red herring,' said Alex. 'To try and prescribe a correct way of approaching it is contrary to the spirit of the music. If you hear the singing of someone like Margaret Barry, the best thing about it is that it is untutored. It has a feral aspect. I realised that if you like this wild, expressive type of singing then it isn't much of a leap to connect it with the free jazz of Albert Ayler, or even with rock'n'roll.'

That's exactly what he did. Alex and his girlfriend Lavinia's duo Directing Hand took Britain's darkest murder ballads and aligned them with frantic drumming, dronesounds, and Lavinia's vocals veering between the glorious and the horrific. She was capable of sounding both like she was giving birth and like she had given up the physical realm as an unnecessary vulgarity. It was about as far from the true-to-the-tradition attitudes I had encountered from the morris men I had met in Oxford as you could possibly find, and yet it revealed a deeper understanding of the old music of Britain, and harnessed the ancient spirit far more effectively than jigging about with bells on in a pub car park ever could.

The big inspiration for Directing Hand were the Edward Ballads, the extremely old songs collected by Francis Child that Stanley Robertson had rejected as revivalist rubbish and which were based on the ancient theme of fratricide. There's an element of sacrifice to the Edward Ballads, as if the light of summer is given to the darkness of winter, and they capture the everyday terror of violence and the unknown. Alex pointed out how much the ballads deal in the supernatural, as well as the reality of one brother killing the other.

'In some of the versions of "My Son David", which is one of the Edward Ballads, the murdered brother speaks from beyond the grave,' said Alex. 'There's always symbolic information in the songs, too, and a linking in with the changing of the seasons. Sometimes the song ends with a conundrum: the dead brother will return, but only when oranges grow on apple trees and the sun and the moon both shine in the sky. I felt that the only way to really understand this music was not to study it and make conclusions about how it should be approached, but to inhabit it as much as possible. The themes that reoccur in these songs – treachery, idealised love, nature worship, death and rebirth – are profound and primal and have nothing to do with the style in which they are presented.'

Alex saw the theme of two brothers warring in the Edward Ballads as elemental not only to British music, and almost definitely stretching back to pre-Christian ritual practice, but to the very fundament of life itself. He cited a song called 'Two Brothers' as an example. One brother kills another in competition for a woman. The murdered man is brought back to life by his true love, thereby establishing the pattern of life, death and resurrection that is at the root of all religious beliefs.

A section in *Where Is Saint George? Pagan Imagery In English Folk Song* expounded on 'Two Brothers'. 'No story could be simpler and yet contain such a wealth of meaning,' writes Bob Stewart. 'Entire religions and vast empires have grown and fallen through manifestations of this one myth as dogma. The two brothers have fought their way through human consciousness through the entire history of man's existence.'

Even in Govan, in this bleak neighbourhood of shell suits and low expectations, the ancient mystery of the two brothers lay just below the concrete. Whether it is Horus and Set or Cain and Abel, the metaphysical pairing of opposites goes to the heart of the perpetual struggle. Life opposes death and dark opposes light. Alex Neilson had understood this, and his journey into British traditional music was really all about searching for this one indelible truth and filtering it through the ark of his imagination. It impressed the girls, too. As he talked, French Mystery Girl gazed longingly at Alex before throwing a shawl across her shoulders and wandering off, eyes flashing redundantly at non-seduceable household items.

It was time to make a recording. Alex suggested doing a rendition of 'The Bitter Withy', an extremely odd song he had learned from a version by Mike Waterson. It tells a story of Jesus as a young boy, meeting three young lords who are having a game of ball. He asks if he can join them, but they tell him that since he's 'nothing but a poor carpenter's son' and they are the sons of 'ladies fair' he can't possibly play with them. So he tells them that he's going to show how he's 'an angel above you all', and builds a bridge with the rays of the sun, leads the lords into a pond, and drowns them.

Three grieving mothers turn up at Mary's house, weeping, saying how Jesus killed their sons. Mary metes out what she believes to be a suitable punishment for a triple murder: she whips Jesus with a willow wand. The petulant infant Christ, in his final act of vengeance, curses the willow tree for causing him to smart. Now the willow is the only tree to perish from the heart. As far as I'm aware 'The Bitter Withy' is not sung in many churches.

Alex had a high, eerie singing voice, a little like how you would imagine a pixie to sound. He didn't appear to mind being recorded, even giving me advice on how to get the best quality out of the Zoom. We recorded the song in the corridor between the living room and the kitchen as French Mystery Girl peered around a door slightly open, eyes rolling this way and that.

'It's hallucinatory,' said Alex, once his rendition of the song came to an end. 'But it also shows how the songs explained the way life was. As far as I'm aware the willow does rot from the inside out, which explains its strange shape. And "The Bitter Withy" is about social injustice. It turns Jesus into a hero in a rather vindictive way. How many peasants dreamed of killing lords?'

Alasdair Roberts arrived. With his T-shaped body, short, tousled hair and gap-toothed grin he looked like an impoverished preacher. He was smiling, and arrived with a handful of his albums for me, but asking him questions meant either getting answers that petered out rather quickly, or just long silences finally ended by statements like: 'I don't know.'

Slowly, though, he warmed up enough to address the issue of how songs in Scotland vary from place to place.

'Different regions produce different types of songs,' he said at last. 'You have the border ballads, like "Fair Flower Of Northumberland", and then you have the bothy ballads about farm life and so on. Social structures give rise to certain styles of music and dance, so the music mirrors the society.'

'How about Glasgow?' I asked him.

'People like stories here,' he replied softly. 'Dolly Parton is huge in Glasgow, as is a lot of country music. There's a lot of line dancing going on. It's a hard-working, hard-drinking town where bullshit isn't tolerated, so folk like music that mirrors their life in ways they can understand.'

'There's a theory that because the west coast of Scotland faces the east coast of America, we like American music,' said Alex, leaning against a wall, filling in one of the interminable gaps in the conversation.

'Glasgow is a tough post-industrial town,' said Alasdair, sternly. 'Edinburgh is more effete.'

That was about as much as I was going to get out of Alasdair, although he did volunteer the information that he once pissed on the guitarist John Renbourn's feet. 'I was only five and I couldn't hold it in any longer,' he said, apologetic at the memory. Then Alasdair and Alex went to the narrow room filled with the drum kit and the bells to do a song for a field recording, with Alasdair on guitar and vocals and Alex on drums. I wasn't sure how this was going to work. So far I had been recording unaccompanied singers or, at the most, people playing acoustic guitars. But Alasdair was playing through a Marshall amplifier in order to reach the volume levels set by Alex's drums. There was a small coffee table in the little windowless room. I put the Zoom on that and, for once, changed the recording setting: there was one called 'electric rock' that sounded like it might suit the situation. I pressed record and told them to get on with it.

They ran through a rendition of 'Two Brothers'. Alex hammered away at the drums in a manner that seemed entirely random, although listening back to the recording a few days later revealed complex patterns that fitted in with the song in ways that were not obvious. Alasdair's guitar was heavily distorted, and every now and then he punctuated the words of the ancient ballad with whoops and hollers. Alex drummed with his eyes closed. They were lost in their own dark communion. French Mystery Girl could do little but glare from the shadows of the hallway.

They followed 'Two Brothers' with a song by Alasdair called 'Farewell Sorrow', and finally a song by Alasdair's late guitarist father called 'Kilmahog Saturday Afternoon'. It was a simple, jig-like guitar riff played over and over. Alex hit cowbells and snare drums, and the whole effect would have fitted in well as incidental music for a chase scene in a children's adventure film. They seemed happy to continue playing these songs, seemingly unaware of my presence or that of the Zoom that was recording them.

Alasdair lost all inhibition. I had seen this before: shy people get in front of a microphone and hold an instrument and are transformed. Often actors can barely string a sentence together when you meet them socially, but give them a script and they come alive. The guitarist Bert Jansch is virtually incapable of conversation and yet he is one of the most expressive musicians this country has ever produced. Alasdair and Alex quickly appeared to forget that I was in the room at all, and were lost entirely in the conversation of music. By the time they got to 'Kilmahog Saturday Afternoon' they seemed like two teenage boys bashing out music in the attic. You half-expected one of their mums to tell them to stop making that racket and come downstairs for dinner, it's already on the table.

They stopped entirely at one point.

'What shall we do?' whispered Alex.

'Shall we just keep going?' said Alasdair.

'OK. Whenever you're ready . . .'

'One, two, three, go!' And they were off again. 'This is Alex Neilson on drums,' said Alasdair, somewhere towards the end of the song, 'Alasdair Roberts on guitar . . . wooh!'

After a hot night in the old town (a few pints in pubs and cigarettes smoked in the shivering cold of the streets outside, Alex and I eulogising the late medieval revivalist David Munrow and French Mystery Girl sipping at a glass of red wine and looking distant) it was time to move on. Stephanie Hladowski was in Bradford, and a call to her revealed another example of the innate hospitality of the British: we had never met but she nonetheless suggested I stay at her parents' house. It had a spare room as her brother was off in Budapest, and her parents were very welcoming people. I gave my thanks to Alex, said goodbye to French Mystery Girl, and turned the key of the Astra, making a silent thanks to it for wheezing into life once more.

Anne Briggs sang 'Blackwaterside'. The Astra passed through small Scottish towns that looked like they had been constructed in a matter of days, the ugliness of the barren pebble-dashed bungalow houses contrasting sharply with the beauty of the rolling fields around them. It went up hills and down hills, through pine forests and heather-dappled plains. I got lost in Ayr and had to ask a man with an impenetrable accent how to get back on track. Somewhere around the Scotland/England border the temperature gauge went more into the red, but only a tiny bit more, so I decided the car would be OK for the while.

The roads seemed to go on forever. Stephanie, who had a rather vague telephone manner, said that it shouldn't take more than four hours to get from Glasgow to Bradford. It was more like seven before the city's industrial silhouettes came into view. She told me that her house was on the main road in Bradford and that I was sure to find it. I didn't. I pulled into an Asda car park in an area of estates and sweat-shops. I called Stephanie, who said that I should drive towards Saltaire into a Muslim area; when the mosque caller could be heard I would be getting close. She would stand outside her house and wave me down.

Over the course of the last few days my image of Stephanie had shifted from Gypsy Rose to latter-day Guin-evere, a little like French Mystery Girl, in a high-waisted dress with billowing sleeves and long hair augmented by a plait crossing the top of her head. She was nothing of the sort. She was small with dark, shoulder-length hair, and pretty in an approachable way. She looked very young indeed – I would have guessed she was still in her teens had she not announced she had recently graduated from univer-sity and was still unsure about what to do for a living. She lived with her parents, first-generation Polish immigrants to Britain, in a large, clean terraced house in the Muslim heart-land of Bradford.

They were remarkably welcoming, given that this strange man who claimed to want to record their daughter had dropped in out of nowhere in a shockingly filthy once-white Vauxhall Astra and was now preparing to stay the night with them. Stephanie's dad, who had taken early retirement and dedicated most of his time to fell walking in the rolling hills surrounding Bradford, offered a selection of real ales from his extensive collection. Stephanie's mum, still working as a legal secretary, asked if I was hungry, before we sat down around a large goulash in a brown earthenware pot. I told them about staying with Alex, and of going to

Fife, and we all agreed that Robin Hood's Bay was beautiful. After supper, Stephanie and I went to her brother Chris's room – neat and sparse, perhaps unsurprising given that he had left home to live in Budapest, but still with a stack of records against a wall and comics on the shelves – to make a recording.

I asked Stephanie how she started to sing traditional British songs. 'I always loved singing,' she said in an uncertain, lispy voice as she sat cross-legged on the carpet. 'I was in the school production of *Grease* when I was twelve. I got a part in *Bugsy Malone* a few years after that. Do you know that song "Tomorrow"? In *Bugsy Malone* a little boy sings it, but at our school I got to do it because none of the boys wanted to. I've never sung professionally or anything like that.'

At sixteen Stephanie went to Leeds College of Music, not because she saw a career ahead of her but because she didn't know what else to do. 'It went well, though. I was Dorothy in a production of *The Wizard Of Oz*.' She stared at the floor and smiled to herself in a shy way. 'It's funny. I never really practise singing, even though I take it very seriously, but when it comes to the final performance it usually comes out perfect. The thing is, I don't really have a path. I mean, I do love singing, but it's not something I've ever taken that seriously. I'm certainly not studious about it because I always feel so free when I do it – it's the opposite of a chore or a discipline, I suppose.'

Stephanie knew little about the old songs of England and Scotland, but her brother Chris was school friends with Alex Neilson and they formed a band called Scatter; needing a singer, they drafted in Stephanie. She was sixteen at the time. Scatter played mostly free, experimental music, but Alex had already begun his discovery of traditional music and suggested that Stephanie and Chris come up to Glasgow in order to record some old folk songs together. 'At that point I had never really heard folk songs,' she remembered. 'I had heard Pentangle's version of "Willie O' Winsbury" and that was about it. All I remember is being nervous on the train up to Glasgow because I didn't know what to expect. It was just me singing and Chris playing guitar and bouzouki in the end because Alex was in a weird mood that day. I did it and didn't really think anything of it, and came back down to Bradford because I had school the next day.'

I asked Stephanie if she would sing 'Willie O' Winsbury', which appears in different versions throughout Scotland and England. She said in a disengaged way that she was happy to, without a great deal of enthusiasm but without reticence either. Then she embarked on one of the most spine-chilling renditions of this strange old song I have ever heard. It tells the story of a king returning to his land after being a prisoner in Spain, and discovering that his daughter is pregnant after sensing that something is wrong with her. 'What ails you, what ails you, my daughter Janet?' he asks her. 'Are you suffering from sore sickness, or have you been sleeping with a man?' (Stephanie sang this as 'soul' sickness.) The daughter denies either, but then he makes her cast off her berry-brown gown and stand naked on a stone before him, and the secret is out. Finally she announces that she's in love with a young man called Willie O' Winsbury. Furious, the king demands that Willie is brought before him to be executed, but then he's so struck by the man's dazzling beauty that not only does he grant his daughter the right to marry her beloved; he goes so far as to tell Willie he'd marry him too if only he were a woman. The king offers Willie land and wealth but Willie rejects the offer, claiming that he has plenty of his own. This last detail has led to theories that the ballad is about James V of Scotland who married one of Francis I's daughters, although there's little else to suggest this.

This is the kind of ballad that was once written on a broadside and sung by the broadside singers. Typically, these singers had a handful of melodies that they applied to whatever broadsides – the carriers of the news and the latest stories – they were trying to sell. That's why the old ballads are so long: they were news stories of a kind. Gypsies, being travelling people, naturally found themselves perfectly suited to being broadside singers, which is one of the reasons why the ballads are still such an integral part of Gypsy culture.

Stephanie sang 'Willie O' Winsbury' in an unaffected way. She had no particular reverence or regard for British folk music and that was her strength. It gave her a freedom that people more deeply involved in it were lacking. She sang without thinking and thereby imbued the song with its true spiritual value, rather than treating it as a precious artefact and so rendering it a perfectly formed empty husk. I found it incredibly moving.

'I suppose I've got a funny relationship with British folk music,' she said in a whisper. 'My family come from Poland and so I'm drawn to a lot of Eastern European music, and a woman from a Bulgarian choir I sing in told me I had a Gypsy spirit, but I was born here and something about these songs does stir up an ancient memory. But then my boyfriend is really into dub reggae. I'm singing a lot of that at the moment.'

The Eastern European songs she sang were lovely, but there was something about the way Stephanie approached the old British ballads that was mesmerising. 'I've noticed that I seem to be drawn to a lot of sad songs,' she said, eyes down-turned. 'I was in France recently and I was listening to a singer called Jean Ritchie do a song called "Derry Gaol", which is about a guy who is on his way to the scaffold to be hung as his sweetheart watches, and I was in floods of tears. You begin to realise how these songs are so relevant to everyone. Anyone who has lost a close relative or someone they love can listen to "Derry Gaol" and feel a kinship with it.'

She sang a version of 'Derry Gaol', which I recorded. Then she sang a Bulgarian song called 'Zalibh Si Edno Libe', which was about falling in love. We talked a little about the singers she admired – Gypsy singers like Jane Turriff, Margaret Barry and Jeannie Robertson – and she talked about her ambitions. She had no intention of becoming a professional singer, nor had she really even entertained the idea, much as she loved to sing. She was thinking about becoming a teacher and was currently applying for jobs as a teaching assistant. In the meantime the family were moving out of the house in Bradford and into a cottage deep in the countryside, and Stephanie's thoughts were focused on that.

We had a game of pool in the basement, which had been turned into a Dad's Den complete with a Dansette record player, a stack of Stephanie's father's old Rolling Stones and The Who records, beer mats on the walls, various sporting trophies and a large collection of real ales. Stephanie won the game.

'It's funny,' she said over a post-match beer as Mick Jagger sang 'Under My Thumb'. 'You hear Arabic music and you realise how much it is a part of life. It's completely tied in with spirituality, and the hopes of everyday people, and the stories that they tell to each other. I don't really know much about British music. I never buy records because I'm completely skint and I don't keep up with what's happening with the new bands because I don't have much interest in them. But when I sing songs like "Willie O' Winsbury" I feel so alive, and so deeply connected to them, even though I'm more Polish than I am English. I wonder if that's unusual.'

In a way it was, although it shouldn't have been. Somehow the music of our shared heritage had become marginalised, yet there were people who had a deep feeling for its beauty, and who imbued it with a feeling that could only be described as spiritual.

The following morning Stephanie's mum and dad wrote down detailed directions to get me out of Bradford and into nearby Sheffield. They said that I should come and visit them in their new house. Perhaps it was a northern thing, but once again I had come across an example of British people waiting for a chance to be hospitable and kind, of welcoming the possibility of celebrating whatever was right there on their doorstep. And what I had found – a Polish-British girl singing old Gypsy ballads – was hardly typical of Bradford, but then I couldn't say what was. Perhaps the kaleidoscopic reality of 21st-century Britain was such that this was as valid a vision of Bradford as anything else. Still in Yorkshire, however, was a city that was famous for two things: steel manufacture and weird music. It was time to visit the concrete haven of Sheffield.

Chapter Twelve

Sheffield

THE BRITISH MOTORWAY EXPERIENCE HAS A SPECIAL flavour all of its own. Once you leave the stretching suburbs of any city the world of Moto and Welcome Break service stations begins, where Costa Coffee, with its regulation armchairs and sophisticated snacks, is enough of a pull to be announced on the signposts. CDs by the operatic Il Divo, a singing quartet with hair gel and rounded unthreatening faces, are on sale alongside oversized packets of Haribo sweets, pornography and petrol.

The soothing consumer portal of the service station can do little to soften the rough ride of life on British roads. Although summertime was now officially well under way the weather told a different story: along the stretch of the M1 that connects Bradford to Sheffield, heavy rain meant that having the windscreen wipers on top speed only resulted in partial visibility. Miniature lakes formed in central lanes and angry lorries flashed their lights for no obvious reason, like bulls kicking the dirt and preparing to charge. It made for a hazy, ominous mood, particularly after hitting static traffic that eventually inched forward to reveal its cause: a small car horribly mangled onto the central reservation by a crushed van. The cold lights of ambulances flashed and yellow figures moved in the rain, and you couldn't help but think that the life of someone who earlier that morning might have been wavering between an Il Divo CD and a bumper pack of

Haribo sour cola bottles was now destroyed. Then the traffic loosened up and the journey continued. Finally the concrete curves of Sheffield's factories came into view.

Sheffield is a hard place to figure out. In the late seventies and early eighties one glamorous, odd, futuristic pop band after another came out of the city, including mainstream groups with an art-school sensibility like ABC and The Human League and underground, cult groups like Clock DVA and Cabaret Voltaire. Phil Oakey of The Human League would appear on television with a curtain of shimmering hair covering one side of his face, singing in metallic, effete tones about someone who was working as a waitress in a cocktail bar or listening to the voice of Buddha as the rest of the band stood over keyboards and poked at them with the kind of enthusiasm generally reserved for filling in applications at job centres. Then in the interview afterwards he would talk in gruff tones about how miserable life in Sheffield was. It was a confusing image for a nine-year-old southerner to process, particularly as The Human League also featured two glamorous and sexy but resolutely suburban girls who, with their bored, vacant stares, gum-chewing lips and wedge haircuts, looked like the best baby-sitters I never had.

In a sense, although I was never exactly a fan, I can now see that The Human League was the ultimate Sheffield band. Phil Oakey sang in his own Yorkshire accent, which is less abrasive and nasal than Mancunian and slower and more considered than Liverpudlian, and he wrote songs about how humanity would survive in the future; a pertinent question given the band was finding fame at a time when the city was imploding around them. Sheffield's electronic-music boom coincided with its industrial collapse, as the city's steel industry, its economic backbone since the fifteenth century, underwent an economic crisis at the beginning of the 1980s that it has never recovered from.

Then there was Heaven 17, who seemed even more directed towards straight pop and yet were even more perverse. When the moment came to spend pocket money on albums for the first time I went for *Replicas* by Gary Numan's Tubeway Army (he looked like a robot and wrote lines like 'Down in the park with a friend called 5'), while my best friend went for *Penthouse And Pavement* by Heaven 17. We didn't know they were from Sheffield then, but we were intrigued by the fact that the album cover featured an illustration of the band as go-getting businessmen, shaking hands and clinching deals outside impersonal office constructions. Something wasn't right about the image. A band with long hair and leather jackets is easy to compute. A band in pinstriped suits singing about being 37 and having an affair with a seventeen-year-old gets rather more interesting, particularly if they come from a city deep in the throes of a crisis.

In the years that have followed, music with a lyrical, observational sensibility has emerged from the city. After a decade in the wilderness Jarvis Cocker rose to become pop's answer to Alan Bennett, while the modern-day crooner guitarist Richard Hawley embodied the northern working-class man's love affair with American rock'n'roll and The Arctic Monkeys captured the tawdry aspects of being young in 21st-century Britain. Alongside this, the city has a history of producing the most out-there music imaginable: free, improvised noise that follows no obvious patterns – and quite often finds no audience.

Singing Knives turned out to be a label that operated on the further fringes of Sheffield's musical community. Run by a couple called Jon and Fiona in their spare time (they had day jobs), it released limited runs of vinyl featuring artists that surely couldn't ever find a huge audience: folk-influenced, guitar-based experimentalism does have a limited appeal, after all. But they were positively mainstream compared with some of the labels operating out of the city. Alongside the long-standing electronic label Warp there was Blackest Rainbow (ear-crushing doom, only without drums or rhythms – chosen format for album releases: the cassette tape) and Free Noise (totally random improvisation). 'Improvisational and experimental music has a big tradition in Sheffield,' said Jon, when I spoke to him on the phone from a service station somewhere between Bradford and Sheffield. 'I could put you in touch with Jonny from Free Noise. I'm sure he'll be happy to get a bunch of musicians together for a recording session. There's an amazing oud player called John Jasnoch. He once performed with the great Derek Bailey!'

I told him that John the Oud Player did indeed sound amazing, concluding that this was not the time to admit I had no idea who the great Derek Bailey was (an influential guitarist on the free jazz scene, I later discovered). I contacted Jonny of Free Noise.

'Would you mind if I recorded a session?' I asked.

'We can do it in my basement,' he replied.

As if this wasn't enough of an introduction, Blackest Rainbow were putting on an event at a place called The Red House. My immersion into the localised phenomenon of weird Sheffield music would be complete.

First it was time to explore the city's pop heritage. Jarvis Cocker is an unlikely star, being a twig-like middle-aged man in National Health glasses and sensible brown shoes, but he's very good at it. It took a decade and a move down to London to make it, but in 1996 Jarvis brought world fame to his band Pulp with 'Common People', a simple but brilliantly constructed song about a wealthy art-school girl living out peasant fantasies with the riff-raff. From then on he's stayed firmly in the public consciousness despite splitting up with Pulp, moving to Paris and swapping hanging around in rehearsal rooms for hanging around the school gates, dropping off and picking up his young son. I had met Jarvis before, and tried to interview him countless times, but he had never shown the slightest interest. Then, out of the blue, a call came to say that he would be in Sheffield to rehearse for a couple of gigs. If I could make it there by ten in the morning he could spare a couple of hours – musicians can't get it together before midday, apparently. 'And if we meet there,' he said in a tone of restrained but noticeable excitement, 'I can introduce you to the best fish and chips in Sheffield.'

Would it be possible to get a field recording out of him? 'I'm not going to have a great deal of time,' he said, cautiously. I didn't press the issue.

I had visited Sheffield once before, to meet Jarvis's friend Richard Hawley. It had been in Fagan's, a tiny womb-like pub where the city's ageing folk musicians get together most evenings to have acoustic sing-alongs, and it was some-thing of a second home for Richard whose childhood was a story of following his steelworker father and uncle around the clubs with their rock'n'roll covers band. This time Richard didn't know if he could meet me. His star was in the ascendant: every album he released was selling well and getting good reviews, he had a second career as a producer, and he was becoming something of a hero figure to young bands like The Arctic Monkeys for his lyrical romanticism and solid musical grounding. But while Jarvis chased glamour – he was married to a beautiful, aristocratic French stylist and moved in a fashionable world of artists, designers and fellow pop stars – Richard steadfastly refused to leave Sheffield. 'The most beautiful thing in the world,' he had told me that afternoon in Fagan's, 'is driving along the motorway and seeing the old factories come into view. And there's nothing I like better than taking kids to the park and pushing them on swings. Why would I want to leave the place?'

I wasn't sure that I could share Richard 's vision of beauty as, the car bonnet steaming dangerously as a result of being stuck in virtually stationary traffic for the last two hours, I drove along the tangle of bypasses and slip roads that lead off the motorway and into the city, which appeared to be in a period of flux. Cranes dominated the skyline. Jarvis had told me to meet him at a place called Yellow Arch Studios in Neepsend. 'It's easy to find,' he told me, adding, 'It's got a yellow arch.'

It might have seemed sensible to check its location on the map before setting off, but that wouldn't have done any good. Our road atlas has had so much rainwater and orange juice spilled on it that most of the pages are glued together. Sooner or later we'll get round to buying a new one. In the meantime I had to utilise the technique we had been relying on for years – leaning out of the window and shouting to the nearest passer-by for directions. A cheerful businessman-type sent me off on the right way and some builders got me to the final destination.

Neepsend is a mostly deserted area of empty ware-houses and builders' yards. Wide, uneven streets are lined with large, faceless buildings and occasional shops. New developments of brown brick and glass look lonely among crumbling buildings so fiercely belonging to a slower age. In the city's steelworking heyday it was thriving, but now it's a rough, barren place with a reputation for prostitutes, drugs and the violence that goes with them. Like so many other former industrial areas it is also an artistic haven. On my visit the developers were yet to move in, the rents were cheap and Neepsend had the air of a place where anything, good or bad, could happen.

Yellow Arch Studios was leading the area's creative renaissance. Entered by a nondescript battered door down a cobbled mews (the arch connects the mews with the street outside) the studios are where The Arctic Monkeys rehearsed before recording their first album and where Richard Hawley has based himself since 1997. I got a call from Jarvis to say he was running late – something to do with having a fried breakfast. I waited under the yellow arch, watching the raindrops make splashing patterns on the broken paving stones of the street, and trying to catch a glimpse of the faces of the occasional lorry drivers that went past, until he arrived.

Jarvis, now in his mid-forties, looked a lot more sombre than the bright pop misfit who became public property back in the mid-nineties. With longish hair streaked with grey, corduroy trousers and a nicely cut if slightly shabby tweed jacket, he looked more like an intrinsically stylish geography teacher than a superstar. He made us both a cup of tea, adding in his dry but warm way that Richard Hawley was the only person he knew who put two bags in one cup but he could do the same for me if I wished. We found a corner of a rehearsal room with a couple of prehistoric sofas, and I told him that it seemed it wasn't the done thing in Sheffield to bolster oneself up too much. 'In Liverpool and Manchester you have to proclaim your band as the best in the world, as Echo And The Bunnymen and Oasis have done,' I added. 'In Sheffield you have a band like The Arctic Monkeys that are clearly huge, yet they seem to do the opposite.'

'One of the biggest crimes you can commit is to get ideas above your station,' Jarvis confirmed, in a low semi-monotone. 'All that "we're the greatest" business gets on my nerves, but then I'm from Sheffield, aren't I? We don't like show-offs. As for why that is, I couldn't really hazard a guess. But it's deep-rooted. If you want to be a pop star here you have to make it look like it just happened. You certainly don't want to be seen as having put any effort into becoming famous.'

Jarvis wore his success lightly. He achieved national-treasure status during the ceremony for the 1996 Brit

Awards when, offended at Michael Jackson's Christ-like performance featuring scores of children apparently worshipping him as the new Messiah, Jarvis got up on stage, wiggled his bum a bit, and ran off before being captured by security guards. The day after the event the nation's tabloids made a serious error of judgement by painting him as a cross between a talent-free spoilsport and the Child Catcher from *Chitty Chitty Bang Bang*, terrifying the stage-school kids and ruining Michael Jackson's impersonation of God in the process. They then made a swift about-turn when it became obvious everyone loved him for pricking the bubble of such a tasteless display of self-importance. I asked him what Sheffield was like to grow up in.

'You don't know any different, do you?' he replied with a shrug, legs poking out of the sofa like corduroy-clad sticks. 'I assumed the rest of the world was like Sheffield. The big moment for me came when I was on the bus going to college in London, it was a wet day, and it was all steamed up. I noticed that people weren't wiping the windows to look outside. They were so insular and focused on making their way through the day that they didn't take an interest in what else was going on. In Sheffield they're wiping those windows like crazy.'

I told him that people seemed friendly, that a woman had smiled and said, 'All right, luv?' while I was waiting for him under the yellow arch. 'That's a social thing here,' he replied. 'I guess because London is a bigger place people tend to hang around with people doing similar things and not really talk to anyone else. It's like that pub Fagan's, where Richard took you. It's quite near the police station, so you get the chief of the serious crime squad sitting next to an old folkie. People don't seem to be so much defined by what they do – that's just how you make some money. It's about what else you've got to offer that's interesting, not just the sales figures.'

Jarvis was 25 when he left Sheffield, close to two decades previously. Having left school at sixteen, Pulp already in a pre-pupal state of existence, he worked briefly on a fish stall in a market but spent a greater portion of his time in the city as an unemployed would-be superstar. There was little family money, his father having deserted Jarvis, his sister and their mother years before, and this was in the mid-eighties when the national miners' strike was coming to a disastrous end and the Sheffield steelworks were closing down. I asked Jarvis, perhaps redundantly, why he left Sheffield at the end of the eighties, first to study film at St Martin's College in London and ultimately to achieve his pop dream.

'I remember feeling that I had to get out otherwise I would be stuck forever,' he said reflectively. 'All the factories had gone . . . not that I was contemplating a career in steel manufacture . . . and there was nothing happening. The band was going nowhere. I saw a film about the Sheffield music scene of the mid-eighties recently and everyone looked like they were clinically depressed. Back then the big thing was leaving Sheffield and moving to London if you wanted to make it. That's not really the case any more, I guess because of the Internet. Now people are interested in a band from a far-flung Outer Hebridean island – it's exotic and not a disability – but when we started we had a bit of a local following and nothing outside of it. We would go to London and play in front of ten people. It was desperate.'

Jarvis's creative voice was born of this void. ABC and The Human League had been and gone, there was very little entertainment laid on and hardly any money around, and so for someone like Jarvis, who wasn't really labouring material, the city's depression forced action – in small doses.

'It was dole culture,' he said on life in the mid-eighties. 'I followed a well-worn path of leaving school and signing on. You did the "dole stroll", aimlessly wandering around town, meeting people by a fountain and doing things that didn't cost anything. You could get a bit of money towards your rent, and you could get things like bedding allowance. Everyone went for that. You said you were going to buy a mattress from DFS, and they gave you the money, and then you went off to spend it on beer. Halcyon days . . . you left school, you formed a band, and you got left alone, subsisting on a low level. Gradually that eroded. I think the bedding allowance might have been one of the first things to go.'

I asked him if, back then, he really thought he stood much of a chance of becoming a pop star. 'That was the general attitude,' he replied with a shrug. 'If you told people you had been in a band for the last five years, you might as well have told them that you spent it wanking off. There was no respect for it and in a way, fair enough. If I think of a gangly kid setting his sights on becoming a pop star it would seem unlikely, but I'm quite glad I did it. It was punk that made it all possible. All of a sudden you didn't have to go to Rock School to be in a band, and as long as a song was about something it had validity. You could write a song about the Neepsend Triangle if you liked.'

It's been argued that the British culture of signing on, of collecting a bit of welfare money each week and doing whatever you can to avoid conventional employment, has been the great artistic patronage system of modern times, allowing musicians, writers and artists to develop their voice or style without pressures of time and money. But the welfare culture in Britain no longer favours the willingly unemployed – and neither, oddly, does Jarvis.

'I have to say, now I'm a family man with responsibilities, I don't really think being on the dole is a great lifestyle option. In fact I'm quite ashamed at all the time I wasted. If you only have to turn up to the benefits office once a fortnight and even that seems to be hard, you just become lazy. The band never rehearsed more than once a week. I made excuses for myself. I was seeking inspiration. I was observing life . . . and it was always at the back of my mind that I should have been doing something. Actually it's my biggest regret. I've been involved in music for thirty years. I've released six albums in that time. It's not exactly a massive work rate, is it?'

ABC, The Human League and all the other Sheffield bands that came before Pulp had suggested an image of the city as a futuristic metropolis, at a time when its great industries were crumbling and nothing was coming in their place. 'When those bands were around everyone said they were a result of the fact that Sheffield is an industrial city,' said Jarvis. 'I always thought that you'd want a rest from it if you've been working at the steel factory all day. But there have been a lot of hare-brained schemes to make Sheffield the city of the future. There are the big brutalist flats at Hyde Park and Park Hill. There's a bus station that won an award for being futuristic. It's fucking horrible. You get mugged there in five minutes. Maybe the Sheffield bands reflected that. Or maybe they wanted an escape from the grind and the grimness of it all by offering a vision of the future.'

Jarvis's Sheffield was a place of cheap laughs and potential danger. Certain parts of town were out of bounds. Weekends were always risky because townies – tough working-class men with cropped hair, moustaches and short-sleeved shirts, even in sub-zero temperatures – were on the lookout for anyone slightly weird. It was a reminder that Britain is still a dangerously tribal place. Boredom, frustration and a need to belong frequently create violence that occasionally spills over into something horrific. A few months previously a goth teenager in Preston had been kicked to death by a gang of fifteen-year-old boys. There can be few countries in the world where so much creativity goes alongside such vicious intolerance.

The West Street area of Sheffield was a safer option, chiefly because that's where the city's many students hung out. 'But they got on my tits as well,' said Jarvis, crossing his arms. 'At least we could crash their parties and drink their beer. So you had the airy-fairy students on one side and the brutal townies on the other, and we were the filling in the sandwich.'

Jarvis lives in Paris. Before then he was a credible pop star in London, invited to all the parties the city's beautiful people could be found at. 'It took moving away from Sheffield to appreciate it, certainly in terms of writing about it, and you realised that it has formed your world-view and that can be irritating because it's inappropriate. You're in some exotic place filled with glamorous people and all you can think is: why don't they have good chips here? I mean, is that really the point? But for better or for worse the place you were born forms you. When I come back here I'm pleased that I still feel comfortable, and that I still have something in common with the people here.'

Sheffield today is a very different city from the depressed dole-culture one of the 1980s. It has chain coffee shops, smart restaurants and countless new developments. Neepsend, with its empty cobbled streets and leaning buildings with tiny blackened windows, looks like a stereotype of a northern industrial town, but it is one of the few reminders of that old world.

'Neepsend is actually one of the only parts of Sheffield I recognise,' said Jarvis, when I commented on the amount of cranes the city skyline is dotted with. 'When I was on the dole I would walk along the river until I came here, and there would be massive derelict warehouses you could sneak into and wander around, and I found it fascinating that I was the only person in this giant place. But it can't last. Sooner or later this whole area will be redeveloped.'

On that reflection, in walked Richard Hawley who, it turned out, was producing an album by the Sheffield crooner Tony Christie in the next room. If Jarvis Cocker had occasional nostalgic pangs for the city he left behind, Richard had built a career on it. His breakthrough album is named *Cole's Corner* after the entrance to the long-gone Cole Brothers department store, which served as a meeting place for courting couples. His singing style combines an obvious debt to the melancholic crooning of Roy Orbison with a professionalism that is part of the Sheffield work ethic, no doubt gleaned from the father and uncle he cites as the men that provided the inspiration for everything he does. He seemed the type to drink a lot of beer and hold his own, but there was something childlike about him, too. He asked Jarvis if he wanted to order anything from the Yellow Arch Studios kitchen.

'I'm thinking about going to the chippy,' he replied, a little sheepishly. 'I'm leaving tomorrow and I haven't had any in two weeks.'

'I've just spent so many hours in here, Jarv, that I don't know if I can face eating chips.'

'I know your body is your temple.'

A change of mood took place when Richard joined us. There's a touch of the fairground worker about Richard, with his greasy quiff and denim jacket, and I had a feeling – I could have been wrong – that Jarvis was slightly in awe of him; even a little intimidated. His Sheffield accent got stronger. He took something of a back seat as Richard held forth.

'I'm a simple man,' announced Richard. 'One of my greatest pleasures is going into Fagan's when there's no one around to have a pint, do a crossword, and chat with Tom the landlord. See, it's a Sheffield thing that people mix. In that pub you get hairy-arsed musicians, rock climbers, drunks, librarians and coppers. I met a man the other day whose job it is to survey the biggest cave in Europe, which is in the Peak District, not far from here. He was telling me about it – goes down there on his own. You're not going to meet someone like that in one of these shiny new boozers.'

I told Jarvis and Richard that I was looking for modern folk music; that there must be, a hundred years on from the first great song collectors, thousands of people writing or singing songs on a localised level. 'You wouldn't think of The Human League as a folk band, but for me they represent the place better than anyone, which is folk music's purpose,' said Jarvis. 'Songs are generally about the same three things – love, conflict and death – but the scenery changes. When people told me I didn't have a cat's chance of getting anywhere I would always think of *Kes*. That's the film that reflected the environment I was brought up in, and it proved to me that you can be specific, and show things that are particular to that social milieu, and still tell a universal story: a kid grows up not knowing where he fits in. That's a very successful film and yet in America it had to be subtitled because nobody could decipher the thick Yorkshire accent. So the period detail and the local detail shouldn't be seen as a handicap because that's what creates a sense of place.'

'I would describe what I do as folk music,' said Richard. 'I was once in a band with people whose goal was to own a Ferrari and a swimming pool in LA. I wanted a Mini and a birdbath at best, which is why we didn't get on. The more remote your ambitions are from what you start off from, the less based in reality your songs are. If you write songs about where you're from you deal with the reality of that. Mind you, if you do write about your immediate environment you have to be careful what you say, especially in Sheffield. You can get smacked.'

Richard had to get on with his production work for Tony Christie – unlike Jarvis Cocker's band, his had turned up bright and early to put a good day's work in. 'The point I make in a lot of songs,' he said as he left,' is that no matter what they do, humanity prevails. The Sheffield skyline does my head in right now. All you see is cranes, and the redevelopment certainly isn't for the benefit of the Sheffield people. They're always trying to redevelop this city. Some knobhead will have his next grand scheme to get the people from the slums into Park Hill and call it Streets In The Sky. I wrote a song about it, and what a bad idea that scheme was when you look at the practicality of it. But you can't kill history dead. The spirit of the people prevails.'

Once Richard was out of earshot, Jarvis admitted that he frequently got lost when he visited Sheffield now. 'I'll go on a walk and it will seem familiar at first, but then I'll realise they've redeveloped something and I don't know where I am,' he said quietly, leaning forward with eyebrows raised. 'But what Richard said is true. You can get dewy-eyed about the old days, but things just move. That documentary on the eighties music scene I mentioned would instantly cure you of any nostalgia. There was no sense of being proud of our musical heritage back then. It was more: who are these doley scumbags who claim to be musicians?'

In the late eighties there were attempts by Sheffield Council to create an official space for musical development. A council-run studio and rehearsal space was set up, available for use through application, with a number of grants handed out to musicians with a laudable work ethic.

'Lo and behold, not one decent piece of music came out of it,' said Jarvis. 'I think Jive Bunny [a horrific attempt to make medleys out of the pop and soul hits of yesteryear] recorded there, and they were from Rotherham. And yet somebody decided to do something with a derelict building in Neepsend and call it Yellow Arch Studios and it becomes the nerve centre of the city's creativity. Maybe nice ideas by the council will never work. Music is more organic than that.'

We went downstairs and around the corner to Jarvis's favourite fish-and-chip shop, presumably an antidote to all that haute cuisine he gets in Paris. One of the women behind the counter told him that a film crew had turned up and filmed her in connection with a documentary about him, and she hadn't even had a chance to do her hair. 'Talk about Common People!' she said with a loud laugh. He ordered cod and chips and mushy peas on the side. Everyone called everyone 'luv'.

It had gone one o'clock. The band had not turned up yet. We went back to the studio and ate cod and chips in polystyrene containers, sitting on amplifiers. Jarvis was going back to Paris the following day, and although his life there did sound idyllic – an elegant flat, a beautiful super-chic wife, a sweet son, plenty of commissions and just enough fame to feel special without so much that popping out for a pint of milk is impossible – he did seem nostalgic, not just for Sheffield but for the British way of life in general.

'We had some friends over to stay from London recently,' he said, jabbing a plastic fork into mushy peas that were a radioactive shade of green. 'They were flabbergasted that you could walk around Paris on a Friday night and not get hassled by gangs of drunken blokes going "Come on, then!" And I could tell what they were thinking: you've got it cushy here. But while I don't miss the feeling that you're about to get beaten up, I do get frustrated that the French aren't very *passionate* about things.'

'What do you mean?'

'The slightly ugly approach to life in Britain makes people create stuff,' he replied. 'France is more cultured. For that reason they don't react violently in the way we do. They'd rather have a nice meal and a glass of wine. I mean, in England if people are into rock'n'roll they dress the part, and call the kids Elvis and Jerry Lee, and go for it whole hog. In Paris it's: "I 'ave an eenterest in many cultural phenomena." They're so aware of their heritage that they can't do anything new. The city is beautiful, and the radio is

243

filled with French singers from fifty years ago, and there's no room for anything to happen. The contemporary art scene in Paris is a joke. But you're tripping over artists in London, aren't you? England, for all its faults, does allow for a sense of possibility.'

What happened later that day served to illustrate Jarvis Cocker's point. Sheffield 7 is one of the city's less brutal neighbourhoods. Large oak trees stand outside tall terraced houses made of bricks in Yorkshire red. There are old cars and camper vans on the hilly uneven streets, giving an arty but familial, welcoming touch. I came to a large house, hidden from the road by a high hedge, and a garden dotted with plastic toys and bicycles. A tough-looking man in his early forties with cropped grey hair and piercing blue eyes opened the door. He stared at me. I stared at him. I wasn't sure where all this staring would lead but I didn't like it.

'Come in,' he said. 'You must be Will. I'm Jonny from Free Noise. Did yer find it all right? Cup of tea?'

Some long-haired children ran into the corridor and ran out again. We went into an airy living room with a pleasant feel of alternative domesticity – there were two well-worn large sofas, flowers on the mantelpiece, but also framed concert posters for the scary industrial art-noise four-piece Throbbing Gristle, whose leader Genesis P Orridge is in the process of turning into a hermaphrodite. Also in the room was a softly spoken, middle-aged man who introduced himself as Glynn, and said that when he wasn't making atonal noise with self-built electronic contraptions he worked at the local hospital. Occasionally, through the door, I would see glimpses of a thin, nervous-looking woman swathed in the Eastern fabrics of someone with a soft spot for alternative therapies. So this was the world of Northern improvisation. I asked Jonny and Glynn why Sheffield had a history of this kind of out-there music.

'The first name to drop is Derek Bailey,' said Jonny, looking very serious. 'He became a household name in the last decade, and he started it all. He was playing in working-men's clubs until he got fed up with it and went off on his own path. Personally, in the late eighties I embarked on a spiritual quest that lasted for the next fifteen years. I gave up all worldly things, and when I came back to Sheffield there was a clean slate for creativity. Improv is all about that moment when something is created out of nothing. So I started Free Noise and we staged concerts.'

'Jonny would put on events where there would be really abrasive noise, and the audience would be walking out,' said Glynn, whose voice reminded me of George, the pink hippo from the seventies children's programme *Rainbow*. 'Around the same time we formed a group called Shad Panic that was electro-based. We wanted to make abrasive noise, but we couldn't do it. We're too poetic.' He made a gentle smile.

'So why do you want to make noise in the first place?' I asked.

There was a silence. Then Jonny said, 'What's noise?' He gave me that cold metallic stare that seemed so threatening. 'You could just say sound. There's a massive spiritual angle in improv that goes back to the Om.'

'Noise doesn't inspire you to do destructive acts,' added Glynn in his mild way. You couldn't imagine him doing so much as stamping on an ant without apologising afterwards. 'Noise is a purging of angst and anger. It's a cleansing.'

They talked of the great heroes of noise. There was Genesis P Orridge, and also a Japanese man called

Merzbow. 'See, he's a spiritual guy,' said Jonny. 'He's into protecting birds and that.'

Just as we reflected on the spiritual side of Merzbow while listening to walls of screeching chaos, John the oud player arrived. He was a thin man of around fifty with white hair, and didn't look like the type to go on too many group-bonding weekends. I asked him about Sheffield's history of musical oddness.

'I've noticed that unlike other British cities, there's a sense of cynicism to any kind of cultural activity here,' he began. 'The local authorities are anti-culture. Anish Kapoor made a sculpture to go on an empty bit of paving down near the market and the council said that we don't have that kind of thing round here. The city is aggressively working class and there's an idea that some things are within your realm of activity and some things aren't. I think we're all reacting against that.'

'You have to toe the line,' said Jonny, slumped into the sofa.

'In Sheffield it's assumed that this is how life is: you go to work and don't complain and if anyone doesn't want to do that, who the hell do they think they are?' said John. 'There were plans for various retailers to set up shops in the city centre, and all these councillors put a stop to it. One of them, I think his name was Ironmonger, said: "If the lasses want to get posh frocks they can go to Leeds." This is the fourth biggest city in the country, but if you look at what's available in terms of art galleries and so on it's incredible. The Millennium Gallery has a few knives and forks in it. All of these little co-operatives spring up throughout the city in reaction to the mainstream philistine mentality.'

'Bloody nightclubs have got a lot to answer for,' grumbled Jonny. 'I put up thirty posters for Free Noise events. Next day there's posters over them for a nightclub offering vodka at a pound for students.'

'These conditions are a breeding ground for doing your own thing,' Glynn piped in – gently.

'There's another reason why improvisational music is a localised, Sheffield thing,' said John. 'It doesn't travel well because it's so marginal. People can't afford to tour because the concerts are always going to be in the back rooms of pubs.'

'Like the one at The Grapes,' said Jonny.

'The Grapes is a pub where Derek Bailey used to play on Saturday lunchtimes for half a crown,' explained John. 'Forty years later we're all playing the same venue.'

I couldn't tell if this was said with triumph or misery. But it was interesting. Here were three men, no longer young, who made music that stood near-zero hope of getting much of an audience. But *they* got a huge amount out of it. We went down into Jonny's dark, windowless basement, which was filled with instruments and amplifiers and had psychedelic murals on the uneven walls. I set up the eight-track in the middle of the room. John plucked at his oud. Jonny hit various percussive instruments, apparently at random. Glynn twiddled with a few knobs and made some electronic warbles. It sounded vaguely Eastern, or possibly like a series of random messages arriving in a kind of musical code, and you couldn't really place any particularly emotion on it. It went on for about fifteen minutes.

'Wow,' said John, after the final bleep, oud string and shimmering bell died out. 'We were really going somewhere.' He pointed his finger backwards and forwards between his fellow improvisation-makers.

'I felt a connection,' said Glynn in not much more than a whisper. 'It was telepathic.'

'It's spiritual,' added Jonny, rubbing his temples, eyes closed. 'I purged a lot of angst.'

I couldn't make head nor tail of it.

Later that evening Jonny and I went for a walk from his house to the countryside, and it only took about five minutes. Sheffield is a unique city in that it is one of the most brutal industrial centres imaginable, and yet is surrounded by glorious English countryside. Woods of beech and plane give way to the hills and dales of the Peak District. There doesn't seem to be much in between. Londoners are used to the sprawl of suburbia that separates the metropolis from rural life, but in Sheffield the city gives way to the glories of nature very quickly.

Jonny explained how he got by. Running Free Noise didn't bring too much money in, but he had various government allowances that meant the rent on the house was paid and there was enough to keep the children healthy and happy. The family had returned to Sheffield at the conclusion of Jonny's aforementioned spiritual journey; before then they had lived in a state of primal ascetic suffering on the Isle of Skye.

'It sounds nice at first, but it soon gets horrible,' he said of life on the island. 'In the winter everybody stays in their homes because it's dark all the time and in the summer the midges are so fierce you have to keep moving constantly or they eat you alive. It wasn't really the spiritual experience that we were hoping for.'

We returned to his home. Jonny's wife, whose name I never did find out, made us rice and dhal. They talked about home-schooling their children, of the example set by Genesis P Orridge, and of adolescence in Manchester (Jonny) and Milton Keynes (wife) filled with wasting years of 'too much of that' (Jonny miming smoking a joint). Then Jonny announced he was going out. His wife asked when he would be back. 'Don't know. Don't wait up for me.'

We arrived at a venue called The Red House, for a night put on by the Sheffield label Blackest Rainbow. It was down a small street alongside a housing estate where bored-looking prostitutes stood on corners, fiddling with mobile phones. The Red House consisted of two small rooms. One had a bar and a stage in it and the other had a few chairs and a table selling Blackest Rainbow merchandise: cassettes, mostly, but also posters, vinyl albums and even, in a nod to mainstream convenience culture, CDs. I thought about buying one by a band named Pukes but decided against it. There was a balcony where you could go for a cigarette; it looked out onto a concrete skyline where nature had been obliterated by ongoing, endless construction.

There were about ten people in The Red House when the first band came on; a duo made up of a drummer with a severe medieval bowl cut and Punch-like features and a guitarist who bent over his instrument without saying anything. They didn't introduce themselves. They launched into a barrage of total chaos. The guitarist was making a screeching squawk while the medieval drummer, who looked as if he was about to either burst into tears or have an orgasm, attacked his drums with untold fury, sometimes actually grabbing one and shaking it like a deranged nanny unleashing her long-repressed frustration onto a screaming baby. This went on for 25 minutes without a break. Then they stopped and walked off. About ten minutes later they were leaning against the bar with pints in their hands, chatting about that evening's football match.

More improvisational noise followed. The audience expanded to fourteen people. There were three middle-aged men that Jonny was chatting to; one was giggling maniacally and another had a permanent rictus grin; the third appeared to be observing the other two with disdainful amusement, although it was slightly hard to tell as his eyes were heading off in opposite directions. Apparently they ran Sheffield's best record shop. Jon and Fiona from Singing Knives arrived. A quiet, apparently normal couple in their early twenties, they politely reeled off the names of various bands and singers I had never heard of. I told them about staying with Stephanie Hladowski in Bradford, and they revealed that her brother Chris was a big name on the northern free folk/weird noise/Eastern/devotional/basically-not-James-Blunt scene. I thought about making an escape back to the cheap hotel I was staying in. Fascinating though this world of totally non-commercial music was, it begins to affect one's mentality after a while, particularly when sleep-deprived after constant travel. I thanked Jon and Fiona, braved the barrage of whatever was coming out of the speakers at that moment, and told Jonny I was heading back.

'Where are you staying?' he asked.

I told him.

'That's got a bar that stays open until 4 a.m.,' he said, bristling his shoulders and rubbing his palms together. 'Let's go.'

My hotel was in the heart of Sheffield's student area, and its bar appeared to be something of a student favourite. It was getting late and I really had to go to bed. 'The night is young, eh?' said Jonny, transforming from intense improvisational spiritual seeker into Northern lad as he looked around at the welter of attractive young students from the vantage point of the bar, pint raised. Then he met someone he knew. It was my chance of a getaway. I thanked him for his hospitality and escaped to the drab hotel room, which was painted in durable pastel shades of institution green and pretend-friendly purple. Much as I liked and admired the place, Sheffield had overwhelmed me with its confusing mix of down-to-earth philosophy and out-there weirdness. Besides, I had to get on with finding an answer to a question that had been bothering me for ages: why is everyone in Liverpool obsessed with Pink Floyd?

Chapter Thirteen

Why Does Everyone in Liverpool Love Pink Floyd?

I LEFT EARLY THE FOLLOWING MORNING, NOT QUITE ABLE to face a breakfast in the hotel bar alongside the other guests (a delegation of photocopier salesmen from Harrogate), and called NJ from the car. Suddenly home seemed a long way away, although in reality it was a few hours' drive down the M1. Otto had just completed a detailed illustration of a weasel's set that he wanted to show me. Pearl was sad that I had missed a ballet performance she had been a part of. NJ was immersed in staging an exhibition on a seventies fashion designer. I had a pang of wanting to be among my people again. But the journey wasn't over yet. I prayed the Astra into activity, pushed a couple of empty crisp packets off the driver's seat, removed a leaflet for deep-pan pizza from underneath the windscreen wiper and headed west along the M62, for a city that appears to occupy a parallel reality to the rest of Britain.

What is it about Liverpool and Pink Floyd? For the last two or three decades one of the toughest cities in Britain has been engaged in a love affair with the biggest bunch of southern softies provincial England ever produced. Liverpool, the place that heard the rock'n'roll and R&B of fifties and sixties America first via a steady influx of sailors bringing records back from their voyages, is the city that gave birth to the most iconic and successful band that ever was and ever will be: The Beatles. Yet it has an ongoing dedication to the glum Cambridge stadium-packers whose intricate, melancholic soundscapes on albums like *Wish You Were Here* and *Dark Side Of The Moon* are a product of a group of men feeling guilty that they're doing something as frivolous as being in a rock group when they should be running architectural practices or becoming partners in law firms. The city's football fans chant 'Fearless', from Pink Floyd's 1971 hippy opus *Meddle*, as they get ready to do battle with rival supporters. There's even a term – Floyd la – to describe the average long-haired, dope-smoking Liverpudlian scallywag. The people of Liverpool also have an obsession with Love, the sixties folk-rock band from Los Angeles led by the late Arthur Lee that never had a hit and aren't particularly famous, and the American recluse Captain Beefheart, as surreal and brilliant an artist as he is obscure to the world at large. Why is this?

Manchester, less than an hour down the road, has a less eccentric if no less defined musical identity. The ongoing influence is the great groups of the sixties: The Byrds, The Kinks, The Beatles and The Beach Boys. The bands from Manchester that have made a worldwide impact, such as The Smiths, The Stone Roses and Oasis, have all had a sound and look rooted in the 1960s, albeit different aspects of it: kitchen-sink Britain with The Smiths, LA folk-rockers The Byrds with The Stone Roses, and The Beatles with Oasis. And, unlike Sheffield, both Manchester and Liverpool share an ability to produce bands and singers that regularly proclaim themselves to be the greatest in the entire world.

Manchester had gone though some sort of economic miracle in the previous decade, but Liverpool was still in the throes of depression. The entire city looked like the Neepsend Triangle. There were boarded-up shop fronts throughout the city centre. The population was steadily decreasing each year as Liverpool struggled to find an industry to replace the ones that had died away in the 1980s, and nowhere was there the crush of people you expect to get in city life. But Liverpool has immense charm. It is filled with grand Victorian architecture, gothic and mysterious, and you are never far away from the cold blue glory of the seafront and the dockyards along it. It is small – you can walk from one side to another in twenty minutes, at a leisurely pace – and you can't go anywhere without someone striking up a conversation.

And they really *are* obsessed with Pink Floyd in Liverpool. Soon after finding a place to stay – an identikit cheap hotel, with a television hammered to the wall and various cardboard sales leaflets boasting unappetising photographs of toasted baguettes with vaguely Mediterranean names – I had lunch in a Formica-laden greasy spoon in the city centre and shared a table with a dockworker with a moustache and highlighted hair. By his second cup of extra-strong tea he was eulogising the vocal solo on 'The Great Gig In The Sky', from 1973's *The Dark Side Of The Moon*.

Before getting to the heart of the Pink Floyd enigma, there was time to visit the scene of some local folklore. Overlooking the Mersey is the Liver Building, which has two domes that are crowned by enormous copper statues called Liver Birds. The story (untrue, as it turns out) goes that these upright, rather haughty but also slightly silly-looking birds were meant to be eagles. They ended up resembling cormorants, which don't have the same gravitas somehow. The artist was so distraught at the failure of his great work that he killed himself.

Ian McCulloch, the lead singer of Echo & The Bunnymen, one of the most famous bands to emerge from Liverpool, shares something of the character of the city, and perhaps of the sculptor of the Liver Birds: proud, but tragic. Throughout the 1980s he regularly announced that Echo &

The Bunnymen was the greatest band in the world, and while some of its fans might have agreed with him, the world did not. One sensed that Ian himself was too intelligent to take such a statement seriously. Apparently he once saw Bono effusively thank an empty concert hall a few hours before U2 were booked to perform there. At that point he knew U2 would go stratospheric and Echo & The Bunnymen wouldn't. And that he would have looked terrible in a cowboy hat anyway.

Ian McCulloch would surely be the ideal person to ask about the Pink Floyd enigma, so after taking a walk back from the Liver Building through quiet city streets I headed to Parr Street Studios, a recording complex owned by Echo & The Bunnymen's managers, to meet him. Pretty much every Liverpool band has recorded in Parr Street, and a few others besides – even hand-wringing mature-rock behemoths Coldplay made a visit – and it's a successful operation that gives hope for better things to come. Occupying an old warehouse at the centre of the city, the studios have hotel rooms much, much nicer than the one I was staying in and a sparsely furnished bar that appeared to be popular with the kind of Liverpool girls who are fascinating yet terrifying: extremely fashion conscious and yet remarkably down to earth. 'Who the fuck are you looking ah?' said one to me, just-stepped-out-of-the-salon hairstyle shining under neon lights, before turning to her friends and cackling demonically. I had only been going up to the bar to ask how to get into the studio below.

I sensed that Ian shared something of an attitude with these girls: a love of glamour combined with a caustic wit and an understanding that proclaiming yourself to be the greatest band in the world, from the greatest city in the world, is all part of the game of creating a fantasy to shield you from the world's cruelty. We met in the studio itself, and as Ian sat on a sofa in the shadow of a grand piano, dark sunglasses never to leave his face, he talked eloquently about how the city has always been his greatest inspiration. He went on to say that Echo & The Bunnymen never wanted to be the biggest band in the world – only the best – and that if it weren't for writing songs and being a pop star he'd spend his days watching *Countdown* and doing the quick crossword. His greatest songs, he claimed, such as 'The Killing Moon' and 'Rescue', came from somewhere beyond the graft of songwriting; they were touched by the divine. There was a charisma to the way his mouth curled up at the edges as he veered between making wild claims to greatness and admitting that he was just a little bit lost.

I asked him why everyone in Liverpool loved Pink Floyd.

'I don't know,' he replied with a sniff. 'They're shit.'

Will Sergeant is Echo & The Bunnymen's guitarist. The band had formed when Will met Ian at the famously squalid Liverpool club Eric's in the late 1970s, reputedly in the ladies' toilets. 'There's no point in talking to Mac about Pink Floyd. He's more into the songwriters like Leonard Cohen and Lou Reed,' said Will, when I told him about this conversation a little later. 'Mac doesn't like any music that reminds him of men with beards.'

Unlike Ian, Will loved the music of bearded men, particularly of the psychedelic variety. He was only too happy to explain the city's unique relationship with Pink Floyd, Love and Captain Beefheart.

'Pink Floyd played at the Liverpool Philharmonic in the early seventies,' said Will, who appeared to be quieter, more grounded than Ian. 'They were all sitting on the floor of the stage, and this was not long after Syd Barrett left. Liverpool's a small place, and because it's so far out of the way most of the big bands don't come here so the city never forgot that Floyd made the effort. Add to that the fact that generations of Liverpudlian kids have sat in their bedrooms getting stoned and listening to *The Dark Side Of The Moon* and the whole thing makes sense.'

Will believed that Liverpool's relationship with music came down to the fact that it was a city of outsiders: a place that saw itself as separate from the rest of the country. For this reason the population related to other outsiders. 'It's the end of the road,' he said. 'Go any further and you end up in the sea. It's got a bad reputation, too. In Victorian times you had the High Rip Gang, who went around with knives and bludgeons mugging the sailors getting off the boats. It's the kind of place most people don't bother going to, so people remember it if you do. Arthur Lee of Love came here early on and was amazed to discover that everyone knew the words to his songs. Captain Beefheart played at a club called Rotters and it was packed, at a time when he was performing to empty houses everywhere else in the world. You could go to anyone's house and find *Unconditionally Guaranteed* by Captain Beefheart and *Forever Changes* by Love in their record collection. It's that outsider thing, la. Liverpudlians pride themselves on being different.'

A lot of bands stopped bothering to include Liverpool on their tour schedule from the 1980s onwards as the city fell deeper into depression. It became even more idiosyncratic as a result, and Pink Floyd, Captain Beefheart and Love became the official music for a city embracing its underdog status. Now it was European City Of Culture, but Will Sergeant couldn't see that making much of a difference.

'There are still loads of boarded-up buildings. They built a load of expensive yuppie apartments on the front but they didn't quite think it through – there are no yuppies in Liverpool. Half the flats are empty. Even Eric's, which is one of the most famous clubs in British history, was a horrible black room with overflowing bogs. It was a dump. But it was *our* dump. And it had " And 7 Is" by Love on the jukebox.'

The next person to speak to about Liverpool's Pink Floyd obsession was the songwriter, producer and occasional pop star Ian Broudie. He too played at Eric's, the forever-flooding club on Matthew Street that gave birth to many of the city's most famous bands in the late seventies, as a sixteen-year-old hotshot guitarist. After getting his number from one of Ian McCulloch's managers I gave him a call when I was back in the lonely functionality of my hotel room. He was in the process of buying a portion of fish and chips. He had just taken a break from his current job as producer on a record by the young Liverpudlian Floyd/Love/Beefheart obsessives The Coral, and after twenty years at the coalface of the Liverpool music industry, writing songs, playing with his own band The Lightning Seeds, producing albums and even having a number-one hit with the football anthem 'Three Lions', Broudie had a strong understanding of the city's musical identity. I asked him to open up on the Pink Floyd question.

'See, after punk, Pink Floyd weren't popular any-where in Britain except for Liverpool,' he said, in between asking for extra vinegar on his chips. 'But then, Liverpool has never cared about what's going on in the rest of the country. It's about being in tower blocks with no money, taking drugs and listening to trippy music. And maybe because it's a small place, but big enough to support a musical community, you hear things for a long time up here. Once songs make it on to the jukeboxes they stay there for years. That's what happened to Pink Floyd.'

As for Love and Captain Beefheart, Ian reckoned their Liverpudlian popularity was circumstantial. He said it was because a load of unsold albums by those artists had ended up in Liverpool and were available throughout the seventies in branches of Woolworth's for 60p. 'For every album by Jimi Hendrix or The Who, there were just as many by Love and Beefheart,' he claimed. 'There were loads of factory seconds that got dumped here, probably because nowhere else would have them, so everyone owned a copy of *Forever Changes* by Love, which is hailed as a classic album now, at a time when the rest of the country had never heard of it. The most unlikely people in Liverpool are fans of Love and Beefheart. Old ladies, schoolchildren, bricklayers . . .'

Ian Broudie had to get back into his producer's chair, but before he went he had time to tell a story about The Coral, whose members are from Hoylake, a seaside town on the Wirral Peninsula, which is near Liverpool. They were only fourteen when they first got the band together, and it came about through very Liverpudlian means. 'When they were thirteen they found this record in a charity shop. They had never heard anything like it and nobody else at school had heard of it. So they formed a band on the strength of finding this record, and thought they were really cool, and that this was their special secret that the rest of the world didn't know about, like they had discovered the Holy Grail. Then they went to Liverpool and discovered that only everyone and his sister had the bloody record.'

'What was it?' I asked.

'*Forever Changes* by Love.'

In my obsession to get to the heart of why Liverpool had such a weakness for soft southern psychedelic progressive rock from the early seventies I had entirely forgotten to make a field recording. So, after a night in the blank hotel where the Polish receptionist had an ability to carry out her job efficiently while giving no clues to her character whatsoever, and a stag party in the rooms next to mine ensured that sleep would be a luxury denied, I headed east. I was pleased for the heavy rain that came that morning. With any luck it would cool down the Astra's increasingly overheating engine. The next stop on the journey was Manchester, where I planned to record a band that captured something of the essence of the city on a grass-roots level: a group of young men from the southern suburb of Chorlton called The Beep Seals.

I had seen the band on the same bill as Pete Molinari had played at a few months earlier, and was taken with them: they combined sixties-style harmonies and a strong sense of melody with a swagger typical of Manchester, and yet they weren't the types to proclaim themselves as the best band in the world. They swapped instruments, seemed to take a relish in the simple joy of making music, and had good tunes. It turned out they all had day jobs and were under no illusions about the likelihood of making it as full-time musicians. I got to know their lead singer, a tall, fresh-faced man called Jack Cooper, and told him about what I was doing. He suggested I come up to Chorlton to record the band above a bar called The Dulcimer, something of a mecca for Manchester's folk fraternity. I imagined it to be full of bearded, long-haired men strumming guitars and willowy hippy maidens wafting about with lutes. It had an upstairs room that was mostly empty on weekdays. It would make an ideal place for the Zoom to capture the innocent magic of The Beep Seals, as long as we did it in the evening after they clocked off from their respective nine-to-five tasks.

I went to Manchester a lot in the early nineties, just after leaving school. Two school friends had gone to university there and one summer I stayed with them for six weeks. We ended up doing night shifts in a post office in a suburb called Didsbury where the local letter-box lothario astounded us with tales of on-delivery conquests that inevitably ended with the line: 'woman's knickers dripping like 'ot teabag'. Manchester was different then. I hitchhiked my way up there, during which I got arrested for walking along a motorway lay-by. Somebody dropped me off on the outskirts of Salford, a suburb with a bleak atmosphere captured by the savage observations of The Fall's Mark E Smith. I got trapped inside an industrial estate and ended up climbing over a high wire fence, attracting the attention of some local kids who wanted to know whether I had nicked anything worth having. The streets were empty and buildings were boarded up. Eventually a bus arrived that went into Piccadilly, the city centre. It was full of elderly people that called me cock.

My friends lived in Fallowfield, a student ghetto of bedsits and cheap curry houses. There was little to do except dress up in silly costumes and feed the ducks in the local park, see how many of us could squeeze into a telephone box, and attempt to buy an eighth of hash in the back room of a spirit-broken pub where the barmaid looked furious at the way things had turned out and the kids flashed knives at one another. This was meant to be the golden age of Madch-ester, when The Hacienda was world famous and The Happy Mondays and The Stone Roses were the coolest bands on the planet, but from the perspective of a penniless student Manchester seemed like a desperate place. Walking into areas like Hulme and Moss Side meant at the best putting up with being shouted at and at the worst mugged, and everything was half-hearted and lacklustre. The Smiths had happened, but it was the bleak, industrial music of Joy Division, long since split up and their singer Ian Curtis long dead, which seemed to best capture the spirit of the city.

What really struck me back then was how empty Britain's second-biggest city was. Where were the people? Even in the centre you never really saw crowds the likes of which you got in London's West End all day and all night. It was easy to meet strangers, and there was a ready humour that presented itself every time you went into a shop or a pub, but Manchester felt defeated. Music was an escape from and a reflection of what was outside your window. Everyone I met seemed to be in a band and they generally sounded like Joy Division.

As the Astra steamed its way into the city centre I could hardly believe this was the same place. The rain was still coming down, of course, but the area around Piccadilly Station, once empty save for a few old pubs and warehouses, had been transformed into a world of smart walkways, coffee bars and hotels. Parking the car to walk into the heart of the city along Oldham Street, the first thing that struck me was how many people were around, and how cosmopolitan the city had become: this was as varied a group of people as you would find in London or New York.

It was fashionable too. There has always been a culture in northern British cities of dressing up and looking your best, but there was sophistication and imagination to the way Mancunians were dressing that was striking. I wandered into a place called The Deaf Institute, which was no such thing – it was a bar and music venue filled with people with challenging hairstyles.

The Beep Seals were a product of this new environment. Their music was full of sunshine and hope, but tinged with melancholy and not given to the fantastical. I was to meet Jack Cooper in a bar called Night And Day on Oldham Street, something of a long-standing hub for the city's musical community. I had been here a few years previously and back then it was the only place of its kind. Now it was one among many. Jack had just finished working for the day – he had a job with the local council – and after making the recording with the rest of The Beep Seals at The Dulcimer he had to start planning a miniature festival of local bands he was putting on at The Deaf Institute. I asked him how he found the time to have a full-time job and keep a band going.

'It's the only way,' he said after we sat down at one of Night And Day's gnarled wooden tables. 'If you want to be a musician these days you have to have two jobs, and it's a slog and a pain in the arse but you do it in spite of all that. I was thinking about this the other day. We're not being paid. We're not getting free drinks and loads of girls. Last time we played in London we only got back at eight-thirty in the morning and our keyboard player was due to start work half an hour earlier. So why are we doing it? Maybe we just love it.'

Jack grew up in Blackpool but had moved to Manchester seven years previously, initially driven by a love of The Stone Roses and a desire to form a band. Like so many of his ilk the music he liked was from America, from the sixties, and sunny: The Beach Boys, Love and The Byrds were his favourite groups. He put this down to climatic conditions.

'What you have to remember about Manchester,' he said, long body folding over the wooden table, 'is that it really does rain all the flippin' time. Blackpool's just as bad. You've got the seaside, and you look out onto the beach and try to figure out why it's not sunny. And in the north of England The Beatles get rammed down your throat when you're young. So you get into bands that sound a bit like The Beatles but come from sunnier places, like Los Angeles. And what else are you going to do but learn guitar and form a band? It rains so much that you can't go out and kick a ball around half the time. You may as well be in a band just to stop yourself from dying of boredom.'

I glanced around Night And Day. The clientele and staff, to a man and woman, looked like they were musicians of some sort or another. And the walls were plastered with flyers advertising gigs of hundreds of bands I had never heard of. I asked Jack what this sixties thing was all about.

'I think that's a reaction to Manchester past,' he replied. 'Manchester had a sound, an industrial gloom, that you associate with Factory Records and Joy Division, but it's a very different city now. I mean, people complain about it not being like it used to. But it was bloody miserable when I used to come here as a kid. It's loads better now. Certainly the old people, who knew Manchester when it was really deprived, don't think it was better back then.'

Then there was Oasis. The most successful band to have ever come from the city, possibly the biggest British live act of them all, had only made two decent albums, but such was the fascination with them that every release was hailed as a return to form before finding its way to the back of record collections and bargain bins the world over. It could have been down to the overwhelming confidence and charm of the Gallagher brothers. They typified a certain type of Northern bravado, of taking on the world with insouciant humour and a lack of preciousness. And they had claimed that Oasis were the best band in the world. I asked Jack why Mancunian bands felt the need to do this.

'I think it's The Stone Roses' fault. Until they came along everything in Manchester was underplayed – the biggest label was Factory, and they didn't seem to care whether they sold any records or not. Then The Stone Roses turned up and said they wanted to be the biggest band in the world and it captured everyone's imaginations. From then on it was Oasis, and The Verve up in Wigan, filled with bravado . . . my girlfriend hates The Stone Roses because of that. That gang mentality, that Northern machismo, is not very appealing to girls.'

It was time to meet the rest of the band at The Dulcimer, over in Chorlton. As the Astra passed the tower blocks and empty sodden streets of Hulme and Moss Side Jack explained to me how the geography of the city affected the music that came from it. 'Northern Manchester is traditional football culture territory,' he said as we passed what looked like two grown men, their faces shadowed by hooded tops, riding along the pavement on BMX bicycles. 'Oasis are huge up there. In south Manchester you tend to get the stoners and the freaks. Maybe it comes from Liverpool, because the Mersey runs up through Chorlton. Do you know that song "Mersey Paradise" by The Stone Roses? It's about a nature park in Chorlton that the Mersey passes through. There's something in the water from up there that affects us lot down here.'

We came into Chorlton. It was a mix of the well-to-do and the rough, with smart Georgian terraces towering over dilapidated kebab shops. 'It's a nice place to live, but it can still be quite dodgy,' said Jack as we pulled up outside The Dulcimer, a new-looking bar on a street corner. 'Half of it is *Guardian*-reading teachers and lecturers, and then you have the old community that has always been there, and then the gangs that spill over from Moss Side and Hulme. Three or four people have been killed on my street alone in the last five years.'

The Dulcimer was a nice place – wooden floors, colourful framed posters on the walls, real ales and Pentangle on the stereo – but it wasn't full of the floaty dress-wearing maidens of my imagination. 'Yeah, it's not really like that,' said Jack as we walked in to witness a pockmarked woman, rendered insane with drink, scream uncontrollably at the bearded barman refusing to serve her.

'It's the best place in Chorlton and I'm glad it's here, but you have this strange mix of a handful of people going there because they love folk and psychedelic music, all the townies going along on weekends trying to pick each other up, and a few old drunks completely oblivious to it all.'

The four other Beep Seals were huddled around a table at the back of the bar drinking pints: a shabby, smiling mass of hair and musical instruments. The band's multi-instrumentalist Sam had just finished teaching his after-school rock club, in which he educated under-twelves in how to get the best out of a fuzz pedal and look mean in photoshoots. Jay, The Beep Seals' drummer, showed people how to use the music-making computer program Logic at the Apple Store and the others had office jobs of one description or another. We went to the upstairs room. Two girls were chatting in the corner. The Beep Seals took out their instruments – guitars, a xylophone, a French horn and beer bottles to tap in the absence of drums – as I put the Zoom on a small round table next to the low stage the band members sat along.

The girls in the corner kept chatting, and you could hear the hubbub rising from the packed bar below, as The Beep Seals played two songs, 'Chariot Song' and 'Biting Glass', perfectly in time and in tune without any practice. This might have been the most authentic field recording so far. These were songs that Jack had written, not learned from his ancestors, but there was something about the words, especially the line in 'Biting Glass' that went 'biting things that smash, wearing clothes that clash' that said something of what it was like to be young in Manchester at that time. Who knows? In the archaeological rubble of pop, perhaps this would be a shard unearthed 500 years from now.

'Does it matter that I started laughing at one point?' asked Jack. 'I couldn't help it. The notes were tickling my throat.'

'I don't think so,' I replied. 'We did record it in a bar, after all. That's going to be fairly obvious.'

It wasn't to be a late night. There was a football match on that Jack and a couple of the other members of the band wanted to get home to watch, and everyone had a job to go to the next morning. I wanted to move on to the final destination on the journey, somewhere with an elemental mystery that stood in stark contrast to the industrial, rain-soaked, concrete-and-brick world of Manchester and Liverpool, but resigned myself to another night in a cheap B&B before setting off in the morning.

None of the young men who gave up so much of their time to being in The Beep Seals had the bravado that has come to be associated with Manchester bands, and you could hear it in the music. Perhaps this was a new side of the city: pluralistic, quietly confident, but still with a strong grounding in a down-to-earth philosophy and approach. Everyone agreed that Oasis ruined Manchester for a while. 'They were so successful that every band in the city thought they had to sound like that, and act like that, to make it,' said Jack, as everyone packed up their instruments while The Dulcimer's upstairs room slowly filled up. 'Now things have swung the other way. People have returned to making music as something to do for its own sake without worrying about whether they end up being the biggest band in the world or not.'

Summer was almost over. My journey, too, had to finish soon. It wouldn't be long before the children started a new year at school and the reassuring routines of very normal life – school runs, botched DIY attempts – took hold. But first there was time to make an exploration into one of the most exotic corners of British musical life: a lush, hilly area in the western tip of Wales.

Chapter Fourteen

The Dyfed Triangle, West Wales

I N WEST WALES THERE IS A STRETCH OF LAND CALLED THE
Dyfed Triangle. It is a place where mist clings to the
earth like a spectral blanket, shrouding the hills
dipping into valleys and the narrow lanes shadowed by tree
tunnels. Rain soaks into the fleeces of the sheep and the bark
of the birches. The rich scent of the air, of honeysuckle and
ferns, is as free as the rooks that rise like clouds from the
woods and the wind that cries along the jagged stone walls
cutting across fields in infinite geometry.

All of this gives the Dyfed Triangle a feeling of unre-
ality that lends itself to the creation of myth. It is imbued
with stories of Druids and power-giving ley lines. There
have been more UFOs sighted in Dyfed than anywhere else
in Europe. In *The White Goddess*, Robert Graves pinpoints
this beautiful land as the wellspring of poetic mythology and
of the invocation of the muse.

With parallels to the westerly tip of Cornwall, the
land, the farming community that lives off it and the outsiders that have come there to shake off the manacles of
society have shaped the Dyfed Triangle. In the early 1970s
it became something of a hippy mecca as escapees from the
cities bought houses for next to nothing, embraced a life
lived close to nature, and made full use of the moist conditions and excess of sheep dung that allow for superb
mushroom harvests.

At the same time the Dyfed Triangle was the traditional heartland of the Welsh-speaking community. After years of subjugation the Welsh were standing up to the domination of English as the Esperanto of the world and reclaiming their own language, and what naturally followed, in a small but significant way, was the growth of a Welsh-language hippy rock and folk scene. These people had children, and those children grew up to be as comfortable speaking in Welsh as they were in English; as familiar with Meic Stevens (the Welsh Bob Dylan, but significantly less famous) as they were with Led Zeppelin. In the early nineties a bunch of West Wales teenagers formed a band called Gorky's Zygotic Mynci. They staged their early concerts in church halls and youth clubs, raided their parents' record collections, and highlighted a renaissance in Welsh identity that was more celebratory and multifaceted than the old, militant approach based around a hatred of the English.

The apotheosis of the renaissance, although they're not from the Dyfed Triangle, is Super Furry Animals. They record albums in Welsh and English, combine the deep understanding of melody that is imbued into the typical Welsh schoolchild with an ongoing quest for new sounds and influences, and form the crux of a community of Welsh-speaking musicians interested in psychedelic rock based in Cardiff – a community that, admittedly, is not very large.

A couple of years previously I had got to know Gruff Rhys, the lead singer of Super Furry Animals, after he had attempted to teach me how to write a song. A gentle, benevolent soul with a thick mop of curly hair who speaks with extended pauses between sentences, Gruff was an ideal subject for a field recording, but so was a young Dyfedite he introduced me to called Cate Le Bon. Cate was singing in Neon Neon, Gruff's electro-pop side project/concept based on the life of the American car entrepreneur John De Lorean, writing and recording her own songs in English and Welsh, and generally enjoying the life of a charismatic singer whose star is in the ascendant. She had written her first song at seven (about her cat Gregory), had guitar lessons from her father (a town planner with a musical past) and had grown up worshipful of Gorky's Zygotic Mynci. With her dark brown eyes and short brown hair she was good-looking in a tomboyish way. She had a lot of the Dyfed about her, a freewheeling toughness that belonged to the lashing wind and the constant rain.

A plan was set. I would meet Cate and her boyfriend Huw in Cardiff, where they lived in Gruff's house in the city centre. Then we would embark on the four-hour drive up to Cate's parents' house in Penboyr In Drefach-Velindre (trans: Small Town With Mill) and make a field recording of Cate, preferably in a field, with a few sheep nearby. Cate said that I could spend the night there, making a welcome respite from the soul-sapping power of another night in a cheap hotel room. The following morning I would head back to Cardiff to make a recording with Jo and Danny, a singing couple, with children the same age as our own, who staged a rock and folk festival in the Brecon Beacons called The Green Man that was on a week later. Then there would hopefully be time to make a recording with Gruff, who spent much of the year in his girlfriend Cat's flat in London but would be coming back to his house in Cardiff *en famille* – Gruff and Cat had just had a baby and they were planning to visit some relatives. All of this would allow a chance to capture the side of Welsh life that fascinated me; that combination of friendly domesticity and cosmic exploration that Gruff and Cate were engaged in, and which The Green Man was imbued with.

It was raining heavily when I pulled the Astra out of a narrow street lined with small terraced houses in Chorlton. I drove over the remnants of a broken pram that someone had left in the middle of the road. Two boys of around ten flicked a V-sign. The car's temperature gauge went quickly up into the red, and I had no choice but to close the windows and turn the heating up to cool the engine.

I cut down through England quickly, first on the M6, then the M5 and finally the M4, taking the toll bridge to Wales and straight into Cardiff, stopping only when I reached Gruff's house. The tape of English folk songs went round a few times and the engine steamed rather a lot. Huw, a tall, curly-haired man with bright blue eyes and an embroidered Western shirt, was inside the house, frantically going at a corner of the living room with a feather duster.

'Got to get it clean,' said Huw breathlessly, shaking my hand and dusting simultaneously. 'Gruff and Cat are coming to stay here tonight, and Cat's a bit of a stickler for cleanliness. I should be finished in an hour or so. You two go on ahead.'

Cate came in a couple of minutes later. She had just arrived in Cardiff, having stayed with Gruff and Cat in London.

'It's all right,' Cate said to Huw as he hopped up to attack a cobweb on the ceiling. 'They're staying at Cat's mum's house.'

Huw stopped mid-dust. 'You mean I've been cleaning the last four hours for nothing?'

We took a miniature tour of Cardiff. 'Charlotte Church's mum owns that,' said Huw, pointing to a nondescript pub on a hilly street. 'Sometimes Charlotte turns up and does a sing-along.' We came upon a large construction site: on one side of the street was a row of rain-grey terraced houses and on the other a wooden wall, beyond which was a vast expanse of industrial activity. 'And over here is what will soon be a new shopping centre. We have one called St

David's, so this is going to be called St David's Two. They're not very imaginative with names in Cardiff.'

Over a café lunch in a shopping arcade we talked about the various branches of Welsh musical culture. 'You have people like Gwyneth Glyn, who is a terrible MOR singer,' said Cate as she poked at a baked potato with a fork. 'She takes lines from famous country songs and uses them in her own . . . "Country Roads" and so on . . . horrible.'

'There's Noel from Hear'Say,' added Huw, brightly, perhaps hopefully. 'Do you remember him?'

With a bit of prompting I did. Hear'Say was made up of the winners on the first of what is now a television phenomenon: the reality-TV pop talent contest. They had one hit soon after the winners were chosen.

'And on the other side of it you have Meic Stevens,' said Cate. 'He's a bit of a hero to the Welsh-language musicians, but most people don't know who he is and he's bitter about it. He had to sell his guitars to pay a tax bill.'

'He hates being a symbol of Welsh identity and he fights against it,' added Huw. 'He played at The Green Man a couple of years ago and spent most of his set insulting the Welsh. There's a line in a song of his called "Gwlad Ar Fy Nghefn" (Land On My Back) that goes: "Living in Wales is like watching the paint dry, watching the grass grow".'

I had a Meic Stevens record. He reminded me of the winsome Scottish singer-songwriter Donovan. The only thing I knew about him – and it may well be apocryphal – was that he was out drinking with Jimi Hendrix on the night he died. Ever since then Meic has blamed himself for the demise of the greatest guitarist of all time because, being American, Hendrix couldn't match the Welshman's capacity for soaking up the booze.

We returned to the Astra. Thinking of the way it was overheating on the way up I decided to refill the radiator again – something I seemed to be doing with alarming regularity – utilising Huw as a bonnet-kicker in the absence of NJ. The radiator was totally dry again. Why did this keep happening? I decided it was best not to think about it too much and hope the car at least made it to Dyfed and back. I was sure that it would. It was a good car, owned by a now-dead mechanic before me. I put the radiator cap on the roof and emptied in an Evian bottle filled with tap water. We got in as Shirley Collins sang 'The Plains Of Waterloo' in the car for the 132nd time that summer and rumbled off.

We had only just left Cardiff when trouble started. The thermometer went up into the red almost immediately – it didn't brush against it, as it had done on the way up from London, but went as far as it could go. The car was steaming ferociously; so much so that it was obscuring my vision.

'Is it meant to be doing that?' asked Cate, languidly revealing doubt in my car's abilities.

'Well, it is raining a lot,' I said, although that didn't explain why all the steam was coming from one place in the bonnet – where the radiator was. But the car had kept going all this time. I couldn't see why it should give up the ghost now. In the past I've found that if you keep moving fast the engine does tend to cool down sooner or later. It's best not to think about these things too much. So I hit eighty as we drove along the M4. But it didn't cool down.

'I think maybe I should check the engine,' I said. 'Something does seem to be wrong.'

We had just turned off onto the A473 by Bridgend when it happened. The steam that had been billowing out of the bonnet turned to a thick fog of smoke, so thick that I could hardly see a thing. And then, when we were doing 70mph and I was working out ways of slowing down without causing the car behind to smash into us, the engine cut out entirely. There was no lay-by so I swerved into the rough space between the road and a line of trees, cars behind honking furiously.

'We'd better get out,' I shouted to Huw and Cate.

The rain was extreme. Cate and Huw huddled under the umbrella of a tree while I inspected the engine. It was giving out the ominous, toxic smell that you get when you burn plastic. 'Luckily,' I said with a placatory smile, 'I'm a member of the AA.'

'Perhaps it's something simple, like it needs more oil,' said Huw. 'I broke down once. It turned out I had run out of petrol.'

We stood amidst the plastic bottles and polystyrene cups of the roadside debris, huddled around a rolled-up cigarette as water cascaded down our faces. Cate and Huw were sanguine about this terrible situation I had put them in. We couldn't sit in the car as it was too near to the side of the road, and besides, it was on fire.

'I hope it doesn't blow up,' said Cate, a little mournfully, as we watched the flicker of a flame on the bonnet rise and die under the sheeting rain.

'I don't think it will,' I said, 'although I'm beginning to wonder if a bit of extra oil is really going to do the trick. Oh my God, all our stuff!'

Not only was Cate's guitar in the back of the car; the Zoom with every recording I had made so far was in there too. I emptied the boot and we stood in the rain with the luggage around our feet.

The AA man was with us half an hour later, swallowed in a fluorescent coat, as helpful as these saviours of stranded motorists always seem to be. He opened the bonnet and asked me to start the engine, but it wouldn't start.

'Where's the radiator cap?' he shouted over the traffic and the rain.

'On the radiator?'

'No it isn't.'

'I remember now,' said Cate, raising a finger. 'I saw it on the roof of the car when we were in Cardiff. You forgot to put it back on.'

273

'Oh.' And then, to the AA man, I said: 'Do you think a new radiator cap will get us to Pembrokeshire?'

'I think your troubles with this car might be bigger than that,' he said, 'but we can give it a go.'

He towed us to a Halfords a few miles away, where he had a lengthy chat with the men working there – they knew his son, who did weekends at Halfords, and he had his first date that night. 'Where's he taking the lucky lady?' I asked. 'They're going to the beach for fish and chips,' he replied, in a tone that suggested the answer was obvious. He filled up the radiator, put the cap on rather than leave it on the roof, and tried to get the car going. It didn't start.

He fiddled around with it. Then he shook his head ominously.

'Your engine is blown. The head gasket is gone and the block is cracked.'

'That doesn't sound good. Will it be expensive to fix?'

'Expensive? I wouldn't bother. Anything can be fixed, but is it worth it? You're looking at a grand at least. How much did you pay for the car?'

'Five hundred pounds, and that was three years ago.'

'There you go, then. I'll tow you to wherever you want to go.'

My car was dead. Despite everything I still had a degree of affection for the thing, with its window of stickers on the side Otto sat, its one tape of English folk music and its Frankenstein's monster appearance. But this was no time for lamentations. We had to work out what to do. If we drove to Cate's parents' house we would be stuck there with no hope of escape. We could return to Cardiff and abandon the trip, but that would be a terrible shame. Huw came to the rescue.

'We can borrow my mum's car,' he said cheerfully. 'She won't mind. She loves helping people.'

It was decided that we would get the car towed to

Huw's mother's house in Cardiff. There we would arrange for a local scrap-metal merchant to take it away – Huw suggested pushing it off a cliff and claiming the insurance, but I wasn't so sure – and then take Huw's mum's car all the way to Penboyr. With the friendly efficiency that does seem to be something of a Welsh national trait, Huw's mum not only loaned us the car but also even arranged for mine to be scrapped. A cup of tea in the living room later we were on our way.

It was only when we had been driving for about an hour, generally upwards of 80mph, that Huw remembered he was half-blind and had forgotten his glasses. 'Try mine,' I said, handing him my Ray-Bans. 'They're perfect!' he said. 'What a coincidence.' He was wearing a corduroy cap and a denim cowboy shirt embroidered with large colourful owls, and with curly hair flapping just above his shoulders and a roll-up dangling from his mouth he looked the image of the kind of Welsh-language hippy I imagined 1970s Dyfed to be filled with.

'Slow down, Huw,' said Cate crossly in her singsong voice. 'You can hardly see a thing and it's pelting it down.'

'But we want to get there before everywhere closes,' said Huw. It was dark already. 'There's the best Indian take-away in the world near to Cate's house. We don't want to miss it.'

'We want to be alive to enjoy it, too,' said Cate, solemnly.

Then came the sound and vision that every motorist fears: the siren and flashing lights of a police car telling us to pull over.

'Now look what you've done,' snapped Cate. 'If anyone has got anything illegal on them throw it out of the window now.'

'Oh, shit,' said Huw, pulling into a lay-by. 'I was doing ninety.'

275

'Speak to him in Welsh,' Cate commanded.

The policeman, whose forearm was the size of my thigh, leaned down and stuck his head through the driver's window. He shone a torch onto our hesitant, best-behaviour faces. 'Good evening, Sir,' he said to Huw. 'This is just a routine check. Is this your car?'

The policeman didn't speak Welsh, so Huw explained in English that the car was his mother's, and that he was insured for it, and that my car had blown up and so on. He told the policeman where we were going. They joked about the terrible weather. Then the enormous man walked slowly around the car, opening the boot and shining his torch onto the back and front seats. He looked at the car from the front and scratched his crew cut before returning to the driver's window.

'Well,' he said with a smile, 'thank you for your co-operation.'

'Is that it?' said Huw, his face shining with a tentative glow. 'Does that mean we can go?'

'Yes, you can. You don't seem to be who I'm looking for.'

Cate leaned forward from the back seat, wide-eyed, and asked, 'Who are you looking for?'

The policeman sighed and looked into the horizon. 'Criminals,' he replied.

It was after ten when we made it to Cate's parent's house, which was at the bottom of a valley and surrounded by fields complete with goats, sheep, horses and the type of heavy wooden country gates that are so hard to close but which farmers go bananas about if you don't. Cate's parents and her little sister were off somewhere so we had the place to ourselves. This was the deepest countryside I had ever been to, deeper even than Cornwall. The roads were tiny and curling, the rain never stopped, and there was an abundance of that relative quality we Londoners are not used to: space. I offered to get the takeaway from this apparently wonderful Indian restaurant. It was a few miles away, in a little high street cottage with low oak beams, and I wondered how the Indian people working there, whose strong accents revealed they were not Welsh-born, felt about this remote, idyllic place.

Over what ended up being a midnight curry Huw and Cate filled me in on a few Welsh localities. Huw was from Prestatyn. 'The pubs are full of dead-heads,' he said of the place. 'They're all really depressed, which is why they're drinking at four in the afternoon. They've often got an interesting story to tell.'

'No, they haven't,' countered Cate. 'They're depressed because they've never been anywhere. Wales is full of people like that.'

'Prestatyn is famous for one thing, though,' said Huw. 'There's a man there who had a full English breakfast tattooed on his head for a bet. He's got a fried egg and beans and everything.'

The pull of the land brought its own problems. Near Penboyr were sweet villages with ornate names like Cum Dwyran (Valley of the Two Crows) and Ilan Pumsaint (Church of the Five Saints) that naturally attracted people with enough money to afford to buy holiday homes in peaceful Welsh valleys. This led to a two-tiered economy, just as had happened in Cornwall, where locals got priced out of the places they were born. Through that situation there developed a Welsh nationalist vigilante group called The Sons of Glyn Dwr, who went around burning holiday homes in a *Straw Dogs*-style retribution against wealthy incomers.

A rather less aggressive celebration of Welsh identity is the Talwrn Y Beirdd, a raucous pub event with roots in the bardic tradition in which poets compete against each other to recite verses of utmost filth in a gorgeous Welsh lilt. Apparently the competition gets quite heated, taking on the character of an MC battle the likes of which Lady Sovereign once engaged in, with rival poets resorting to all kinds of dirty tricks – personal slurs, merciless use of iambic pentameter – to destroy their opponents.

'There are all kinds of rules,' explained Huw. 'A basic verse is called an *engynn* and a line is called a *cynghanedd* – each line is divided in the middle with each side of it balanced out by consonants and vowels. You get professional poets that can make up these complex, highly constructed verses off the top of their heads.'

This goes back to the ancient rites of the Welsh bard, an official title that stands in contrast to the more unorthodox role of the minstrel. By the tenth century, by which time Christianity dominated Wales, ecclesiastical discipline was mirrored by the ossification of the nation's official poetic forms. Mythological imaginings were frowned upon and only certain metaphors and similes were allowed. Themes were restricted and metres fixed. Master-poets became court officials whose duties included praising God and honouring in verse the king who was giving them a chair at his royal table. The nature worship and the mythical, quasi-historical stories the Welsh minstrels recited from memory had no place in this new, structured approach to poetic expression.

This led to the Eisteddfod. Apparently this is a very famous event; a kind of poetry death match, now combined with early nineteenth-century concepts of what Druidic practice involved, that dates back to the fifteenth century.

'It was officially invented in the eighteenth century by an opium-smoking madhead crazo called Iolo Morganwg, although its roots go further back than that,' explained Huw. 'All the different poets compete for a chair. They have a massive sword, which they sit around in a big tent. They play trumpets, take it in turns to recite poetry, and have virgins doing flower dances in front of them. Now kids from all over Wales compete in the Eisteddfod. They have singing competitions, dramas, science tests, musical recitals –'

'All the bad boys do the *gwerin*, which is a type of folk dancing,' added Cate, demolishing the remnants of a chicken jalfrezi. 'They wear waistcoats and three-quarter-length trousers. They do it because it's a great way to meet girls.'

Cate wasn't enamoured with the Eisteddfod. If its champions were the bards of latter-day Wales, she and her ilk were its minstrels: accorded far less status but perhaps more poetic in their untutored way. When I mentioned how good it was that every child in Wales sang, she replied, 'School choirs are full of squares. In England people sing because they like singing. In Wales it's a competitive thing and that's because of the Eisteddfod. All the squares desperately want to do their school proud by winning in it, and it's suggested from an early age that if you are a member of the choir your teachers will like you a little bit more.'

Mention of the Eisteddfod brought up painful memories for Cate. 'There was this thing called the *cerdd dant* (tooth music),' she said quietly. 'One person plays a harp and the other person sings a different melody over it. It sounds shit. It sounds like the people have been given the wrong piece of music.'

'Did you ever sing the *cerdd dant*, Cate?' I asked her.

'No, I didn't,' she replied firmly. 'I wasn't in the choir. At my school the people that could sing got preferential treatment, and they decided that I couldn't sing. That was why me and the bad boys formed a band – to beat the squares at their own game.'

279

Cate's entire musical career might have been a result of this early, traumatic experience.

———— ◆ ◆ ◆ ————

The following morning I came down from a book-filled attic room to find Cate cooking scrambled eggs. It was raining heavily and the wind was wailing through the stone chimney of the old house. 'It's great, isn't it?' she said, nodding towards the window as she stirred the yellow mix in the saucepan.

At first I thought she was being sarcastic.

'I'd really still like to record in the fields, if you don't mind,' I said, peering out of the little window to survey the force of the rain outside.

'Mind?' she replied, doling out the scrambled eggs. 'Why would I mind?'

Cate claimed to love this kind of weather. Equipped with heavy Wellington boots and a large waterproof coat she led the way to a nearby field where a three-week-old foal, sheltering under the twisting lines of a gnarled oak, was the star attraction of a clutch of horses. We climbed over a gate into a field of sheep that made a chorus of baas as they clambered around Cate as if she was the returning Messiah. 'Wow, it's going to be great to get you singing with them in the background,' I said, and took the Zoom out of its plastic bag as Cate got her guitar out of its case and prepared to perform a song bang in the centre of a sheep-strewn, sloping field, surrounded by ragged trees and uneven low stone walls, the bottom half of her legs obscured by the long watery grass.

The rain was so heavy that the Zoom, a complex if compact piece of technology, had rivulets of water running across its various buttons and levers. That could be damaging. But it was a risk I had to take. I held the machine at chest height before Cate as she sang a song of her own called 'Byw Heb Farw' (Living Without Dying). She had a great voice – melodic, unforced and tinged with melancholic resignation – but tough. There was something about her strong West Wales accent, with the syllables of the words so clearly defined, that had both sweetness and defiance to it; it was as steadfast and exotic as the land itself. It didn't matter that I didn't understand a word of what she was saying, since to be honest I didn't really understand her songs in English anyway. When she sang a line like 'I'm on a train it's overrun, I fought like I'm not the only one' on a song called 'Shoeing The Bones', I could appreciate the tender mood she creates without knowing what the hell she was on about. She claimed to have written a lot of her songs as therapy to deal with the trauma of childhood pets dying, but I couldn't see the connection.

The only problem was the sheep. Perhaps in respect to this woman they appeared to worship they were entirely silent throughout the performance.

They started bleating soon after the song ended. 'Is there any way you can tell them to do that while you're singing?' I asked, irritated. She sang a song called 'O, Am Gariad' (O, For Love), but once again the sheep were uncharacteristically quiet the moment I pressed play and record. I suggested we change our position and move to a hedge at the bottom of the field, not least because it was pelting it down and the hedge might offer a little bit of shelter. I also suggested Cate sing a song in English. Perhaps the sheep would object to that.

Cate sang 'No One Can Drag Me Down', an ode to self-preservation in the face of heartbreak, and the sheep finally bleated. We did another version of the Welsh-language songs in the field with the horses to see what they made of them. They didn't respond.

As we sloshed back to the house in the constant rain I asked Cate more about her relationship with singing, given that she felt so strongly about the choir culture of Wales. I had briefly met the former superstar choirboy Aled Jones a couple of years previously and, charming though he was, I had the feeling that he was the type of Eisteddfod-winning choral stiff she was talking about.

'The thing is, I always loved singing,' she said, her guitar under her arm. 'We all do in my family. My mum is forever breaking into a rendition of "Total Eclipse Of The Heart" by Bonnie Tyler and my little sister keeps getting told off for singing in class – she's not trying to be naughty, she doesn't even know she's doing it. So I didn't like the fact that the school turned singing into this point-scoring exercise. I wasn't technically good on any instrument either so ultimately I decided it would be better to go my own way and take inspiration from bands like Gorky's and Super Furry Animals rather than my fellow classmates winning trophies in the Eisteddfod.'

Cate appeared to be remarkably positive about her situation, and about living in a world of rain. 'I'm happy at the minute,' she said as we came up to the house and shook sodden Wellington boots off at the heavy oak front door. 'I like singing my own stuff and I like singing with Gruff in Neon Neon and I don't have any ambition right now beyond continuing with what I'm doing. I don't understand people who wear music as a burden, or think of it as a means to some unlikely end involving wealth and fame. If you're going to do it you're going to do it anyway.'

Now being without a car, the only way to get back to Cardiff was by train. Huw and Cate drove me to the nearest station, at a town called Gowerton. They very much wanted to take me to the wool mill for which Penboyr is famous. 'You get wicked Welsh blankets there,' said Cate, nodding. 'You don't want to miss this premier local attraction.' The mill was a source for Cate's eighties-style wool jumpers emblazoned with scenes from nature, which looked somehow stylish on her but undoubtedly terrible on everyone else. But the destruction of the Astra had thrown my schedule out and I had to get a move on. I thanked Cate and Huw for their kindness and got on a train that went along by the sea and through lush valleys, and through tiny stations it only stopped at if somebody made a request to the conductor.

Jo and Danny met me at the station. We drove to their house in Cardiff and I felt a twinge of lifestyle envy for this couple the same age as NJ and myself and with a son and daughter the same age as Otto and Pearl. They lived in the kind of tall, elegant Georgian terrace you find in cities throughout Britain; the type with high ceilings, stone floors and a large fireplace surrounded by ornate tiles in the living room. It was so much nicer than our pokey Peckham semi. But then, NJ and I could never leave London. The capital was the only place we felt safe.

After years of working in the music industry in London, forming a reasonably successful acoustic duet and staging scores of concerts, Jo and Danny moved in 2000 from a one-bedroom flat in North London to a house in Brecon, deep in the Welsh countryside, because the double whammy of becoming parents and facing prohibitive house prices made staying in London very difficult indeed. That year they got signed to a major label, were dropped the year after, and began to wonder what they were going to do for the rest of their lives.

'We were feeling isolated and we missed our friends,' said Danny on the genesis of The Green Man. 'By 2003 we were getting desperate, and had the idea of starting a little festival. So we called a friend whose wife is from Brecon to see about organising it. Three months later we found a castle owned by the opera singer Adelina Patti, who had fallen in love with Wales and built a miniature Drury Lane theatre in the castle grounds. James Yorkston played, there was a cinema tent, and we put on a few kids' games.'

'We lost nine pounds ten pence,' said Jo.

Jo and Danny persevered, and the following year they expanded the festival to attract a thousand people to the new location of the grounds of a stately home called Baskerville Hall. In 2005 Will Oldham, the American singer who my Govan chums Alex Neilson and Alasdair Roberts performed with, headlined on the main stage in his guise as Bonnie 'Prince' Billy, while a Californian singing harpist called Joanna Newsom was the other major attraction. There was a power cut just as the sun turned orange and Oldham and his band started one of his most famous songs, an ode to friendship called 'I See A Darkness'. The band kept playing – through the silence and the darkness.

'I just lost it,' said Jo. 'I went backstage and screamed at the soundman, "What the fuck is going on?" It turned out that there was a trip switch between the two generators and it kept flicking from one to the other, cutting off the power supply in doing so. The power came on just as Will Oldham finished the song. In a way it was good because it's the one moment of the festival that everyone remembers.'

'2005 nearly killed us,' said Danny. 'We built the stage with a local scaffolder a few hours before the festival was due to start. Then two three-year-old girls went missing.'

'Everyone was freaking out, thinking they had been abducted,' said Jo. ' It turned out that they had met each other and decided to go and see Joanna Newsom together.'

'Then the speakers caught fire.'

'We went into the red that year.'

You couldn't help but wonder, given nervous-break-down-inducing incidents like these, why Jo and Danny continued with The Green Man at all. But the following year they moved the festival to an emerald valley called Glanusk

Park near Brecon, where it is now. It began to turn a profit and make a name for itself as the best festival in Britain, so different from the raft of corporate-run three-day events that were now a major part of the live-music calendar and so different from the nightmare that Glastonbury had become. The collapse in album sales as a result of downloading and a changing cultural climate had been paralleled with a growth in live music, and Jo and Danny were finding their template – an alternative rock and folk festival with an organic, egalitarian feel – copied and commercialised elsewhere. The Green Man still held a deep appeal, though, probably because one could tell it was a product of a love of music and of a belief in the positive power of like-minded people coming together.

Jo and Danny sang two songs for me to record. I placed the Zoom on the sofa, put on the headphones, and told them to start whenever they wanted. Jo's voice reminded me of Sandy Denny, the late, hard-living lead singer of the folk-rock group Fairport Convention. The children came in to see what was going on, found that it was their parents singing and playing guitar as usual, and went off again. It was the evening, and too late to go round to Cat's mum's house and make Gruff Rhys do a recording when he probably should have been helping out with putting-the-baby-to-bed duties, so I decided to head back to London by train. As Danny drove me to the station I asked him how he was feeling about that year's Green Man, only a week away.

'It's very odd,' he said as we passed through the neon lights of the city centre. 'For the first time ever it all seems relatively under control. But that might be the calm before the storm.'

'Still, it'll all be over soon and you'll be able to relax, eh?'

'You would think so, wouldn't you? But when you spend all year preparing to entertain ten thousand people for three days it's very hard to wind down. As soon as this festival ends we have to start thinking about booking bands for the next one. It's funny to think that all of this came as a result of our wanting to get a few friends to do a gig in the Brecon Beacons.'

———————◆————

A week later Otto, Pearl and myself – NJ, who generally prefers walking on surfaces suitable for high heels, was not joining us – were in our new car, an old Saab a hundred times nicer than the Vauxhall and a remarkably generous and timely gift from a friend who didn't want it any more, heading for Glanusk Park in Brecon for The Green Man festival. The Astra was officially deceased: documents came from a Cardiff breaker's yard to confirm that Huw's mother had arranged for its destruction. Gruff Rhys assured me he could find the time to do a field recording over the course of the weekend, even if Super Furry Animals were head-lining on the main stage on Saturday.

'I know the perfect place to do it,' he said over the phone in his faltering tone. 'There's a cave about half an hour's drive and then a half-hour walk away from the festival site. You get excellent acoustics in there.'

It was raining, of course. It rarely stopped for the entire weekend and the mud got thicker and deeper with each passing hour. Otto and Pearl offered to help carry the gear from a field outside the site where the car was parked to a field inside the site where we could pitch our tent, but good intentions gave way to fatigue within a few feet amidst announcements of hunger and tiredness. Somehow we got the tent up, the children leaped about inside it for a bit, and then we trudged through the mud to try and watch some bands. Otto and Pearl lasted for a few minutes before yanking at my kagoule and announcing they were bored and couldn't see anything. From then on the festival experience chiefly consisted of non-competitive games in the children's field.

Still, the atmosphere was inspiring. The Green Man had a democratic ethos. There was no major separation between artist and festival-goer – the reformed seveties folk-rock band Pentangle were about the most famous band going, and that's not saying much – and no big backstage area to make the ticket-payers feel like they were missing out on the action. My dislike of the big festivals is that they turn rock music into a spectator sport in which the audience dumbly consumes as the on-stage acts earn. At The Green Man you felt that being there meant being involved; that this was a community.

Nailing Gruff Rhys down to a field recording did prove tricky. We had arranged to meet in the beer tent on the Saturday afternoon, from where we would head off to the cave – Otto got excited about the idea and Pearl was happy to go along with it – but Gruff had his extended family in tow and was feeling the pressure of keeping them all happy. 'I think the cave is looking unlikely,' he said hesitantly, as two middle-aged Welsh women tugged at his arm. He suggested we meet behind the main stage at eight that evening. Wouldn't he have other things on his mind, given that he would be performing in front of 10,000 people two and a half hours later? 'Our tour manager says we're not allowed to do anything until ten, so I'll just be hanging around,' he replied. 'We can find a quiet place to do the recording then.'

This sounded hopelessly optimistic. But Cate Le Bon, also doing a set, offered to come along to look after the kids while Gruff and I did the recording, so after an afternoon's sleeping in the tent – the rain was so heavy there was little point in doing anything else – we met her in a small marquee marked 'Howling Bells'. This wasn't some sort of pre-gig psychotherapeutic exercise but the name of the Australian rock band occupying it. They ignored us.

'I'm sure he'll turn up,' said Cate in a low voice. But the minutes passed and Gruff did not appear, while various Howling Bells sprayed beer at each other. 'He's a man of his word. A very late man of his word, admittedly . . . why don't we talk to Howling Bells while we're waiting?'

I don't think the children were too enamoured with the idea, given the way they kept pushing into my legs and asking if we could go now, and if we were still going to the cave, and when could we go and get the fish and chips I had promised them, and was Mummy warm and dry at home, watching television, going to sleep in a bed that night? I finally got through to Gruff some time after nine. He was in the middle of putting the baby down in a nearby bed and breakfast. By the time he had done that it would be time to blow the minds of thousands in his role as the star of a psychedelic-rock band. He was apologetic. He said that if I could be in the same place at ten the following morning he would definitely be there.

'I can't keep dragging the kids through the mud to do this,' I told him, admonishingly. 'The whole idea of the cave was fun, but all this hanging around is boring.'

'I promise to turn up tomorrow,' he said – and he did. We all stayed up until after midnight to watch Super Furry Animals, the children transfixed by the flashing lights and electric atmosphere of a concert under a starry sky and a full moon, and the next day we waded through the Sunday morning mud to meet Gruff, standing alone, lost in the expanse of space behind the main stage.

'I might have to sing a cappella,' he said, looking like a displaced farmer in his Barbour jacket and Wellington boots. 'The tour manager packed all our equipment on the bus . . .'

'I've got a guitar in the boot of my car,' I replied. 'If you don't mind doing it in the car park, we could do the recording there.'

We walked over to where the car was parked, trudging through a field of tents. Every few minutes somebody that knew Gruff, or wanted to know him, came over and told him about their latest project, or how good his last album was. Each time he stood and listened politely, patiently, before eventually saying, 'Well, I've got to go and do this recording now . . .'

It was raining, of course, and the kids fought over who carried the umbrella they were sharing. Then Pearl began to sing: 'Under my umbrella-ella-ella . . .' Otto joined in. The fighting stopped. The umbrella went backwards and forwards in time with the singing, negating its protective properties somewhat.

'What's that?'

' "Umbrella",' Pearl replied with a giggle. 'All of my gang sing it all the time. We love it.'

'Umbrella' was a massive hit for a pop princess from Barbados called Rihanna. If all the little girls were singing 'Umbrella' in the playground that summer, perhaps it would become a nursery rhyme – and part of the fabric of British life – in years to come.

We crouched on the wet grass behind the boot of the car, just next to a path where a procession of people trudged past. Gruff sang a song in Welsh, 'Cryndod Yn Dy Lais' (The Quiver In Your Voice) as Otto and Pearl sat quietly and the sound of boots stomping through mud kept up an irregular rhythm nearby. Luckily, nobody spoiled the recording by coming up to tell Gruff how much they loved everything he did. Pearl tapped at the Zoom, and tried to get my attention to whisper something in my ear about having more fish and chips, but otherwise there were no interruptions.

Gruff had an easy talent. There was nothing precious

about what he did, and yet these songs that he came up with were so accomplished – 'Cryndod Yn Dy Lais' had a haunting, eerie quality, and I got a feeling of poetic yearning from it even though I couldn't understand a word. Something about his lyricism reminded me of the riddle-filled confusion of 'The Battle Of The Trees', the ancient Welsh myth, beloved of minstrels, that concerns willows, rowan trees and 'a toad with a hundred claws' going into a battle that may well be a metaphor for the ongoing challenge of Druidic intellectual rigour. Gruff could switch from the whimsical to the hard-bitten in a line, and filled his songs with imagery that may or may not have deeper metaphorical meaning depending on your reading of them. He claimed that one of Super Furry Animals' most famous songs, 'Rings Around The World', was about the global connectivity of mobile-phone networks. It could equally have been about a more metaphysical, eternal power.

'What do you think of that, kids?' I asked Otto and Pearl, who had been bribed into silence by a KitKat.

'It was all right,' said Otto, tearing at clutches of grass and watching them as they scattered in the wind. 'Are we still going to the cave?'

Pearl looked up with big eyes and said, 'I liked it.'

I asked Gruff about how he found his musical voice. He said that it all came from the internal and external forces making up the culture of Bethesda, the industrial slate-quarry town in the north where he grew up.

'There were a lot of hippy dropouts. They introduced freaky music to the industrial workers and the Welsh-speaking population, and filled the charity shops with records people like me would later buy, like The Velvet Underground and Neil Young. A lot of them had been students at Bangor University and then bought cheap houses in the mountains. It was the kids of hippies that taught me to speak English.'

The first hippy in the area was a Londoner called Joe Hatt. He had moved to Bethesda after seeing a classified ad for a Hammond B12 organ for sale in Holyhead. A price was agreed, and not being a believer in four-wheeled char-iots of destruction (cars), Joe borrowed a cart and a dog and set off for Holyhead from London, walking along the A5. It took him three weeks, and he slept in hedges and barns along the way, and by the time he got to Holyhead the organ had been sold. But on the way Joe had passed through Bethesda, where he had seen an advertisement for a house for £200. He bought the house, moved his family up from London, and introduced the local slate-mining boys to the joys of psychedelic rock in an attempt to stop them from kicking his head in.

It worked. Joe and the slate-quarry boys formed a rock band and the Welsh underground movement began. Before long acid-fried stalwarts of the drug-drenched free-festival scene like Hawkwind and The Pink Fairies were staging outdoor concerts in this tiny, Welsh-speaking, rural quarry town. According to Gruff they went down reason-ably well. 'People were just pleased of some activity,' he explained.

Alongside his Bethesda neighbours, the other key figure in Gruff's education was a giant anteater called Caleb. Caleb was a popular character on Welsh children's television throughout the 1970s. 'In many ways he was the first rock star I came across,' said Gruff. 'He was always on TV when I was growing up, and he was very cool – rather like the Fonz – despite being a man in a giant anteater costume. He lived in a cave.'

'Who lived in a cave?' asked Otto, a little sulkily. I think he was feeling short-changed by the way events were panning out.

'I had the good fortune to see Caleb appear live at a festival in 1975, when I was five, which is my first abiding memory,' Gruff continued. 'He was amazing. So cool . . . And he released a single. I've got a copy. What's more, he spoke Welsh.'

Gruff claimed Caleb as the single biggest influence on his entire life. Surely his band – Super Furry Animals – was named after this phallus-nosed cool guy, although he wouldn't open up on this.

One hundred and twenty years ago the Welsh language was spoken by 100 per cent of the population. Now it is spoken by 20 per cent, but that is a huge improvement since the mid-twentieth century, when Welsh was seen as a working-class language – NJ's grandmother was Welsh but certainly wouldn't speak a word of the language and went so far as to pass herself off as English – and the teaching of it was discouraged in industrial areas. It was unusual for someone of Gruff's age to speak Welsh as his or her first language, but he was of the generation that fought hard for its survival. In his teens he followed militant Welsh-language punk bands, the most famous of which were called Datblygu (Develop). I said to him that it seemed like the fight had been successful, given that there was now a generation of young people like Cate Le Bon and Huw Evans that took speaking Welsh for granted.

'There has been a resurgence in Welsh language education,' he said, scratching his head and crunching up his eyes, as he did when taking consideration over his sentences. 'There are now Welsh-language schools, so kids are learning it from a young age. But in the natural heartlands of the language, which are the rural areas, people are being priced out of their houses and the communities are falling apart as a result. There's a real danger of Welsh becoming a heritage language, a media language, rather than a living one.'

Gruff played another song, 'Ffrwydriad Yn Y Ffurfafen', which means something like explosions in the extended sky, or explosions in the atmosphere, the horizon, the stratosphere and the cosmos all rolled into one. It was very pretty, and captured that mix of the familiar and the exotic that Gruff did so well.

'Thanks for being patient, kids,' said Gruff to Otto and Pearl. I think they were just grateful not to be dragged around through the mud any more. We finished the festival experience by eating fish and chips around a large campfire, going to a puppet show, and even watching a couple of bands.

Despite (or perhaps because of) the car exploding, Wales had been the best trip yet. Cate Le Bon and Gruff Rhys wrote songs that reflected a place and a reality grounded in experience, and as such they made modern folk music that was as relevant to the tapestry of the land as the old songs collected by Cecil Sharp and Francis Child. Whether they made a living from it or not, and whether those songs would be strong enough to be soaked up by the community, was another matter. This was what I had been hoping to find.

Now I had to think about how to turn this rough collection of field recordings, from the indistinguishable noise in a Sheffield basement to the ancient purity of Stephanie Hladowski's 'Willie O' Winsbury', from the gospel joy of Tendayi's rendition of 'Amazing Grace' to Gruff's Welsh poetry in a festival car park, into a discernible entity; a collection of musical snapshots that fashioned a portrait of Britain in the 21st century.

Chapter Fifteen

The Ballads of Britain

I T WAS AUTUMN. THE CHILDREN WENT BACK TO SCHOOL
and the skies darkened. The brown mulch of fallen
leaves mingled with the acid colours of crisp packets,
sweet wrappers and fried-chicken cartons in Peckham
gutters. In the school playground Pearl and her friends sang
'Ring-A-Ring O' Roses', a nursery rhyme with roots in the
Great Plague of London that killed up to 100,000 people in
1665, dropping onto the stone floor in their winter coats in
imitation of death at the rhyme's conclusion. Otto lost and
sometimes found a combination of hat, gloves, homework
and coat each afternoon before walking home to draw
pictures of manga monsters and mythical creatures until it
was time for supper. NJ and I worried about money.

A sense of guilt took root and budded. Making field
recordings had become something of an addiction. There
was always the feeling that just around the corner lay
someone with a song that would encapsulate the times, or a
piece of living history that stretched back a thousand years.
I began to understand why Doc Rowe had dedicated his life
to collecting fragments of folk history, relying on the good-
will of others to get by: the search never ended. The pot of
gold at the end of the rainbow was forever in sight but
always out of reach. It couldn't continue. I was no longer
sleeping at night. On one side of my mental television screen
was a charismatic Gypsy, sitting on the steps of a hand-

painted wooden caravan, singing the most exquisite version of 'My Son David' anyone had ever heard. On the other was a team of grim-faced bailiffs turning up at the door of our house with a repossession order.

In attempting to create a portrait of Britain through these recordings I had come up with a subjective, organic, random piece of oral history; a series of snapshots reflective of the people that made them and the places, times and communities they came from and certainly not of the history of British music as a whole. One person led to another and that shaped the journey. Some of the songs, like 'Oft Have I Sigh'd' by The English Ayre, were fantasy visions of England's distant past. Others, like Stephanie Hladowski's 'Willie O' Winsbury' and Alasdair Roberts and Alex Neilson's 'Two Brothers', were invocations of something ancient and mysterious that was still among us; songs that held their power through so many anonymous people that had sung them. Lewis's inner-city busking songs that dreamed of the countryside and Pete Molinari's cry of help from the depths of a dull market town were expressions of a present reality inspired by eternal sentiments. These were just a handful of stories in the millions that stitch together the fabric of British life, but I began to see the role they served. They helped illustrate that everything we need is right there in front of us. It's in ourselves, and in the people we know. All of this art, history and culture is out there, free for all, owned by everyone and possessed by nobody.

There was a comment that came back more than once when I told people of my plans to make a series of field recordings around Great Britain: folk music is all over. Everything has been written down, recorded and universalised and there is no such thing as a local, oral culture any more. All that is left are the remnants; a few old Gypsies still singing the songs their parents taught them. What I found, over a spring to autumn of making field recordings, negated this. The combination of down-to-earth humour, belligerence and far-out experimentation the improvisational Sheffield musicians revealed in their basement was something unique to the city. The stark, unadorned way Alex Neilson and Alasdair Roberts approached traditional Scottish ballads made sense in one of the toughest neighbourhoods of a tough town like Glasgow. The Beep Seals had a very Mancunian combination of sixties sunshine pop and lyrics about doing stupid things like biting on glass bottles. Pearl learned the words of 'Do-Re-Mi' and 'Ring-A-Ring O' Roses' through hearing other kids singing them in the playground. The cultural theorist Marshall McLuhan predicted electronic communication would create a new kind of oral culture and he was proved right. There might not be too many Shropshire stonewallers out there singing the unwritten ballads their grandmother taught them, but in the age of instant global communication the land is awash with people using song as a basic vehicle for nuggets of social history, whether that means carrying fragments of the past into the present or writing about whatever is happening to them at the time or sharing with their community a story or a piece of music that belongs to them all. 'Tango' by Lady Sovereign might be taught in schools as an illustration of notions of beauty at the beginning of the 21st century. Judging by Keith Allen's shocking rendition of it at the little festival in Devon, 'Anarchy In The UK' by The Sex Pistols is well on its way to becoming a British folk song. The organic process by which culture forms is continuous and eternal, ever shifting and as uncontrollable as the ocean.

Singing was ubiquitous in pre-industrial Britain. It was solace and recreation, and the amount of the old songs about sex, drinking, the changing of the seasons, murder and death reveals how little the basic preoccupations change. Perhaps singing and storytelling take the place of consumerism when the chips are down, and help to foster a sense of community when fewer people spend weekends travelling to second homes or weekend breaks abroad, and go down to the pub for a sing-along instead. Like having a game of Monopoly by candlelight because the electricity has been cut off, it is a joy born of a situation.

The journey ended where it began: with 'The Seeds Of Love'. Soon after returning from Wales I visited a young singer called Tim Van Eyken, who was making a living by travelling around the country singing the old songs of Britain. He had the one that first opened Cecil Sharp to the glories of British traditional music in his repertoire. 'My mum was a folk singer, so I grew up going to folk festivals and pub sessions,' said Tim, when I went around to the garret he rented in a tall Islington town house on a bright Sunday morning to make a recording of him singing 'The Seeds Of Love'. 'I like to think that if more people had better access to folk music there would be more people engaged with it, because these songs are beautiful.'

I had 75 recordings. They all fitted onto a little card, the type that a digital camera uses, which slotted into the back of the eight-track. After an afternoon of technological frustration that almost ended up with my throwing the laptop against a wall I worked out how to get the recordings from the card onto the computer. Now it was possible to turn them into an album that might find its way to people's collections, and stick them up on a website for anyone in the world to hear. Whether anyone in the world actually wanted to was another matter. But it still felt remarkable that something so casual, so intimate and so localised had the potential to be universal.

Inspired by something Philip Larkin once wrote – 'the English have become poor caretakers of Englishness itself' – I decided that my goal for these recordings was for Cecil Sharp House to keep them in their archive. So I spoke to its long-standing librarian, a man called Malcolm Taylor, who rarely mentions that his services to the preservation of the history of everyday people have garnered him an OBE. I asked Malcolm if it would be possible to have the songs stored within this great bastion of British folk music's myriad vaults.

'It's interesting to hear about people's ideas of what folk music is,' said Malcolm, after I told him about what I had been trying to do, of recording people singing old, anonymous songs as well as self-composed ones. 'I'm doing a talk about it at a school in Bermondsey next week. When the teacher told the kids about it they replied, in all serious-ness: "Do folk music people wear bells and ribbons?" Can you believe it? I'm going to have to tell them that only 90 per cent of us do . . .'

I made two CDs containing most of the recordings. On one were all the renditions of traditional ballads. On the other were the songs that people had written. Then I took the tube to Camden Town and made the short walk up to the red-brick monolith on Gloucester Avenue that is Cecil Sharp House.

Sam Lee met me by the door, an oversized scarf underlining his broad, big-toothed grin and wire-brush hair. He had spent much of the summer volunteering on Forest School Camps and the weeks of relentless rain had made them hard work, but the singing around the campfire had kept him going. 'It really was a reminder of what it is that excites me about all this,' he said, gesturing an arm around the hallway of Cecil Sharp House, which, with its leaflets for folk clubs and reinforced glass doors, looked like the community hall of a reasonably vibrant English village. 'It's the reason why I'm so passionate about folk songs in the first place. The most precious experiences of my childhood were round a campfire, singing songs I didn't understand but got a great sense of their importance in creating a community. That was a deep feeling I got that had nothing to do with my love of Michael Jackson.'

A vision of Sam attempting to do a moonwalk around the campfire, a fingerless glove dotted with glitter glue on one hand, dodging burning embers and cider-filled tin cups, suddenly brightened the institutional drabness of Cecil Sharp House's hallway.

We went into the wood-panelled library, a single high-ceilinged room that, save for a pair of computers, looked like it could have belonged to any decade from the beginning of the twentieth century onwards. There was a shelf marked 'Nursery Rhymes' and another marked 'Gypsy Songs'. At the far end was Malcolm Taylor, a short-haired, sharp-eyed man with a southeast London accent and a tweed jacket who had spent the bulk of the last thirty years of his life in this room, and one on the floor above that housed the field recordings that had been bequeathed to Cecil Sharp House from the early twentieth century onwards.

We all sat down at a desk. I laid the CDs down on the space before Malcolm and asked if Cecil Sharp House would have any use for them.

'We tend to look at the continuum, and the way traditional songs have evolved,' he said, picking up the CDs and running his eyes down the names of the songs and the people contained within them. 'So while this one is useful' – and he raised up the CD containing the traditional songs – 'this other one might not be just yet. You or I might write a song in our bedrooms and try to put it into an institution like this. But most of what we deal with here is a product of community, and that's why it's called folk music. What function does it have? Some of these songs you've collected are going to play an important part in someone's bedroom, but beyond that they may not have any value at all.'

'It's very hard to know what is currently useful,' added Sam. 'We can't know what role this material will play in ten, twenty, fifty years, so I differentiate the acts according to their intention. Are they doing it for the love of the song, or to become rich and famous?'

I couldn't imagine any of the people I had recorded getting it together sufficiently to become rich and famous, but stranger things had happened.

'Bob Dylan is an example of that process,' said Malcolm. 'In the early days he was called a folk singer because he was grounded in traditional music and wrote anthemic songs that meant something for a lot of people. But his songs really need to be around a bit longer in order to belong to that canon; they need to develop to a point where they're not wholly associated with him. To me, it's the idea of a community adopting something and shaping it that counts. For example, I've come across singing games in East London that are done to the tune of "That's The Way I Like It" by KC And The Sunshine Band. For some reason that disco hit has gone into the collective consciousness and it's adapting as a result. That's how traditions are created.'

I asked Malcolm if, in that case, the songs I recorded in Anstruther could be called folk songs. The people I had either met or heard of, like Kenny and Gordon Anderson and James Yorkston, had written them, but everyone in the village seemed to know them. They sang along to 'Blue Mantle' and 'Going Gone', songs that I had recorded on that trip up there, at The Ship Tavern in the way people in other pubs might sing along to 'The Wild Rover' or, for all I know, 'Wonderwall' by Oasis.

'I would say that, in that context, they do become folk songs,' said Malcolm.

'Songs like that don't exist separately of the environment from which they came,' added Sam. 'It's great that you documented them.'

This all added up to a roundabout way of hedging the question of whether they were going to take my recordings or not. Meanwhile, Sam and Malcolm entered into some sort of an argument about whether it was the narrative or the melody that was more important in traditional song. This tends to happen when two people talk about folk music. Mention the term and heated discussions follow, I think because it is actually something that's impossible to define. The question of what is folk music is a question that can't be answered because, having no particular form, it is forever changing.

Here was the paradox at the heart of my travels with a Zoom. Britain is nothing more than a landmass. Generations of immigrants bring their own influences and inaugurate subtle shifts in the collective consciousness, as do forces of economy, industry, technology and morality. From Cecil Sharp to Alan Lomax to a limited collection of recordings made from spring to autumn with the help of an eight-track and a disgusting Vauxhall Astra, any attempt to document it through song is only going to offer up a tiny part of the story. But it's hopefully a tiny part with value. And it seemed that Cecil Sharp House *was* going to add the recordings made on the Zoom eight-track portable home studio I was yet to learn how to use properly.

'Snapshots are *so* important,' said Sam, giving credence to my project through a subtle gesture. 'That's why we've got to keep making them.'

———————◆◆◆———————

A few days later, on a bright, cold October morning, NJ and I were in the kitchen of our house in Peckham. The high light of the autumn sun shone down from above the hedge outside and in through the window, illuminating the shifting twists of steam that rose from the coffee. Playing on the spillage-stained portable CD player was an album called

From Gardens Where We Feel Secure by Virginia Astley. The sound of birds singing, children playing, church bells ringing and the wind dancing through the trees of a wood tangled up against the chirps of a flute and the stirrings of a bass. Virginia made it over a couple of weeks in Oxfordshire, walking through fields and along country lanes with a microphone to capture all the sounds she needed to create a late-twentieth-century take on the folk-inspired classical pieces of Vaughan Williams and Elgar. It was the perfect evocation of the dream of English life.

'I don't think this is the best thing to begin a Monday morning with,' said NJ, who had just finished curating an exhibition and was suffering from the inevitable despondency that comes at the completion of a long-gestating project.

'What do you mean? It's beautiful.'

'It is,' she said, resting her head on a palm, 'but it makes you want to retreat.'

In the springtime, the seeds of a musical journey through Britain were sown as the songs of Heron, an obscure folk-rock band from the seventies, clashed with the soundtrack to 21st-century urban London in our kitchen. By the autumn the journey was over and the harvest was in. The snapshots of Britain were collected and recorded and Virginia Astley's meditative, plaintive compositions gave a quiet, sadly hopeful vision of a small island. Finally, I had an answer to the question of what British music is, because it was right here in this unheralded, largely unknown album. British music, like the British character itself, is melancholic, localised, tragicomic, and averse to the grandiose. The circle continues, with Britishness – an idea, a feeling, a corner of the imagination – enduring and returning, again and again.

Bibliography

Ackroyd, Peter, *Albion: The Origins of the English Imagination* (Chatto & Windus, 2002)

Armitage, Simon (trans.): *Sir Gawain and the Green Knight* (Faber & Faber, 2008)

Boyd, Joe: *White Bicycles: Making Music in the 1960s* (Serpent's Tail, 2007)

Bracewell, Michael: *England Is Mine: Pop Life in Albion from Wilde To Goldie* (Flamingo, 1998)

Bracewell, Michael: *Remake, Remodel* (Faber & Faber, 2007)

Burchill, Julie and Parsons, Tony: *The Boy Looked at Johnny: An Obituary of Rock and Roll* (Pluto, 1978)

Chambers, Robert: *Hares on the Mountains* (Boosey & Hawkes, 1960)

Child, Francis: *English And Scottish Ballads Vols I–VIII* (Little, Brown, 1858)

Copper, Bob: *Early to Rise* (William Heinemann, 1976)

Du Maurier, Daphne: *The House on the Strand* (Arrow, 1992)

Du Maurier, Daphne: *Vanishing Cornwall* (Gollancz, 1981)

Farson, Daniel: *Soho in the Fifties* (Pimlico, 1993)

Gammon, Vic: *Desire, Drink and Death in the English Folk Song Vernacular* (Ashgate, 2008)

Giuliano, Geoffrey: *Behind Blue Eyes: Life of Pete Townshend* (Coronet, 1996)

Grainger, Percy: *The All-Round Man: Selected Letters* (Clarendon, 1994)

Graves, Robert: *The White Goddess* (Faber & Faber, 1948)

Green, Thomas A (ed.): *Folklore: An Encyclopedia of Beliefs, Customs, Tales, Music and Art* (ABC-Clio, 1997)

Harker, Dave: *Fakesong* (Open University Press)

Harper, Colin: *Dazzling Stranger: Bert Jansch and the British Folk and Blues Revival* (Bloomsbury, 2006)

Henderson, Hamish: *Alias Macalias: Writings on Songs, Folk & Literature* (Polygon, 1992)

Hood, Grahame: *Empty Pocket Blues: The Life and Music of Clive Palmer* (Helter Skelter, 2008)

Karpeles, Maud: *Cecil Sharp: His Life and Work* (Faber & Faber, 2008)

Karpeles, Maud: *An Introduction to English Folk Song* (Oxford Paperbacks, 1987)

Palmer, Roy: *The Sound of History: Songs and Social Comment* (OUP, 1988)

Pollard, Michael: *Discovering English Folk Song* (Shire Publications, 1982)

Sachs, Curt: *World History of the Dance* (WW Norton & Co, 1937)

Sacks, Oliver: *Musicophilia: Tales of Music and the Brain* (Picador, 2007)

Sawyer, Miranda: *Park and Ride* (Little, Brown, 1999)

Sharp, Cecil: *English Folk Songs: Some Conclusions* (Simpkin; Novello, 1907)

Stewart, Bob: *Where is Saint George? Pagan Imagery in English Folk Song* (Moonraker, 1977)

Val Baker, Denys: *The Sea's in the Kitchen* (Humdrumming, 2006)

Westwood, Jennifer and Simpson, Jacqueline: *The Lore of the Land* (Penguin, 2005)

Williams, Ursula: *RVW: A Biography of Ralph Vaughan Williams* (Clarendon, 1998)

Yates, Mike (ed.): *Traveller's Joy: Songs of English and Scottish Travellers and Gypsies 1965–2005* (EFDSS, 2008)

Acknowledgements

THIS HAS BEEN A COLLABORATIVE PROJECT AND IT HAPPENED through the generosity of the following people. Thanks, in chronological order, to Simon Benham, Mike Jones, Tom Bromley, Malcolm Croft and all at Portico, Simon Tong, Lee Dorian and all at Rise Above, Malcolm Taylor, Daniel Pemberton, Johnny Trunk, Ian Anderson, Lawrence, Laura Coxeter, Will Lee, Stacey Williams, Bill Partridge and all at the Headington Quarry Side, Gary Carpenter, Ben and Lydia, Tiffany and Jarvis, Steve Jarvis, Ham and Gill Stevenson, Charles Stevenson, Wizz Jones, Donovan, Clive Palmer, Martin Val Baker, Zoe and Murray Young, Bert Jansch, Gina Val Baker, Jarvis Cocker, Richard Hawley, all at Yellow Arch Studios, Sheffield, Jon and Fiona at Singing Knives, Jonny Drury, John Jasnoch, Glynn Heppenstall, Blackest Rainbow, Chris Goodwin, Jeni Melia, Kathryn Hamilton-Hall, Charles Hazlewood, Michael Tyack, Will Summers, Sam Lee, Harriet at Glass Ceiling, Ildiko and Cosmicorus, the Penfold Family, Stanley Robertson, Ed, Will and Ginger, Martin Carthy, Norma Waterson, Marry Waterson, Olly Knight, Doc Rowe and Gill, Johnny Lynch, Kenny Anderson, James Yorkston, Alex Neilson, Alasdair Roberts, Stephanie Hladowski and the rest of the Hladowski Family, Pete Townshend, Arthur Boulton, Coco, Declan and Charncle at the Brit School in Croydon, Andy Hank Dog, Tim Siddall, Lewis Floyd Henry, Trevor and Hannah Moss, Martin Ledner, Gabriel Olegavich, Lady Sovereign (in absentis), Jazzie B, Pete Molinari, Pete's mum and dad, Tandayi, Zoe Williams, Gruff Rhys, Cate Le Bon, Huw Evans, Huw's mum Erica, Ken Lower at Hermana, Jo and Danny at The Green Man, Jenny Sjoholm and Jake Hawkes, Guy Garvey, Jack Cooper and all of The Beep Seals, Paul Toogood, Mick Houghton, Ian McCulloch, Pete and Peasy at Parr Street Studios, Liverpool, Ian Broudie, Will Sergeant, Pat Long and Jarin Tabata at Heron Recordings, Tjinder Singh, Ben Ayres, Leo Smee and Chrome Hoof, Tim Van Eyken and Richard Vine.

My biggest thanks of all to NJ, Otto and Pearl.

Tracklisting

available through Heron Records

1. *Mabe Cloud* — The Rosemarie Band (Cornwall)
After a disastrous attempt to capture morris dancers in Oxford — they almost trampled on the Zoom — the first proper field recording session happened in a cottage in Mabe, Cornwall, where Jarvis and Tiffany of The Rosemarie Band make music in the evenings after they have finished working on the local farm. Something about the meandering but earthy feel of this flute-led instrumental captures Cornwall's wild spirit.

2. *The Lakes Of Shallin* — Sam Lee (Devon)
In a church in Lynton, a pretty coastal town connected to nearby Lynmouth by a water-powered cliffside railway, a fresh-faced man stood before the altar and sang this old supernatural ballad with great passion and conviction. The fact that he was a Jewish boy from north London and not one of the Gypsy singers with which the ballad is usually associated in no way takes away from the power of his rendition.

3. *Edi Be Thu, Heven-Queene* — The English Ayre (Hampstead, north London)
Back in London, the journey brought me to the rarefied world of early music. Chris Goodwin is the secretary of The Lute Society and a devotee of the instrument ever since falling for its charms in his teens. Jeni Melia is a pure-voiced soprano. Together they make up The English Ayre, and this thirteenth-century ode to the Virgin Mary is among their repertoire. When we were recording this in the flat of a charming actress called Kathryn her enormous dog Jupiter was affected by its spiritual

power and started howling. This one was recorded when Jeni's daughter took Jupiter out for a walk on nearby Hampstead Heath.

4. *Summer Is Icumen In* — The Princes In The Tower (One Tree Hill, south London)
Elizabeth I herself is said to have planted the one tree at One Tree Hill, making it the ideal place to record this theatrical medieval duo made up of Michael Tyack (cittern) and Will Summers (crumhorn, rauch pfeifer). The chorus of birds in the background certainly adds to the atmosphere. Fans of cult film *The Wicker Man* may recognise this thirteenth-century medieval smash: the islanders sing a rousing version of it as they roast the virginal Sergeant Howie to death.

5. *John Barleycorn* — Ed, Will and Ginger (Selling, Kent)
The story of how barley is turned into beer and whisky, this ale celebration imagines John Barleycorn as a heroic character that goes through all kinds of horrific events in his journey from cereal crop to alcoholic brew. It offers a seamless blend of the pagan myth of the recurring king with the single, resurrected Christ figure: John Barleycorn is the vegetable king that must die for the harvest. Ed, Will and Ginger are three polite young men that were walking across Britain, singing for supper along the way, and we recorded this in the Kentish orchard they were staying in before they set off on their next mammoth journey. It was suitable for the land we were in, where hops and barley are the agricultural mainstays and beer takes on an almost sacred importance.

6. *Black Town* — Pete Molinari (Chatham, Kent)
Pete Molinari is a Cuban-heeled greaser of Egyptian/Italian/Maltese parentage whose American-influenced songs are the product of a man dreaming of escape from life in the tough dock town of Chatham. Pete had told me of the dangers he faced in Chatham. I felt he was exaggerating until I went there to make this field recording, and a large woman threw a chair at us. After attempts to record on the high street ended in violence we

retreated to the safety of the family kitchen and his mum's wonderful cooking, where Pete sang this sad, lonely ode to his hometown.

7. *Summertime* — Tandayi (Chatham, Kent)
Shortly after being attacked by the woman with the chair our spirits were lifted by the sight of a beautiful, smiling young woman sitting on a bench on the high street, having lunch with her mother. Pete knew the girl, whose name was Tandayi, and said she had an amazing voice after having learned to sing gospel in church. Sure enough, she did, and Tandayi gave us her elegant rendition of this standard in the garden of her parents' house before she had an appointment to keep with the optician.

8. *Ayres The Bakers* — The Boycott Coca-Cola Experience (Peckham, southeast London)
Residents of Nunhead in southeast London will know all about Ayres The Bakers, which has been serving the bread-based needs of the community for 100 years. The Boycott Coca-Cola Experience is a Peckham father of three who travels about the place performing pedal-powered concerts here, there and everywhere — sometimes outside Ayres The Bakers.

9. *The Bedmaking* — Martin Carthy (Robin Hood's Bay, Yorkshire)
It was very nice of folk hero Martin Carthy, who had never met me before, to let me record him in his living room, singing this saucy tale of a servant maid used and abused and getting her revenge. Martin's wife Norma Waterson made scones, and their niece and nephew Marry and Olly, children of Norma's late sister Lal Waterson, dropped by. There are many Yorkshire songs that would have been long forgotten had The Watersons, one of Britain's great singing families, not revived them.

10. *Blue Mantle* — King Creosote, James Yorkston, The Pictish Trail (Anstruther, Fife)
Half of the little Scottish fishing village of Anstruther seem to fill their spare time by writing songs. Everyone from the postman to the guy driving the delivery van for the Co-Op is busy getting

up at The Ship Tavern and knocking out a rendition of their latest number. Here, three prominent members of Anstruther's Fence Collective perform a song about an alien coming to Earth, which was written by Kenny Anderson's (King Creosote's) brother Gordon. At the beginning you'll hear Kenny's daughter Beth making her own contribution to this rich creative tapestry.

11. *The Bitter Withy* — Alex Neilson (Govan, Glasgow)
In this ancient tale Jesus is a spiteful little boy who kills three young lords that refuse to play with him. Perhaps not exactly making the punishment fit the crime Mother Mary beats Jesus with a willow wand, or withy. So he curses it, and now the willow is the only tree that perishes from the heart. The eerie, reedy voice of Leeds-born, Govan-based singer and drummer Alex Neilson perfectly fits the strange mood of this folkloric interpretation of the Christ story.

12. *Kilmahog Saturday Afternoon* — Alasdair Roberts and Alex Neilson (Govan, Glasgow)
Over an afternoon in the less than bucolic neighbourhood of Govan Alex Neilson and his friend, the Glasgow singer Alasdair Roberts, performed this spirited version of a song written by Alasdair's father. There's something about it that makes me think we're going to hear their mum calling them down for tea at any minute, telling them their beans on toast is getting cold.

13. *Willie O' Winsbury* — Stephanie Hladowski (Bradford)
This one really gets to me. Alex Neilson told me to visit a young woman he knew in Bradford, of Polish parentage, living with her mum and dad in the heart of the city's Muslim area, with a wonderful singing voice. So I turned up at the family home of this person I had never met before, sat down with them for a hearty goulash, and then went upstairs, where Stephanie calmly sang this chillingly beautiful version of an old Scottish ballad. She felt a deep connection to it, even though her blood was Polish.

14. *Biting Glass* — The Beep Seals (Chorlton, Manchester)
South Manchester seems to have a feeling for the sixties, The

Beach Boys in particular never being too far away from stereos and pub jukeboxes. The Beep Seals are redolent of this, and also of the city's working ethic. Understanding that making a living from being in a band is unlikely, this highly musical five-piece all have day jobs. We recorded this upstairs in a neighbourhood bar called The Dulcimer one extremely rainy autumn night before The Beep Seals all went back to their respective homes. I think there was a match on.

15. *Byw Heb Frw* — Cate Le Bon (Penboyr, Dyfed, Wales)
Cate Le Bon is a young woman from Dyfed, South Wales, where it always seems to rain and the green valleys are shrouded in a spectral mist. At the back of her parents' house in Penboyr is a field full of sheep. This seemed the ideal place to record this pretty song by Cate, which translates as Living Without Dying. To me it sounds exotic yet steadfast, much like the place itself.

16. Sheep in a field in Penboyr

17. *Ffrwydriad Yn Y Ffurfafen* — Gruff Rhys (Brecon, Wales)
The title translates as Explosions In The Outer Sky. This was recorded in the car park of The Green Man Festival in Brecon, the morning after Gruff's band Super Furry Animals headlined on the main stage. If you listen carefully, you can hear the crunch of mud under Wellington boots and the occasional shout from my children, who were sitting patiently, waiting for Gruff's song to finish so we could get fish and chips.

18. *Sea Shanty* — Cosmicorus (Leytonstone, east London)
The creation of a young teacher called Ildiko, Cosmicorus are like a church choir that has been listening to Pink Floyd and forgetting its holy purpose. Recorded in Ildiko's former rail shed home in Leytonstone, this haunting ode to a wayfarer features eleven voices, a guitar and a saxophone. 'I was really ill last year, and doing Cosmichorus got me through,' I remember one member telling me. Everyone in the chorus has a job; everyone sings together because they love it.

19. *Fresh Air* — Lewis Floyd Henry (Blackheath, southeast London)
Wild man Lewis is a local legend, southeast London's own Jimi Hendrix; although he reminds me more of a sharply dressed southern blues man like Robert Johnson. We recorded this in Lewis's van, which was parked near the council house he grew up in around the corner from Blackheath. Lewis dreams of open spaces as he plays guitar, harmonica and drums at the same time.

20. *The Seeds Of Love* — Tim Van Eyken (Islington, north London)
Here is the song that started Cecil Sharp off on his journey to capture the essence of England through folksong, over a hundred years ago. Sharp was staying at a vicarage in Somerset when a gardener sang this poetic ode to the pleasures of love. Young Tim Van Eyken learned the old songs of Britain from his mother, and now sings them with great sympathy. We recorded this in Tim's garret in Islington, north London, shortly before he was giving a music lesson.

21. *Do-Re-Mi* — Pearl (Peckham, south London)
One day my five-year-old daughter Pearl was singing this Richard Rodgers classic around the house. She had learned it in the school playground. I asked her if she would mind my recording her, and she gracefully agreed. Proof, I hope, that oral history, the process by which folk music exists, is alive and well and moving into the voices of a new generation.

Heron Recordings is a London-Based indie record label run by two people on a shoestring and dedicated to the promotion and dissemination of music in a psychedelic progressive pop, rock or folk vein.
www.heronrecordings.com